Praise for the Author

D0746877

"Brian Jackman is a passionate b...
who lives surrounded by reminders...
relish for the experience he is recalling and for the language in which he
sets it down. His prose is clean and uncluttered, his sense of history acute."
The Sunday Times

"The author has that priceless gift of imparting his own enthusiasm
without over-emphasis… it is a pleasure to be in his company."
The Sunday Telegraph

"Brian Jackman not only writes well, but has that rare gift of
communicating his own sensual perceptions."
Birds Magazine

"Few writers are able to evoke a sense of place as effectively
as Brian Jackman."
In Britain

"Vivid and real. His fine descriptive writing brings
the sights and sounds of Africa to life."
Robin Page on *The Marsh Lions* in *The Daily Telegraph*

"Absolutely stunning, both from the point of view of the photography and
the writing. It reeks of Africa. It smells of Africa. The whole thing is just
living Africa. It's a lovely book for the armchair naturalist."
Living World (BBC Radio 4) on *The Marsh Lions*

About the Author

BRIAN JACKMAN is a freelance journalist and author with a lifelong passion for travel and wildlife. For 20 years he worked for *The Sunday Times*, during which time he was voted Travel Writer of the Year in 1982. In that same year he also won the *Wildscreen '82* award for the best commentary script, *Osprey*, at the first International Wildlife and Television Festival in Bristol.

Today his work appears mostly in *The Daily Telegraph*, *BBC Wildlife Magazine* and *Travel Africa*. Although his travels have taken him around the world, he is best known as Britain's foremost writer on African wildlife safaris, and has spent more than three years in total under canvas in the bush. He is also a Fellow of the Royal Geographical Society, a trustee of the George Adamson Wildlife Preservation Trust and a patron of Tusk Trust.

His other African books include *The Marsh Lions* and *The Big Cat Diary* (both with Jonathan Scott) and *Roaring at the Dawn*. He also edited *My Serengeti Years* by Myles Turner and *Battle for the Elephants* by Iain and Oria Douglas-Hamilton.

He is married, with one daughter and two grandchildren, and lives in Dorset.

🐾   🐾   🐾

savannah diaries

A celebration of Africa's big cat country

By
Brian Jackman

Illustrations by
Jonathan Truss

Foreword by
Virginia McKenna

Bradt

First published in book form in the UK in February 2014 by

Bradt Travel Guides Ltd
IDC House, The Vale, Chalfont St Peter, Bucks SL9 9RZ, England
www.bradtguides.com

Print edition published in the USA by The Globe Pequot Press Inc,
PO Box 480, Guilford, Connecticut 06437-0480

Text copyright © 2014 Brian Jackman
Photographs (digital edition) copyright © 2014 Brian Jackman
Illustrations copyright © 2014 Jonathan Truss
Edited by Rachel Fielding
Proofread by Janet Mears
Designed and typeset from the author's files by Adrian McLaughlin
Cover design: illustration and concept by Neil Gower, typesetting by Creative Design and Print
Digital conversion by Scott Gibson

This collection is drawn and adapted from articles previously published in *The Times*, *The Sunday Times*, *The Daily Telegraph* and *Travel Africa* – please see acknowledgements.

ISBN: 978 1 84162 493 8 (print)
e-ISBN: 978 1 84162 789 2 (e-pub)
e-ISBN: 978 1 84162 690 1 (mobi)

British Library Cataloguing in Publication Data
A catalogue record for this book is available from the British Library

Production managed by Jellyfish Print Solutions; printed in the UK

Contents

Foreword

I have just finished a very English journey: travelling by train in December from Yorkshire to London. On the way north the skies lowered in shades of deep purple and grey, the clouds moved chaotically in a kind of frenzy. Returning the next day, a brilliant sun and clear skies make yesterday seem like a dream. A great cloth had wiped the sky clean.

But, in truth, what I really have been seeing through the train windows are not the fields and woodlands of my homeland, but the plains, forests, skies and deserts of East Africa – so uniquely and vividly described in Brian's *Savannah Diaries*.

I am biased, of course. Since sailing to Kenya in 1964 with my husband Bill Travers and our children, these lands of wild animals, endless vistas, ever-changing cloud patterns, short twilights, magical dawns and warm, welcoming people, have been my spiritual home. And this book holds so many echoes of my own feelings and experiences that I often felt I was a part of Brian's mind and heart and walking in his footsteps.

I have been privileged to meet several of the people he writes about and have travelled to some of the places. I am moved by the same feelings of wonder, excitement, exhilaration and sadness. I feel the same admiration for, and gratitude to, those early visionary 'pioneers' who turned from hunting to conservation, their dedication and determination needed more now than ever before.

Some people experience moments when their lives change forever. But few have Brian's extraordinary skill in bringing them to life for the reader. His vivid descriptions lift us effortlessly into sharing some of these moments: whether he is watching a pride of lions, being confronted by a huge bull elephant, listening to birdsong, absorbing the harsh environment of the desert, sitting in camp in the stillness of the night, hearing the stories of men and women for whom the protection of wilderness has become their mission in life, or reflecting on and mourning those now gone, who unconsciously pioneered a new way of thinking.

One of those, deeply valued by Bill and myself as a close friend, was George Adamson. The life George led from 1965, when the filming of *Born Free* in Kenya ended, was unique. He asked for nothing except to be allowed to live with some previously captive lions and to teach them to be free and independent. This he achieved with many, first in Meru and then in Kora. But George was a realist – as well as one of the kindest, most loyal and modest people I ever met. His heartfelt cry for the future of Kora and its animals still echoes around us: "Who will now care for the animals in the reserve, for they cannot look after themselves? .... Who will raise their voices, when mine is carried away on the wind…?" This cry is more telling and more poignant than when he first wrote it in 1986. Brian knows that. All of us do who care about wilderness, respecting wild animals for what they are, recognising that they too are individuals who can suffer, feel joy, tenderness, anger and jealousy.

The wild world of Africa that Brian experienced 40 years ago now exists only in small scattered fragments. As human footsteps tread in ever greater numbers on wilderness soil the footprints of lion and leopard, elephant and rhino, wildebeest and antelope, meerkat and monkey fade. Perhaps forever.

Like Brian, lions have always had a special place in my heart. Through The Born Free Foundation, started by Bill, our eldest son Will and myself 30 years ago, we try to answer George's cry for help: "We will, we will, we will." And there are many others, mentioned in this book, who feel as strongly.

This is a book everyone who loves Africa should read – as well as those who have yet to experience its beauty and magic. But this is more than a reliving of memories, more than an encouragement to visit unknown places and open new horizons. By including the vulnerability of Africa's wild places and its animals in such a poignant way, Brian has presented us with a powerful and inescapable warning.

If we cut down forests, pollute rivers, treat the land and its creatures with indifference, kill wild animals for 'sport', poach them for their body parts, then there will be no 'wild'. No wilderness. No birdsong, no balance, no moments when our hearts beat faster when we glimpse an eagle soaring, hear a lion's roar in the night, watch wild flowers explode on the plains after the rains.

'The Spirit of Elsa' is not only in Meru where that famous lioness is buried. It is out there in the African skies, in the hearts of all wild creatures and the hearts of people who strive with such passion and determination to protect Africa's unmatched legacy.

Brian, who so evocatively tells us of his 40-year fascination with, and love of, this beautiful continent – and tells it with such deep understanding and feeling – has not only allowed us to glimpse a long-gone past, he has surely awakened those who slumber from their indifference, and encouraged all those who already care to try a little harder.

I said, at the start, that this is a unique book, so personal and yet so all-embracing. I feel enormous gratitude to Brian for taking us on his many journeys, for sharing with us his delight and wonder, his warm encounters with the people, and for the sensitive yet profound way he warns us that, because of us, the trumpeting, the roars, the cries and the calls may, one day, be silenced. Brian is proof, if proof were needed, that the pen is indeed mightier than the sword. The pen creates life, the sword ends it. I wonder where his next travels will take him – one thing is sure, I am not the only person who will long to read about them and be immersed once more in the wonders of Africa, seen through his heart and mind and all-seeing eyes.

VIRGINIA MCKENNA
The Born Free Foundation

For Tony Fitzjohn and Charlie Mayhew – conservation heroes

Hii nchi ni ya nani? Hii nchi ni ya nani? Yango, yango, yango!

"Whose land is this? Whose land is this? It is mine, mine, mine!"

(Swahili rendition of the lion's roar.)

Introduction

Lions at First Light

DAWN comes up fast in Africa. In Botswana, far out on the Selinda floodplains, a cheetah stands atop a termite mound above the melting mist. In Zambia's Luangwa Valley a leopard climbs into a sausage tree to warm itself in the rising sun and in Tanzania's Serengeti National Park, as the low light pours across the plains it picks out a pride of lions on their way back to the woodlands after a good night's hunting.

The habitats may vary widely, from Kalahari sandveld to the classic East African savannah of billowing grass and flat-topped thorn trees, but the common bond that unites them is always the same. What lifts them out of the ordinary, what fills them with a tingling sense of heightened awareness are the big cats whose mere presence is enough to dominate the landscape for miles around.

What we are talking about is Africa's awesome trinity of top predators – lion, leopard and cheetah. Revered for their beauty, held in awe for their role as natural born killers, they have a universal appeal that transcends all barriers.

Sharing their wild domain is an entire cavalcade of picture-book animals: giraffes and zebras, elephants and rhinos and all kinds of antelopes from one-ton elands to diminutive dik-diks no bigger than a hare. But it is the big cats that everyone most wants to see.

Who can fail to be moved by their hypnotic presence? Even in repose they exude an aura of imminent drama, of latent power barely suppressed, and the certainty of unimaginable violence never far away. You don't even have to see them to feel the tension in the air. All it needs are fresh pugmarks in the dust or the deep-throated cough of a prowling leopard to set the nerves jangling with anticipation.

In big cat country the eye is never still. One is constantly on the lookout for the silhouette of a leopard sprawled along a bough, the flick of an ear in the grass that might betray a cheetah, or the way in which prey animals raise their heads to stare alertly in the same direction, revealing the hiding place of a hungry lion.

It was in Kenya's Maasai Mara National Reserve that I saw my first wild lion 30 years ago. I had set out at first light from Governors' Camp and found a huge shaggy-headed male silhouetted on a termite mound with the early morning dew around him. The sun was barely above the horizon, and with every roar his breath condensed like smoke from a dragon's nostrils.

In East Africa they translate the song of the lion into Swahili. "*Hii nchi ni ya nani?*" cry the territorial pride males, "Whose land is this?" And as their tumultuous challenge dies away, they answer their own question with a rhythmic coda of deep rasping grunts that make the air vibrate. "*Yango, yango, yango.* Mine, mine, mine."

And it is true. Lions are indeed lords of this land, and ever since I first heard them they have never ceased to walk through my life and inhabit my dreams. At Kora in the thornbush country of northern Kenya George Adamson introduced me to his famous lions, and for five unforgettable years in the Mara I followed the fortunes of the Musiara Marsh pride with the photographer Jonathan Scott.

Often, following the Musiara pride in Kenya's Maasai Mara National Reserve, I would try to imagine what it must feel like to be a lion. Like me, they would have heard the wind in the grass and the sad cries of wood doves in the noontide luggas. Did I not feel the same sense of pleasure when the sun warmed me on a cold morning? Thirst, hunger, aggression and fear, many sensations we must have shared, but what else went on behind those inscrutable eyes would forever remain a mystery.

Long since perfected in evolutionary terms, these glorious carnivores live in a parallel universe far older and wilder than ours, one that we all sprang from but have long since forgotten. Theirs is an ancient story with no beginning and no end, marked only by golden dawns and blood-red sunsets, by the rhythm of the seasons and the movements of the wandering herds as they chase the rains across some of the greatest wildlife strongholds on earth.

Wherever big cats are found, in the Okavango and in Luangwa and above all, perhaps, in the great Mara-Serengeti ecosystem, the sense of space is intoxicating. The light, the distance, the feeling that you could drive forever through this lovely country and never come to the end of it, or ever have enough. All it takes are a few days for the spell of the bush to work its magic, a kind of madness, like the beginning of a love affair in which you cannot take your eyes away from the splendour of the vast horizons.

🐾   🐾   🐾

Africa changes you forever, like nowhere else on earth. Once you have been there, breathed its dry air, watched distant storms trailing across its immense horizons, been awakened by a dawn chorus of purring doves, you will never be the same. But how do you begin to describe its magic to someone who has never been? How can you explain the fascination of a land whose oldest roads are elephant paths? Could it be because Africa is at the heart of all our beginnings, the cradle of humankind, where our species first stood upright on the savannahs of long ago? Maybe that was what led Karen Blixen to say, in *Out of Africa*: "Here I am, where I belong."

Africa is so big. Here, far from the 21st century, you come face to face with uncluttered space and distance on an unimaginable scale. Many of its national parks and game reserves – Kruger, Kafue, Serengeti, Selous – are the size of small countries. You could fit the whole of Yorkshire into the outermost contour of Mt Kilimanjaro and still have room to spare.

Love is altogether too feeble a word to describe what I feel for this ancient continent. As a boy growing up in the London suburbs I dreamed of Africa. I would open my school atlas and there it lay, vast and mysterious, shaped like an elephant's ear and littered with names that spoke to me like talking drums – Zambezi, Okavango, Ngorongoro.

From the library books my father brought home I learned the beautiful Swahili names of all the animals – *chui* (leopard), *simba* (lion) – and slowly a picture emerged, of Africa as a heat-stunned wilderness of dust and thorns and sun-dried grass, as indeed it can be in Tsavo and the Kalahari thirstlands. I knew I would be happy there because it was the fulfilment of my childhood dreams. Yet even then, having read Blixen and Hemingway and the rest, I was totally unprepared for its impact.

For a start, I never knew Africa could be so green. When thunderclouds pile up in the late afternoons, when you can smell the earth after rain and the dust is laid and the plains turn to emerald there is nowhere on earth so verdant. And that is how I first saw it.

❧   ❧   ❧

I'd flown to Kenya in early May, first to Nairobi and then on down to the Mara in a six-seater Cessna. The long rains had just ended, leaving the plains greener than Ireland, the endless rolling savannah covered in waist-high grass that rippled in the wind like ocean waves.

That night, as I lay under canvas beneath a sky seething with stars, I heard for the first time the song of the lion. Not close enough to feel the air vibrating, as I would in years to come, but powerful still – the most thrilling sound in Africa. That did it. I listened and listened and was hooked for life.

Since then I have been back more times than I can recall. Not only to Kenya but Tanzania, too, and all the way south to the Cape by way of Zambia, Zimbabwe, Botswana and Namibia, looking for anywhere that offered a comfortable tent under a tree and the sound of lions at first light.

The backdrop varies from country to country, and from one park to another. In Zambia there are oxbow lagoons beside the Luangwa River with buffaloes trooping in to wallow. In Namibia you will find waterholes strung out along the margins of Etosha's burning saltpans, with zebras quivering like mirages on the horizon.

At Mana Pools in Zimbabwe are giant glades of winterthorns in whose shade elephants take their ease, huge ears flapping like sails in the windless air. And in Botswana, herds of red lechwe antelope leaping and plunging over half-drowned floodplains with a pack of wild dogs in hot pursuit.

Wherever you stay, rustic bush camp or glitzy lodge, the location is seldom less than spectacular and in no time the days slip into a comfortable pattern dictated by the heat of the sun and the movements of the game.

How I adore the stripped-down safari life, the absence of clutter and trivia, the dawn starts that begin in East Africa with a friendly "*Karibu*" ('Welcome') and a big smile from the man with a tea tray at the door of my tent. How I love the early morning game drives, the dew on the grass, doves in the thorn trees and the squeal of zebra stallions in the sharp highland air. I love safari bread, baked daily in a bed of hot ashes to accompany the hearty bush breakfasts, and the languorous noontide siestas followed by an afternoon game drive that stretches into the golden hour before sundown when cheetahs hunt in the last of the light.

For me, the most compelling reason for going on safari has always been to see game. Not just the classic picture-book animals – elephant, lion, giraffe, zebra – but also the antelopes and smaller nocturnal animals: porcupines, honey badgers, spotted genets.

All these and more, together with chameleons and fishing owls, forest butterflies the size of bats, flamingos by the million and baobab trees older than the Pyramids. Nowhere else can you encounter the diversity of nature in such extraordinary abundance. In Africa, every day heaves, buzzes, shrieks and pulsates with life.

And now I must make a confession. In the early years, so complete was my obsession with Africa's wildlife and wild places that I barely noticed its people. The camp staff who brought me food and drink; the cooks and safari drivers; the women hoeing the fields; even the haughty Maasai herdsmen with their red robes and shining spears merely hovered at the edges of my consciousness, as if they inhabited a parallel world whose customs would always remain impenetrable.

How wrong could I be? Now I consider Africans to be among the friendliest people on Earth, the most welcoming and eager to please, with a natural dignity and respect for the elderly that is sadly lacking in our own society.

How I love the melodious Swahili language – its wise proverbs and the way in which every word ends in a vowel – and wish I were more fluent. But at least I have learned enough to break the ice. "Oh," strangers cry with a smile of delight. "You speak our language."

❀   ❀   ❀

Today, tragically, the long shadows of extinction are reaching out even further across the savannah. The elephants I thought safe after the international ivory trade ban of 1989 are again at the mercy of the poaching gangs. Rhinos – their horns now worth more than their weight in gold – are being butchered in unprecedented numbers; and lions are in decline almost everywhere except in the Serengeti. It is now believed that no more than 20,000 lions are left on earth, of which only 3,500 are males, and George Adamson is no longer here to campaign for their survival. "Who will raise their voices" he wrote, "when mine is carried away on the wind?"

As a travel writer, first for *The Sunday Times* and more recently for *The Daily Telegraph,* I have been lucky enough to see it all when the going was good. If I were to add up all the times I have been on safari it would amount to at least three years of my life in the bush – much of it spent in the company of wild Africa's most distinguished individuals.

What follows is an account of those journeys, based on the copious notes I kept for my stories. Together they carry a message, and it is this. I truly believe that eco-tourism, provided it is operated at a sustainable level, holds out the greatest hope for the survival of Africa's wildlife and last wild places. Therefore, if this book persuades you to go and see it for yourself despite the cost, it will have achieved is purpose.

And if you are like me, when your safari is over and you are safely back home, not a day will pass when you don't think of Africa. Even now, looking out of my window on the green hills of England, I cannot help but wonder if it is raining in the Serengeti, and if the lions are roaring across Musiara Marsh.

❀   ❀   ❀

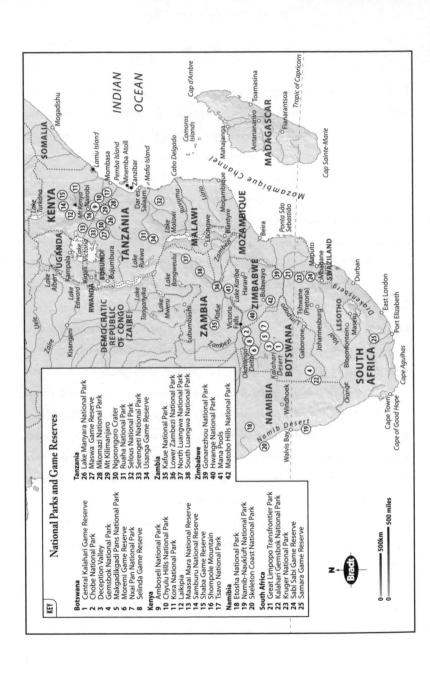

KEY

National Parks and Game Reserves

Botswana
1 Central Kalahari Game Reserve
2 Chobe National Park
3 Deception Valley
4 Gemsbok National Park
5 Makgadikgadi Pans National Park
6 Moremi Game Reserve
7 Nxai Pan National Park
8 Selinda Game Reserve

Kenya
9 Amboseli National Park
10 Chyulu Hills National Park
11 Kora National Park
12 Laikipia
13 Maasai Mara National Reserve
14 Samburu National Reserve
15 Shaba Game Reserve
16 Shompole Mountain
17 Tsavo National Park

Namibia
18 Etosha National Park
19 Namib-Naukluft National Park
20 Skeleton Coast National Park

South Africa
21 Great Limpopo Transfrontier Park
22 Kalahari Gemsbok National Park
23 Kruger National Park
24 Sabi Sabi Game Reserve
25 Samara Game Reserve

Tanzania
26 Lake Manyara National Park
27 Maswa Game Reserve
28 Mkomazi National Park
29 Mt Kilimanjaro
30 Ngorongoro Crater
31 Ruaha National Park
32 Selous National Park
33 Serengeti National Park
34 Usanga Game Reserve

Zambia
35 Kafue National Park
36 Lower Zambezi National Park
37 North Luangwa National Park
38 South Luangwa National Park

Zimbabwe
39 Gonarezhou National Park
40 Hwange National Park
41 Mana Pools
42 Matobo Hills National Park

Chapter One
Maasai Mara

May 1974–2013: The World of the Marsh Lions

EVEN before the six-seater bush plane has touched down on the Governors' Camp airstrip I spot a lioness at rest on a termite mound. As the plane comes to rest, fat African raindrops the size of Kenya shillings begin to drum in the dust, but I don't care. I step down onto the wet murram, thrilled to be back in the oh-so-familiar territory of the Musiara lion pride whose lives I had chronicled three decades ago.

Here in the Maasai Mara National Reserve is where my lifelong love affair with Africa was born. The year was 1974 and I had arrived in May, just as the long rains were ending and the plains were a dazzling emerald green. Flying in over Miti Mbili Plain I watched spellbound as herds of buffalo galloped away through the endless waves of waist-high grass. Elephants turned and shook their ears in defiance as we zoomed overhead and farther off I could see giraffes moving solemnly among the flat-topped acacias beyond Musiara Marsh. From that moment I was hooked, and although I have been back to the Mara more times than I can remember, the magic is as strong as ever.

The Maasai Mara has been called the greatest slice of wildlife real estate in Africa. Bounded in the west by the steeply falling folds of the Siria escarpment, its 1,672 square kilometres of riparian woodlands and rolling savannah are threaded by innumerable *luggas* (seasonal watercourses) whose dense thickets provide shade and cover for the Mara lions.

When I first arrived I used to wonder how the safari guides ever found their way around the bewildering maze of rutted tracks and winding luggas. Now, 30 years on, driving over Rhino Ridge or searching for cats along the Ol Keju Ronkai watercourse, the Mara is as familiar to me as the hills of home in England.

In those early days I used to stay either at Governors' Camp in the forest beside the Mara River, or higher upstream at the Mara River Camp. Governors', built in 1972, was Africa's first permanent luxury camp and Aris Grammaticas, its owner, could not have chosen a better location. This is where the territories of five lion prides converge. Stick a compass point into it and within a five-mile radius you'll find the best game viewing on earth, with leopards in the riparian woodlands and cheetahs hiding on Rhino Ridge.

Mara River Camp was altogether smaller and more informal. It belonged to Jock Anderson, the genial owner of a company called East African Wildlife Safaris, and whenever he was in camp, bush babies would appear after dark, tempted by titbits of chopped-up banana.

Among Jock's safari guides was a hawk-eyed Kipsigis driver called Joseph Rotich – better known as Bwana Chui ('Mister Leopard') because of his extraordinary ability to find Africa's most elusive big cat. Back in the 1970s before the trade in leopard skins was banned these handsome carnivores were rare even in the Mara, but if anyone could find them it was Joseph.

One morning, on a game drive together, I saw a lion far off in the shade of a tree. Eagerly I pointed it out to Joseph, thinking I had spotted it before him and feeling rather pleased with myself. "Yes," he said, "and in the tree above there is a leopard."

Jock's other guide was a young Englishman with a passion for photography. His name was Jonathan Scott – now known all over the world as one of Africa's finest wildlife photographers.

He wanted to show me a pride of lions he had been studying. The core of their territory was Musiara Marsh, which lies not far from Governors' Camp. During the dry season when the migrating wildebeest and zebra trekked in from the Serengeti they would come to drink at the Marsh every day; and there in the reeds the lions would ambush them, providing endless moments of high drama. The Marsh Lions, Jonathan called them, and when we decided to write a true-life story of their triumphs and travails, that was its title. Neither of us knew it then, but three decades later the Marsh pride would become the world's most famous lions, having appeared for week after week in the BBC's hugely popular *Big Cat Diary* television series.

Those days spent in the company of the Marsh Lions were among the most carefree of my life. Tourism in the Mara was still in its infancy. The grasslands were not yet criss-crossed with tyre tracks or overrun with vehicles, and we could be alone with the pride from dawn to dusk.

What an extraordinary privilege it was to enter their world and come to know them as individuals, each one as recognisable to us as an old friend, in the same way that a shepherd knows his sheep.

By following them every day we got to know their hunting ground almost as well as they did; not only the reed beds of the Marsh itself, but also the winding seasonal watercourse called Bila Shaka Lugga with its shady acacias and croton thickets. *Bila Shaka* is Swahili for 'without fail' – so-called by the Governors' Camp drivers because if you couldn't see lions anywhere else you were sure to find them hidden somewhere in the lugga's bank-side tangles of acacia scrub and croton thickets.

Sometimes, as we followed the pride males onto the plains beyond, they would turn and pad towards us to seek the shade of our vehicle and slump down beside us, tongues lolling in the heat. There they would sprawl with their heads on their paws while the life of the plains went on around us. From time to time the magnificent old warrior we knew as Scar would wake up and look at us, and I would remember the words of Myles Turner, the legendary Serengeti warden: "There is nothing in the world as pitiless as the baleful stare of a lion."

Scar was the epitome of a male lion in his prime. From his threadbare muzzle to his black tail-tuft he measured nearly three metres long. His mane was so thick it almost hid his ears, a glossy rug of tobacco-coloured hair, shot through with auburn glints. He was everything a pride male should be: deep in the chest and immensely powerful, with an aura about him, a way of walking with an insolent swagger that reflected his fearless self-confidence.

🐾　　🐾　　🐾

Looking back now I can see that the life of the Marsh pride in those glory days was a golden age for lions. That time is over. In the past 20 years Africa's lion population has halved, and even the Mara prides are in decline. Yet for me this will always be the land of the lion, the iconic carnivore that stands for all that is best about wild Africa.

What you may hear about the Mara sometimes being overcrowded is true; but it is not the whole truth. If you find yourself in one of those unfortunate situations with dozens of vehicles parked around a lion pride or some hapless cheetah, just ask your driver to move on, and within minutes you can be swallowed up by acres of silence.

As for Scar and his companions – they are long gone. But their offspring are still there, keeping watch from the same termite mounds and roaring at the gates of dawn as they await the coming of the wildebeest.

January 1999: To Heaven by Picnic Hamper

IN the Mara, two things strike you about the landscape and your place in it. Driving over its boundless savannahs, you find yourself either gazing up at the wide rolling skylines on which animals – zebra and wildebeest or perhaps a herd of elephants – are outlined against the blue. Or else you are up on those same ridges, looking out over a wide-screen Africa of waving grass with immense views in every direction, of blue faraway hills and the Oloololo escarpment reaching down into the Serengeti.

But for the best views of all there is nothing like a hot-air balloon safari from Little Governors' Camp, lifting off at sunrise to float up and away across the Mara Triangle, heading towards the Serengeti.

Ngambo is a Swahili word meaning 'across the river', and that is how you reach Little Governors', ferried over the Mara River from the main camp on the eastern bank. Location is what Little Governors' is all about. Its 17 tents are spaced around a natural theatre-in-the-round of whispering reeds and glittering pools where elephant come to drink and wallow, and the balloons take off every day at dawn from a grassy meadow nearby.

As the sun comes up I step into the chest-high wicker basket. Above me floats the multi-coloured balloon, tall as a ten-storey building. Then, with a blast from the propane burners, we have lift-off. "Farewell, mere earthlings," cries our pilot, Robin Bachelor, with a wave to his ground crew of Maasai helpers.

Bachelor, a veteran of more than 3,000 flights, is not just a Richard Branson lookalike; he also turns out to be the man who taught the Virgin boss how to fly a balloon.

What happens next is best described as going to heaven in a picnic hamper. From the air you can see it all, just as it must appear to the keen-eyed vultures aloft in the blue. From 500 feet below comes the gleam of the Mara River and its hippo pools, coiling between tall forest trees where green pigeons are feasting on ripening figs. On the plains beyond, zebras are drifting between the neatly clipped parasol shapes of the desert date trees.

Somewhere ahead of us, the ground crew are setting up tables and chairs in readiness for our champagne breakfast in the bush. "We're the biggest consumers of champagne and propane in Africa," says Bachelor.

Thinking about breakfast induces hunger pangs but I don't want this flight to end. We sail past a startled fish eagle in a treetop, spot a cheetah on an anthill, drift over a breeding herd of elephants.

Too soon we are swishing through the long grass to land with a bump that puts the basket on its side and leaves us giggling in a heap. Then, to the popping of champagne corks and the sizzle of fried eggs and bacon, bush breakfast is served.

July 2010: The Great Migration

EVERY year in the Mara, when the long rains have ended and the dry *kiangazi* winds begin to blow across the rolling seas of grass, the migrating zebras and wildebeest arrive from Tanzania. Over the Nyamalumbwa plains they come running, pouring into Kenya across the Sand River as if glad to be free of the Serengeti's northern woodlands with their lurking shadows and swarming tsetse flies. The Mara is their dry season refuge and here they will remain for the next four months, trekking back and forth over the national reserve and spilling out into the dispersal area beyond as far as the Aitong Hills until the onset of the short rains in late October lures them south again.

By the time they reach the Mara in early July the red-oat grasses have already set their seeds. On Paradise Plain the grass is so tall that the cheetahs must lift their heads above it on their endless wanderings. After six weeks without rain it is as ripe as an old English hay meadow, rippling all the way to the horizon under the dry season wind and galleon clouds, waiting for the zebras to chomp it down.

The zebras are usually the first to arrive, like the advance guard of a conquering army, but the wildebeest are never far behind with their calves bouncing along at their side.

Their coming is eagerly awaited by the predators: by the leopards in their trees along the Talek; by the keen-eyed cheetahs of the Mara Triangle; and above all by the hungry Mara lions, who can easily put away 70 pounds of meat at a sitting. For them the arrival of the great migration spells an end to the hardships of the wet season when they fought and quarrelled over warthog kills. Now, lying on the ridges with their manes streaming in the wind, the old pride males catch the distant grunting chorus of wildebeest on the move and sense the time of plenty is at hand.

But lions are not the only perils the migrating wildebeest must face, and by far the greatest are the river crossings that claim thousands of lives every year. Some of the most dramatic crossings take place on a mile-long stretch of the Mara River to the northwest of Mara Serena Safari Lodge.

This is no place for the squeamish. At times, in the wake of a major crossing the air is thick with the stench of death and the riversides resemble the aftermath of a battle, with corpses piled up at the foot of the banks. Other bodies have come to rest against sunken branches or float in the shallows where vultures dance on the bloated bellies.

With the vultures come more carrion-eaters: spotted hyenas, tawny eagles, black kites and ghoulish marabou storks with leprous skulls and pendulous throat pouches – all summoned to the feast by the billowing dust clouds that invariably accompany a big river crossing.

At first the animals hold back, all too aware of the waiting crocodiles. But through the day the numbers swell and the noise is overwhelming – a constant honking, grunting chorus that bursts in waves upon the ears. Occasionally there comes a lull in which other sounds can be heard: the chatter of Ruppell's long-tailed starlings as they swoop through the dust on violet wings; the squeal of zebra. Then the wildebeest begin to moan again, a doleful choir thousands strong, giving voice to the rising tension, and still their numbers grow until those standing on the brink have no option but to take the plunge.

At first they cross in ones and twos, eyes rolling in fear as they leap headlong into the water and strike out for the opposite bank. But soon the trickle becomes an avalanche, a heaving tide of bodies driven by the genetic imperative that has brought them so far from their calving grounds – migrate or die.

Some die anyway, dragged under by the crocodiles. Others are drowned or trampled underfoot in the wild stampede. And even among those that survive the crossing there are the luckless ones – the lost, the lame – whose migration will end when darkness comes and the hyenas close in.

No matter. The rest roll on, unstoppable, unvanquished. Across Olmisingiyoi they pour, rocking through the grass at a steady canter, sweeping around Rhino Ridge and Musiara Marsh and eastwards all the way to Keekorok and beyond, caught up in a story as old as Africa itself.

October 2011: Where Wilderness is the New Luxury

OUT in the acacia woodlands of Naboisho the old order is changing. Here on the edge of the Maasai Mara National Reserve, the Enesikiria lion pride is about to trigger one of those regular and bloody revolutions that reverberate through lion society. Between them its three territorial pride males – Saitoti, his brother Sadala and the veteran Saruni – have produced six feisty sons, all of whom are fast approaching the time when they will be ejected from the pride. And when that happens, provided this fearsome band of brothers stay together, they will become an unstoppable coalition, able to terrorise the neighbouring prides for miles around.

Naboisho is one of a handful of private wildlife conservancies that have sprung up on the adjoining Maasai rangelands in recent years. Initiated by the Maasai themselves, it came into being as a result of the dramatic changes that have rocked the Mara since my first visit three decades ago, and is a partnership forged between 500 landowners and a handful of eco-tourism investors. Today, with a core area of over 200 square kilometres it is helping to preserve a crucial part of the wildlife corridors upon which the Mara-Serengeti ecosystem and its world famous wildebeest migration depend.

As the Maasai are now discovering, wilderness is the new luxury. The scarcer it gets, the more sought-after it becomes. And the glory of it all is that you don't have to rough it to enjoy rubbing cheeks with the natural world. That is why vast tracts of overgrazed rangelands adjoining the Maasai Mara National Reserve are being transformed into born-again sanctuaries for Kenya's big game, with cosy camps for stressed-out Westerners who want to chill on a soft adventure in lion country.

Ever since the winds of climate change threatened to blow away the Maasai's pastoral lifestyle, the entire Mara ecosystem has been at risk, with large areas being fenced off for commercial cultivation. While many Maasai still cling to their old ways, others are moving out of their dung-plastered huts and into the cash economy. Nowadays it is no longer surprising to see a red-robed *moran* ('warrior') with a spear in one hand and a cell phone in the other.

These changes in local land tenure have severely restricted the mobility of wildlife in the so-called dispersal zone outside the reserve where wildlife moves in the dry season and the Mara is estimated to have lost well over half of most species in the past 25 years. Some animal populations have suffered catastrophic collapses, with buffalo numbers down by 75 per cent, warthogs by 80 per cent and giraffe losses as high as 95 per cent. Most disturbing of all, lion numbers inside the national reserve have fallen by almost a third in the past 20 years, reflecting a trend that is taking place right across Africa.

At the same time, the Mara is under growing pressure as new safari camps spring up year after year: today there are at least 25 permanent camps and lodges inside the reserve compared to a mere handful three decades ago.

In those days the reserve was still relatively unknown, its existence eclipsed by the fame of the adjoining Serengeti. But all that changed when Kenya and Tanzania fell out and closed the border in 1977. Until then, Nairobi had been the main tourist gateway for both countries. Now, denied direct access to the Serengeti, visitors began to head for the Mara in ever increasing numbers. What they found was a big game sanctuary without equal.

🐾   🐾   🐾

From the rocky summit of Rhino Ridge you can see it all. To the south are the crossing places where the migrating wildebeest ford the Mara River. Across the river lies the Mara Triangle, its plains speckled with the clipped parasol shapes of desert date trees, and the shadowy folds of the Siria escarpment reaching down into Tanzania. Closer still are Governors' Camp and the reed beds of Musiara, where for five years I lived among the Marsh Lions; and I suddenly realise this is not just a familiar landscape spread out below me, but a major part of my life.

Paradise it was when I first came here, and paradise it remains. But nothing stays the same. In the early 1980s it was still possible to witness the migration storming across the Mara River below the Serena Lodge with scarcely another vehicle in sight.

But in the boom years that followed the 1985 box-office success of *Out of Africa*, the Mara began to creak at the seams as its popularity grew.

Those like me who knew the Mara in its age of innocence find it deeply dispiriting to see how the world is closing in, and nowhere is this truer than at Mara Rianta, where you cross the Mara River in order to enter the Mara Triangle. Here on the very edge of the reserve a shantytown has sprung up where Jonathan Scott and I used to search for leopards 30 years ago.

But it is important to remember that the national reserve itself makes up no more than a third of the Mara ecosystem. The rest of it – the area at greatest risk – lies in the dispersal zone where changing land use combined with a succession of severe droughts was threatening the very existence of the Maasai and their pastoralist lifestyle. At one time it even seemed as if the greater Mara might be lost forever, its plains fenced off, its rich black cotton soil ploughed up and sub-divided to oblivion. Then a miracle happened.

In the mid 1990s Jake Grieves-Cook, a far-sighted safari tour operator with a passion for conservation, persuaded 70 Maasai families to set aside 8,000 acres of their land exclusively for wildlife. This was the Ol Kinyei Conservancy – the first community-owned sanctuary to be established on the rangelands adjoining the national reserve – demonstrating how Maasai landowners could earn a decent income from sustainable tourism by pooling their resources.

The idea caught on fast, and other, bigger wildlife conservancies followed in quick succession, including Olare Orok and Mara North, whose 50,000 acres include Leopard Gorge, featured regularly in the BBC's *Big Cat Diary* television series. The results have been hugely encouraging, with tourist numbers strictly controlled and wildlife increasing.

Of the remaining conservancies, by far the most important is Naboisho, a 50,000-acre wilderness whose lion population currently stands at 70 – one of the highest densities anywhere. Naboisho is also the home of the Koiyaki Guiding School. Established in 2005 with the help of Tusk Trust, the school and its affiliated Wilderness Camp teach young Maasai students to become professional wildlife guides, and more than a hundred of its graduates are now fully employed in the Mara and elsewhere.

Looking back over the past three decades it is impossible to ignore the physical changes that have overtaken the Mara. Aerial photographs, and the personal observations of old-time game wardens and safari guides all bear witness to the manner in which the very fabric of the reserve has undergone a major transformation.

Bush fires, elephants and the trampling of seedlings by the migrating wildebeest herds have all played their part in causing the woodlands to shrink. In earlier times the Maasai shunned the Mara because its thorny acacia thickets were a haven for tsetse flies. But years of regular burning have opened up the bush, displacing the flies and extending the grasslands. Even tourist vehicles have played a part by breaking down the croton thickets in their constant search for lions.

Yet for all its problems the Mara is still Kenya's finest wildlife showcase. It is Hemingway's *Green Hills of Africa* hoisted 5,000 feet into the sky together with its woodland glades and immense sweeps of chest-high oat grass, its endless herds of wandering herbivores and nights that echo to the rumble of lions.

As to the future, the success of private wildlife conservancies such as Naboisho has helped to preserve a crucial part of the dispersal zone. Talk of a Mara-Serengeti trans-frontier national park remains a pipe dream and the Mara National Reserve itself stumbles on from year to year without its long-awaited management plan.

Yet miraculously, despite three decades of change there is still no better place to observe Africa's big cats, and the Marsh Lions continue to occupy centre stage in what is still one of the world's most treasured wild places.

November 2011: Maasai First and Last

SITTING at the wheel of his Toyota long wheelbase Land Cruiser, Jackson Ole Looseyia is looking for the Enesikiria pride. The bush is thick in this wild corner of the Naboisho Conservancy on the edge of the Maasai Mara National Reserve, but Jackson is a Dorobo Maasai, born and bred in this area. He knows exactly where we are going, and if anyone can find lions here then he can.

Sure enough, as we approach the edge of an acacia-fringed lugga, he stops the vehicle and points to where a young male lion is watching us from the shade of a croton thicket. In a little while the lion emerges into the open, followed by one, two, three, four of his brothers and pride companions.

Although not yet full-grown they already have handsome manes and make a splendid sight as they slowly move off in single file. Soon the time will come for them to be ejected from the pride. "Then, if these boys stay together, they will make an awesome coalition," says Jackson admiringly. "They will be the new lords of this land."

Although the Mara is a national reserve, the land belongs to the Maasai pastoralists whose livestock have traditionally co-existed with the migratory herds of East African plains game. Wrapped in their red blankets, adorned with beads and ochre dreadlocks, the Maasai *morans*, or warriors, still use their spears to good effect against lions and cattle rustlers alike. For many, the only concessions to the 21st century are their 'thousand-milers' – makeshift sandals cut from discarded car tyres. But now, unless eco-tourism can give them greater benefits, their land could be claimed for agriculture and their semi-nomadic lifestyle will vanish along with the wildlife they have tolerated for so long.

Increasingly, Maasai families are moving out of their dome-shaped, smoke-filled, dung-plastered huts into solid buildings with corrugated iron roofs, swapping their tribal dress for suits and sending their kids to school to become doctors, teachers or – in Jackson's case – one of Kenya's most sought-after professional safari guides.

"I think I was born in 1967," he says, "but nobody knows for sure." What is certain is that at the age when most British youngsters are starting school, Jackson was out in the bush all day, herding his father's livestock in country where lions and other dangerous game are common. "For my father's generation that was the norm," says Jackson casually. "Most of my relatives were killed by wild animals. Two of my uncles were killed by the same buffalo."

When he was still only 16 he went hunting with his father and watched helplessly as he, too, was nearly killed by a buffalo. It was soon after this that he met Ron Beaton, one of Kenya's most respected safari tour operators, and began working for him as a spotter at Rekero Safari Lodge. "That is when Ron encouraged me to become a professional guide," says Jackson. "He was like a second father."

Now the herd boy who wore nothing but animal skins is a man: urbane, witty, worldly-wise, a natural raconteur who would grace any dinner table. What he doesn't know about the Mara is not worth knowing; and not only is he fluent in three languages – English, Swahili and Maa (the Maasai tongue) – but he can also name every bird, beast and plant in Latin.

Since becoming a guide he has travelled widely in Britain and the USA – always dressed in his traditional Maasai clothes. "I live with one foot in both cultures," he says. "I have my own blog site, laptop, cell phone and video camera, but wherever I go I am a Maasai first and last."

July 2013: Campfire Stories

ON the banks of the Mara River a mobile bush camp has been set up under the trees with old-fashioned green canvas tents to re-create the atmosphere of safari life as it was in the 1960s. Hippos honk from the river below. Swallowtail butterflies flit about our heads on emerald and black velvet wings, and every now and again, above the liquid voices of forest orioles, there comes the yelping cries of fish eagles.

To reach it we have flown from Nairobi by private charter and then driven across miles of lion-coloured plains on which herds of zebras – advance guards of the Serengeti migration – were chomping at the chest-high grass. Now, seated by the river on canvas chairs in a shady grove of African greenhearts, Geoffrey Kent is telling me about his extraordinary life.

Lean and fit – he still goes for regular three-mile runs – his swept back mane of long blond hair frames deeply tanned features that belie his 70 years. Dressed in a green bush shirt, with legs encased in faded jeans, he looks every inch the World Cup polo champion he became. "I was practically born in the saddle," he says. "I've been riding horses since I was two years old."

Geoffrey Kent was born in 1942 while his parents, Colonel John and Valerie Kent, were on safari in Northern Rhodesia (now Zambia), and spent his childhood running wild on the family's 3,000-acre farm on Kenya's Kinangop Plateau.

"I was a real *kaburu* – a Kenya Cowboy and proud of it," he says. "We wanted to be like all the tough Afrikaner boys who used to run around barefoot, killing elephants and doing all sorts of wild things out in the bush."

While still at school he discovered he could make money by selling elephant hair bracelets to an Indian trader and had soon acquired enough to buy a motorbike. But by doing so he had broken the school rules and was expelled as a result. "I didn't care," he says. "I just got on my bike with a sleeping bag and some biltong and set off from Nairobi to Cape Town, 5,000 miles away. I was the first person to make that trip by motorbike."

The year after he returned from South Africa his father decided the Army should be his future. He excelled through his prowess at polo and shooting, and soon found himself in the Middle East as Aide-de-Camp to General John Frost, the legendary airborne officer who commanded the 2nd Parachute Battalion at Arnhem in 1944.

It was in 1962, home on leave from Sandhurst, that he helped his parents to set up Abercrombie & Kent after they were forced off their farm in the run-up to Kenya's independence. "Those first safaris were modest affairs," Kent recalls, "conducted with little more than my mother's silver ice bucket and the farm Land Rover. I still remember the number plate – KBH 482."

Even in those early days the game plan was to become the best high-end tour operator in the field of luxury adventure – hence the company name they chose. "We wanted a name that would put us at the top of the Yellow Pages. Aardvark was a hot contender but in the end we settled for Abercrombie because it sounded so aristocratic."

Today he divides his time jet-setting between Monaco and Belgravia, but Kenya remains his spiritual home, and that is why he decided to celebrate A&K's 50th anniversary by going back to the Mara.

The tents behind us with their weather-beaten canvas and hessian floors are leftovers from the 1980s – the best A&K could find to re-create a 1960s bush camp complete with long-drop loos and bucket showers. "In those days," says Kent, "the first thing you looked for when choosing a camp site was a suitable branch from which to hang your shower."

How life has moved on since then. The Kent formula of providing a luxury cocoon from which to explore the world has attracted more than 200,000 clients, including the likes of Hilary Clinton, Richard Burton, Robert De Niro and Bill Gates, who told him "Geoffrey, you changed my life."

He loves to tell the story of how he once met the Duke of Suffolk on an A&K safari. "Suffolk," said the Duke, extending his hand. "Kent," Geoffrey replied, trying not to smile.

Over the years he also got to know most of East Africa's old-time game wardens including David Sheldrick, the legendary head warden of Tsavo National Park. "They were like gods to us," he says.

"One day my vehicle got bogged down in a waterhole in Tsavo and I'd forgotten to tell anyone where we were heading. I had clients with me and so when night came I rigged up a makeshift bed in a tree. There were lions all around, but eventually Sheldrick found us. He gave me such a bollocking but we still became friends afterwards."

Inevitably the talk gets around to what Kent calls 'laxative moments', like the time when he was on safari with Richard Burton and a buffalo crashed into their campfire with four lionesses on top of it. "When it was all over Burton was so impressed he asked me if I could arrange the same thing the following day."

In mid-morning we break off our conversation to welcome an old friend of Kent's. It is Dr Richard Leakey, a scion of Kenya's famous fossil-hunting family, who has flown in to join us for the next two days. Leakey is the man who gave up his search for the bones of our hominid ancestors to protect his country's living heritage of endangered wildlife. That was in 1989 when he set up the Kenya Wildlife Service, ordered his rangers to shoot elephant poachers on sight and torched 12 tons of confiscated ivory worth millions to ram home the message that trading in tusks was a dirty business.

His reward was a plane crash in 1993 – almost certainly sabotage – in which he lost both his legs below the knees. But his grit and determination survived, along with a restless mind and a wry sense of humour.

Walking slowly but unaided on his artificial legs he joins us in the clearing where the two men greet each other warmly, having known each other since they were children. "As kids growing up in those days, Richard and I thought nothing of going on 20-mile horseback rides," says Kent. "Our farms were so far apart, and so that's how people got around."

When at last the sun goes down, the campfire is lit and the pair of them sit, Tusker beers in hand, continuing to reminisce as lions roar on the distant plains and the sparks fly upwards into the vast African night. This is the time Kent loves best, after a day in the bush, when you end up swapping yarns in the firelight's glow.

Over dinner – a candle-lit feast of pumpkin soup and grilled lamb chops with South African wines in cut-glass goblets – Leakey tells the story of how, after the plane crash, he had his legs embalmed with a ten-year guarantee and kept them at his home on the edge of the Rift Valley until one day he decided he'd had enough of them and buried them under a tree. "Having had a funeral for one half of my body," he adds with a puckish grin, "I'm not worried about what happens to the rest of me."

He is pessimistic about the future of Kenya's wildlife, complains that the government is not doing enough to look after it. "I say to them, this is your oil and we should do everything we can to protect it if someone is trying to steal it."

But Kent remains upbeat. "Kenya is my country," he says. "Its wildlife is our heritage and I have a huge belief in the ability of the Kenyan people to succeed."

Chapter Two

Serengeti

February 1991: The Road to Ndutu

ALL the way from Arusha the land is dry. Beyond the banana groves of Mto-wa-Mbu, where the road toils up the Rift Valley wall, clouds of dust boil up in our wake, drifting away to where a snowdrift of pelicans is slowly turning in the hot air thermals over Lake Manyara.

But an hour later, entering the montane forests of the Ngorongoro Highlands, the air grows cooler and we drive on between huge mossy trees and banks of brilliant yellow canary bush. At the summit, arriving at Ngorongoro's crater rim, we break our journey to look down into the vast sunken caldera, 2,000 feet below. Was it only six months ago that I had watched the lions of Ngorongoro hunting zebras in the yellow grass? Now the grass is green again and from everywhere comes the gleam of water. There is no time to descend into the giant amphitheatre, but there will be predators enough where we are heading and, with mounting anticipation, we drive on.

Soon we are passing Lemagrut, its rounded slopes as green as Sussex, riven with dark gullies of juniper forest. And then, descending towards Olduvai comes the moment that never fails to lift my heart – the first glimpse of the Serengeti, a sunlit ocean of grass and cloud shadows rolling away past the distant Gol Mountains to the ends of the earth.

When it comes to national parks, Serengeti is simply the best. At upwards of 5,000 feet the light is dazzling. The air smells of dust and game and grasses that ripple for mile after mile in the dry highland wind, with seldom a road and never a fence in sight and nothing to break the distant skyline except for the kopjes – the granite inselbergs whose beckoning outlines seem to float on the horizon like fleets of battleships turned to stone.

Now only one question fills my mind. Where is the migration? Every year in January and February the Serengeti wildebeest gather in tens of thousands to produce their calves on these short grass plains. What draws them here is an unusually fertile soil, the result of fine ash spewed out by long-dead volcanoes. For half the year the land is dust, forsaken by all living things except a few kori bustards and Grant's gazelles, and underlain by a limestone crust that few roots can penetrate. But when it rains these barren plains produce a lush carpet of succulent grasses, attracting the heaviest concentration of grazing animals on earth.

At this time you can expect to see more than a million wildebeest, half a million gazelles and more than 200,000 zebras, together with their attendant predators: the lion, cheetah and spotted hyena whose presence, combined with the massed herds, gives these great open spaces of the Serengeti such a powerful sense of impending drama.

Yet in Africa nothing is certain. The grass rains of November had failed. Without grass, without water, the wildebeest would soon be forced to move on. And in a park the size of Holland, even a million wildebeest can be hard to find.

I need not have worried. Despite the drought the herds had come south as expected and were camped on the plains from Ndutu to the Gol Mountains and all the way down to Olduvai. There, since their arrival some weeks earlier, in the miraculous way of the wildebeest, they had been holding back the moment of birth until the rains began. Now it is mid-February and at last the skies have opened. All day long the rain bird, the red-chested cuckoo, cries 'it-will-rain, it-will-rain' in the acacia woodlands around Lake Ndutu. And every afternoon, sudden, violent storms trail across the greening plains.

This is the moment the herds have been waiting for since their time of conception during the full moon of May. Until now, newborn wildebeest have been few; but within a week, like a pent-up flood that can be contained no longer, the plains are alive with pale, gangling calves.

Many will not survive. Some will fall prey to lion and cheetah. Others will be drowned or crushed in the mad stampede across the Grumeti and Mara rivers when the herds trek north to Kenya in the dry season. But the rest will march on, an invincible army moving in long columns that might take three days and nights before the last stragglers pass over the horizon – a spectacle I had witnessed on a previous visit to Ndutu Safari Lodge.

❀   ❀   ❀

At Ndutu, the only lodge in the southern Serengeti, Aadje Geertsema, the Dutch-born owner, puts me in the picture. "It's been a strange migration," she says. "First, the El Niño rains disrupted the rut as the herds went north. Then the November rains failed, so the wildebeest stayed in Kenya until Christmas and Ndutu was still bone-dry until ten days ago."

To see the migration in full swing, she said, I should head out to Miti Mbili – Swahili for 'Two Trees' – a landmark on the open plains. And here, true to her word, the grasslands are black with wildebeest. As we drive forward into the midst of the herds they part to let us through, then close behind us like a tide.

Out on the plains the distances are so vast I feel we could drive right off the edge of the world. Ahead I can see the immense curve of the earth rolling through space, and the blue faraway hills of Lemuta, Lemagrut and Naabi hull down on the eastern skyline.

Against the light the plains are green velvet, strewn with white drifts of taka-taka flowers and the remains of old kills showing where the predators had claimed their tithe from the herds. In the Serengeti, beauty and danger go hand in hand; but when the herds are gathered for the season of birth there is nowhere else on earth so vibrantly alive.

Animals are moving in every direction. Not just wildebeest and zebra but Maasai giraffe and golden jackals, one-ton eland and delicate little bat-eared foxes. Swarms of fleet-footed Thomson gazelles dart this way and that like fishes. Zebra stallions squeal to their mares, and from all around us there rises a mournful, mumbling, grunting chorus – the contact calls of a million wildebeest.

From time to time a cheetah lifts its head from the grass to stare with burning agate eyes; and once we spook an African wild cat, the ancestor of our fireside tabby, which flees like a whiff of smoke.

Other migrations are also in full swing. White storks – elegant birds born on the church towers of Extremadura – stride among the grazing wildebeest in company with sudden flurries of European barn swallows, and the skies are alive with eagles and vultures.

Back at the Ndutu woodlands we stop on a ridge overlooking the swamps where, earlier in the day we had watched a serval cat hunting in the reeds. Now it is hot and the wildebeest are streaming in from the plains to drink. Over the rise they pour, like the US Cavalry, thundering along under a banner of dust. We watch for an hour and still there is no end to them.

In his novel, *The Roots of Heaven*, Romain Gary saw the African elephant as a giant symbol of liberty; but for me the wildebeest migration is a far more potent metaphor. To watch that living mass of animals swarming over the plains, to live under canvas in the sun and the wind and to wake at dawn to the song of the lion is to breathe the air of a vanishing freedom and hope that whatever happens to the rest of the world, Serengeti must never die.

August 1991: Looking for Leopards

L YING across the main migration route in the very epicentre of the Serengeti, the Seronera River Valley is renowned for its large lion prides. But sharing this corner of the park is another top predator whose existence is a prime reason for coming here.

Along the river and its brush-choked *korongos*, or seasonal watercourses, grow dense stands of wild date palms, yellow-barked acacias and shady kigelias – a tree highly favoured by leopards.

Notoriously shy, solitary and largely nocturnal, the leopard is hard to find. But it is also the most beautiful of all African animals, and therefore the one every visitor wants to see.

It is Ben Kilule, my Tanzanian driver, who guides us to the leopard. The safari grapevine had spread the news. The elusive *madoa-doa* ('spots') had been seen earlier by a group of tourists from Seronera Safari Lodge, and we set off in pursuit straight away. To my surprise we find it not by the river but far out on the plain in a solitary acacia, draped along a branch six metres above the ground.

She is also asleep, which in leopard terms means that even when her eyes are closed her ears twitch and turn, constantly monitoring the sounds of the savannah; the keening kites, the crooning doves, the grassland cries of pipits and longclaws.

It is still early afternoon, so we decide to leave the leopard and return to it later after a game drive to Banagi, where a large breeding herd of elephants has been reported.

The presence of elephants in the Serengeti is good news. Poaching in the 1980s had decimated the Serengeti elephants and driven the survivors to seek refuge across the border in the more intensively patrolled sanctuary of Kenya's Maasai Mara National Reserve. But now, two years after the world had decided to ban the ivory trade, the tuskers are beginning to return to their former haunts.

In the end we never catch up with the elephants although we find where they have been feeding, the broken branches stripped of bark, the trampled grass and smell of fresh dung; but the herd itself has marched on into the fathomless thickets of the northern woodlands.

So an hour before sunset we return to Seronera to find the leopard still in its tree.

Thunder rumbles across the plains. A storm is brewing. In the intervening silence a solitary Cape turtledove pleads with Africa to 'work-harder, work-harder', and still the leopard sleeps.

The sun passes down. The storm draws closer. At last the leopard awakes, stands, stretches luxuriously, digging her claws into the bark, then slides headfirst down the trunk in a single fluid movement. There she pauses, sniffing intently at the base of the tree, pees against it to leave her own pungent calling card, and then walks out into the oncoming rain with the white tip of her tail raised like a flag above the waving grass-heads. Then she vanishes, as leopards do, melting away into the fast-falling dusk.

February 1992: The Nomad of Naabi Hill

THE Gol Kopjes have always been one of my favourite parts of the Serengeti; an African Dartmoor expanded to infinity, its every skyline pricked by the horned silhouettes of antelope and gazelle. Here year after year I would come with Baron Hugo van Lawick, the great East African film maker, setting out before dawn from his camp at Ndutu to record the lives of the big cats that roam across these rock-strewn plains.

The kopjes themselves have a life of their own. Each one is a citadel, haunted by Cape rooks and barn owls, a watchtower for cheetahs, a refuge where lionesses can give birth to their cubs, where red-and-blue agama lizards bask on the bare granite and lanner falcons hang in the up-draughts.

To set out into the deep silence of the plains is to know the solitary joys of the long-distance yachtsman. Adrift in this wild and lovely country you feel you could drive forever and never have enough of it. The land has a swell to it, a slow rise and fall like the sea, and each new fold hides a fresh surprise; a carpet of vultures on a kill, a female cheetah and her cubs, a herd of eland running from some real or imagined danger.

Today's richest prize is a solitary male lion resting in the shade of a lone thorn tree not far from the park's southern entrance at Naabi Hill. The tree's twisted trunk forms a natural arch beneath which the old lion sprawls, his huge forepaws clutching a dead gazelle. As I watch he begins to feed, rasping away the white belly fur with his tongue before biting into the flesh.

This lion is a nomad, an old warrior cast out from his pride, living by robbery and intimidation. I later learn from another driver that he had earlier stolen the dead gazelle, having chased away the two Naabi Hill lionesses that had killed it.

His broad muzzle bears the scars of many battles. Maybe twelve times in his life he must have witnessed the annual arrival of the great migration on these short grass plains. Now his race is almost run. He has lost all his lower incisors and one of his bottom canines, so that when he eats, crunching through bone and gristle, he must lay his head on one side in order to bring his powerful carnassials to bear. But he is still a splendid specimen, with a black mane falling like a rug around his shoulders, and for now and a little while longer, this is his land, his kingdom of the grass.

March 1995: Chasing Shadows in the Grass

FOR so many years I have known the Serengeti and its magic never palls. The skies are huge. Colossal thunderheads trail shawls of rain across horizons that seem like the edge of the world. Larks and plovers cry on the wind. Flights of sandgrouse rush overhead, and the plains are smothered in constellations of gazelles.

Bu this is also the land of the quick and the dead. Among the gazelles roam murderous clans of spotted hyenas, the hunchbacked gangsters of the grasslands, armed with the most powerful jaws in Africa; and even as I watch, a Thomson gazelle fawn is run down and dispatched with ruthless efficiency, attracting vultures from miles around.

We camp at Nasera Orok – the Black Rock of the Maasai – a granite monolith the size of York Minster. Rising abruptly from the grass, it guards the entrance to Ang'ata Kiti, the main pass through the Gol Mountains to the Saleh Plains beyond.

Fig trees sprout from its weather-stained flanks. Olive baboons scale its 330-foot-high cliffs, and lanner falcons – the birds that Richard Knocker calls 'the cheetahs of the air' – nest on its inaccessible ledges. It is one of the sacred places of wild Africa, and at its feet our tents have been miraculously assembled, looking out into the immensity of the Ngorongoro Conservation Area.

Knocker is acknowledged as one of East Africa's finest professional safari guides. He describes his life as "a charmed existence, doing what I love best, looking at awesome animals in beautiful places." Time spent in his company is a priceless education in the lore of the wild, but he is also great fun to be with. "You need a sense of humour for this job," he says. Hence his perfect description of a scrum of vultures we had seen near camp, waddling towards a hyena kill with their 'John Wayne' walk.

His favourite animal is the cheetah. "It's that extraordinary blend of grace and vulnerability that gets to me," he says; and so it is cheetahs that we go looking for when we set out from Nasera Orok, chasing cloud shadows across an ocean of grass. In places the skyline is broken by kopjes whose tumbled rocks and shady fig trees are a favourite hiding place for all manner of creatures. But of cheetahs there is no sign.

By now the sun is up. We cross a seasonal watercourse, the Ngare Nanyuki ('Red Water'), where zebras are drinking from shallow pools, and find ourselves a sheltering kopje where we stop for breakfast – fresh mango, toasted egg-and-bacon sandwiches and a flask of coffee – before resuming our search.

There is no shortage of prey. We drive all morning, past herds of Thomson's gazelles, yet still the cheetahs frustrate us.

But Knocker is not to be denied. He simply quotes an old safari saying: "Patience is the key to the larder." And so in the afternoon, with storm clouds towering on the horizon, we try again.

Rain sweeps towards us, obscuring the Ngorongoro Highlands, then passes on, leaving the air pure and fresh-minted. The sun reappears, washing the plains in a golden light, and as we come over a rise we almost run down a mother cheetah with three small cubs.

We do not pursue them as they race away, but watch from a distance as they settle down beside a kopje, where the cubs romp and chase each other over the rocks. Entranced, we stay until the sun goes down.

In the morning we go looking for them again, circling every lonely kopje, praying for a repeat performance; but, like the restless spirits they are, they have vanished into the boundless plains.

July 1996: The Pools of Kirawira

HERE in the Serengeti's Western Corridor tourists are fewer, the animals are still shy and the land still wild, its stony hills framing immense vistas of whistling thornbush and open plains strewn with the bones of old lion kills.

In places the entire landscape resembles a charnel house of bleached bones and horned skulls; yet butterflies dance over the dismantled skeletons and chaste white taka-taka flowers spring from empty eye sockets, underlining the eternal truth of the Serengeti, where life and death walk hand-in-hand.

At the edge of the plains, two lionesses sleep outstretched in the grass. Having just killed a wildebeest and eaten their fill they have abandoned the carcass to a seething mass of white-backed vultures. Even as I watch, more vultures come planing in. These are bigger birds, lappet-faced vultures with livid heads.

They fall across the grass like shrouds, and then goose-step forward with necks outstretched, hissing at the smaller white-backs who reluctantly give way before them. Gruesome they may be, but vultures are a vital part of nature's sanitation squad. Each year in the Serengeti they dispose of about 12,000 tonnes of carrion.

When at last the carcass has been stripped bare the birds lumber into the air to digest their feast in the treetops along the banks of the Grumeti, where drought has reduced the river to a chain of stagnant green pools.

These are the pools of Kirawira, home of the infamous Grumeti crocodiles, which are among the largest in Africa. Some are man-eaters and the biggest of all is Edgar, an 18-foot monster with bulldozer jaws and a beer-drinker's paunch big enough to hold the best part of a wildebeest.

According to Alan Root, the doyen of East African wildlife film makers, Kirawira was named after a poacher who disappeared after trying to swim across the crocodile-infested river to evade capture by a ranger patrol. A year later, when the river dried up, the buckle of his boy-scout belt was found, its motto still legible: 'Be Prepared'.

Even without their man-eating reputation these terrible old murderers are the stuff of horror movies. For most of the year they live in a state of suspended animation, waiting for the migration to arrive. When the wildebeest come to drink, the crocs explode from the water like Exocet missiles to grab them. For a few brief weeks they gorge themselves. Then the wildebeest move on, the river dries up and the crocodiles resume their months-long sleep.

Kusini, July 1996: The Cheetah that Came for Breakfast

IT is two months since the last rain fell at Kusini and the dry season wind brings the smell of bush fires from Maswa Game Reserve outside the park, where hunters have fired the grass to encourage new growth and entice the herds when the rains return.

Every day the huge Serengeti skies are filled with a pall of smoke, and at night the flickering red necklaces of flame draw ever closer. All over Africa it is the time of burning.

In the mornings, after the fires had died down overnight, solemn processions of bustards and ground hornbills stalk through the ashes, snapping up the incinerated corpses of lizards, snakes and locusts.

Up at first light on an early morning game drive our route lies along the banks of the Simiyu River, a seasonal watercourse in whose undergrowth the big cats love to conceal themselves. Up ahead is a dead tree filled with waiting vultures, and sure enough, as we draw closer I catch the twitch of an ear in silhouette under a thornbush.

Three lionesses of the Kusini pride are sprawled around their prey – a young giraffe they must have ambushed in the night and dragged into the bushes to devour at their leisure.

Next morning they are still there, but accompanied this time by three small cubs. While their mothers tear at the half-eaten giraffe, shearing through skin and sinews with their sharp carnassials, the cubs romp around the carcass, hiding in its cave of ribs and then rushing out to pounce on each other in the flattened grass.

Later, driving on across the fire-blackened plains, we find a shady spot under a tree and stop for a picnic breakfast, and then an extraordinary thing happens. No sooner had we set out chairs and tables and begun to munch into our bacon sandwiches than a cheetah appears on the skyline, a taut and quivering creature whose presence seems to dominate the land for miles around.

We sit still and wait as the cheetah draws closer, still walking unhurriedly in our direction. It must have seen us, yet it seems totally unconcerned at our presence and passes within a few metres of us without even turning its head. Instead it walks on at a steady pace, as if intent on a mission, until eventually it is lost to view behind a ridge.

My breakfast encounter with the cheetah reminded me of a story told to me in Arusha by David Keith Jones, the East African wildlife photographer, of when he had taken his father on safari for the first time. "In Africa you don't have to exaggerate what you have seen," said his father, who was clearly overwhelmed by the experience of coming face to face with big game. "Even if I tell the truth, nobody back home will believe me."

Back in camp at the end of the day I take a cold beer and climb up a nearby kopje to watch the sun go down, and later still, when a full moon hangs over Kusini and the whole world is wrapped in black-and-silver darkness, I lie in my tent and listen to the war-whoop of hyenas, the grunting of the Kusini lions somewhere out on the open grasslands and the gunshot cracks of burning thorn trees as the flames continue their relentless advance through the surrounding woodlands.

January 1999: Ngorongoro Crater

AT six in the morning Ngorongoro is still a mystery wrapped in darkness. But half an hour later the red light of an East African highland dawn is already pouring over the crater rim, shining on Lake Magadi far below and illuminating the delicate calligraphy of game trails and water courses on the floor of this stupendous 100-square-mile amphitheatre.

Three million years ago when Ngorongoro was as high as Mt Kilimanjaro, the ash spewed from its enormous crater created the mineral-rich Serengeti plains at its feet.

Then the volcano died. Its cone imploded and Tanzania was left with the world's largest unbroken caldera.

As always, I follow the old familiar mountain road through the Lodoare Gate and into the cloud forest, past the hollows gouged into the red earth banks by elephants tusking for mineral salts, and on up between the graceful stands of pillar-wood trees and gnarled old *Nuxia* (wild elder) festooned with moss to emerge at last on the very lip of the crater.

There is a viewpoint here, and a memorial surmounted by a buffalo skull, honouring a long line of conservationists and including the names of two Tanzanian rangers shot dead by poachers in 1978; and beyond and below lies the immense bowl of the caldera, a lost world entire in itself, complete with acacia forests, flamingo lakes and green-gold plains where 10,000 wildebeest, 5,000 zebras and 3,000 buffaloes provide food for the famous Ngorongoro lions.

Today the crater is protected as part of the Ngorongoro Conservation Area, which stretches from Tanzania's Great Rift Valley to the Serengeti. The whole area, including the lesser-known craters of Olmoti and Empakaai, covers 2,500 square miles and is home to 40,000 Maasai pastoralists and their herds, who live side by side with the wildlife.

Down on the crater floor, driving over the open grasslands towards Engitati – a flat-topped hill known to the Tanzanian safari guides as the Golan Heights – everything is as I remember: avocets stepping over their pin-sharp reflections in the Goose Marshes; flamingos shuffling in candy-floss clouds around the soda-crust rim of Lake Magadi and hippos wallowing in Mandusi Swamp.

Zebras run squealing through the morning sunshine and spotted hyenas slouch past in the background, heading home to their dens after a night of butchery. But where are the lions? On previous visits they have always been so easy to find.

Not so today. El Niño, it seems, is to blame. So much rain fell at the beginning of last year that the crater flooded and was closed to tourists. Washed out from their pride territories, a ranger tells me, many lions were forced to flee and take their chances in the Serengeti. Now, a year later, they have still not returned and the resident population has fallen from 60-plus to just 32 adults.

At least the surviving prides are all busily producing cubs to fill the vacuum, and one of the highlights of my visit is watching a lioness suckling her three tiny cubs in a patch of reeds and then leading them into the open to meet the rest of the pride – perhaps for the first time – as they sprawl at the edge of a hippo pool.

Other predators have been quick to take advantage of the reduction in lion numbers, and I spot two male cheetahs moving with infinite stealth towards a small group of Grant's gazelles. What neither the cheetahs nor I have noticed is that one of the gazelles has just given birth. Its fawn is hidden in the long grass, but as soon as it stands up the cheetahs see it, and a life that has barely begun is snuffed out before the sun is halfway across the sky.

In the late afternoons huge storm clouds pile up, trailing dark veils of rain across the crater, and if Ngorongoro could be said to have a springtime it is surely now in this season of renewal when white flowers appear overnight, stippling the greening plains with their delicate blossoms, and the crowned cranes pair off, facing each other with fluttering wings as they rise and fall through the elegant ritual of their courtship dance.

On one such afternoon I come upon five rare black rhinos – almost one third of Ngorongoro's entire population. Thirty years ago it might have been possible to see a hundred rhinos in the crater. But that was when the whole of Tanzania had more than 20,000, before the poaching holocaust of the 1970s and 1980s all but finished them off. Since then they have slowly edged back from the brink. None has been poached since 1995 and there are now maybe 18 or more roaming across the crater floor.

January 2003: The Big Empty

OUT on the Serengeti Plains a wildebeest licks her newborn calf. Its ginger fur is still wet from the womb, yet already the youngster is striving to stand. Now, with vultures dropping in to feed on the placenta, there is no time to lose.

Even as I watch, three hyenas come loping over the rise, maybe half a mile distant.

They run slowly, sniffing the air as they rock over the grass with heads held high. Is this a tragedy in the making?

By now the mother wildebeest has seen the hyenas and is urging her calf to run. But the youngster can manage only a few wobbly steps before its spindly legs buckle and it falls in a heap. Anxiously the mother nudges the calf to its feet again, and all the while the hyenas are gaining ground. Then inexplicably they lose interest and go lolloping away through the assembled herds.

Having watched the calf tumble into the world only moments before, I am hugely relieved to see it survive its first day. But the episode demonstrates a profound truth about wildebeest: from the moment they are born, every day is a race for life.

The wildebeest, it has been unkindly said, is an antelope designed by a committee: a mad, cavorting, capering beast with an ashen coat and an old man's beard and a head that looks too big for its body. It has the horns of an ox, the mane of a horse and the sloping hindquarters of a hyena. But look again and what you see is a miracle of endurance, the most numerous and the most successful of all African plains game.

Every year the Serengeti wildebeest travel more than 1,200 miles, chasing the life-renewing rains. The only constant in their lives is their return each rainy season to the place where they were born. Every year, 600,000 calves are dropped on these short-grass plains in the south of the park. Most arrive in February, at the rate of about 8,000 a day, and in a land with little or no cover it is a crude but effective survival strategy; for there are so many that the lions, cheetahs and hyenas simply cannot eat them all.

The wildebeest remain on the southern plains throughout the rainy season. With them are 350,000 zebras and a similar number of gazelles. But in May, when the grass turns to stubble and the last waterholes dry up, they stream away to the north and west on the long trek that will eventually lead them to their dry season refuge in Kenya's Maasai Mara National Reserve.

Along the way all kinds of perils lie in wait. Every year, thousands of wildebeest and zebras die cruel deaths in meat poachers' snares. Many are killed by lions, which can easily put away 70 pounds of meat at a sitting, or are pulled down by hungry clans of spotted hyenas; and others fall prey to the notorious Grumeti River crocodiles.

But the great majority come through unscathed. Led by an advance guard of zebras, they arrive in the Mara like a conquering army, crossing and re-crossing the treacherous Mara River in their constant search for grass.

At least fifteen times in the past three decades I have witnessed this extraordinary spectacle and two things above all I have learned. No two migrations are ever the same; and timing is crucial if you want to see it.

November 2005: The Ruwana Plains

WHAT a difference a week can make in Africa. Five days earlier the Serengeti was a dustbowl. The wildebeest herds had long since trekked north to Kenya, and along the Grumeti River in the park's Western Corridor, hippos were dying for want of water.

Hippos need water in which to submerge. Without it they are at risk of dehydration and heat exhaustion, and as the river ceased to flow they crammed together in the last remaining muddy hollows in a desperate bid to survive. After dark they would emerge from the riverbed, following their well-worn hippo highways out onto the margins of the plains, where they would walk for up to six miles every night in search of grass. But a full-grown hippo needs to chomp its way through at least 40 kilograms of grass a night to stay alive, and the grazing areas along the river had been all but exhausted by the drought.

Now at last, the *kiangazi* – 'the dry season' – has ended. The November rains have broken with a vengeance and the Grumeti hippos are wallowing to their hearts' content in the pools beyond my tent.

Almost overnight, the Serengeti has been transformed. Already the acacia trees that grow along the river had burst into blossom in anticipation of the rains. Now the air is heavy with their sweet scent and iridescent sunbirds flit like green and scarlet jewels among the flowers in search of nectar.

Across the river lies the Ruwana Plain, a classic Serengeti landscape of grass and gazelles and flat-roofed thorn trees, and I love driving out there in the early mornings to look for lions on Masira Hill.

From its rock summit in every direction the Serengeti stretches to infinity. This is true parkland, graced by widely spaced *Balanites* trees whose parasol canopies cast dark shadows in the morning light; and wherever I look the grasslands are teeming with life; not only the ubiquitous wildebeest and zebras, but giraffes and topi, eland and impalas, jackals, baboons, bat-eared foxes and ground hornbills whose muttering voices carry far in the windless air.

Then back to camp for breakfast: eggs and bacon, Kilimanjaro coffee and fresh raspberries flown in from Arusha – and paradise flycatchers with rufous tails darting among the acacia branches above my table.

November 2005: Kogakuria Kopjes and the Lamai Wedge

"THIS is as far as most visitors get," says Paul Oliver as we head into the Serengeti's northern woodlands. Oliver is an Englishman from Norfolk who moved to Tanzania 30 years ago and is now one of the country's foremost professional safari guides. We had arranged to meet at Seronera, in the heart of the park, and from there we set off in his distinctive coffee-brown Land Rover.

He was right. Once we crossed the Orangi River we did not see another vehicle until we hit camp seven hours later. We could have flown – there is an airstrip nearby – but only when you travel overland does the sheer size of the Serengeti impress itself upon you.

In coming here I had realised a lifetime's ambition. The Kenyan border is just a few miles from camp, and on the other side is the Maasai Mara National Reserve, an area as familiar to me as the hills of home in England.

For years I had longed to follow the migrating wildebeest as they poured back into Tanzania after their sojourn in the Mara; but the border had been closed to visitors since 1977 and I could only watch with envy as the herds thundered south into the boundless Serengeti.

Now, miraculously, here I am, on a granite hill called Kogakuria, surrounded by ancient fig trees and giant kopjes that pierce the infinity of plain and sky, and at this moment, with the migrating wildebeest all around us, there is nowhere else I would rather be.

You couldn't design a better big cat habitat than this tumbledown chaos of cottage-size boulders. Every night echoes to the hacksaw cough of prowling leopards, and not a day passes without lions posing against the blue on a granite dome or else staring sphinx-like into the distance where Mlima Saba – 'the Seven Hills' – mark the beginning of the Maasai Mara. No wonder Myles Turner, last of the old-time Serengeti wardens, loved this area above all others. ·

Lions are not the only creatures to seek the shelter of the kopjes. Agile klipspringers – small antelopes that stand on tiptoe like ballet dancers – keep watch from these enigmatic rock castles, and fig trees rooted among their weathered crevices provide fruit for green pigeons and deep shade for eagle owls.

Kogakuria is the highest point for miles around, and what you get from its boulder-strewn slopes is a vulture's eye panorama of yellow plains mapped with the green veins of seasonal watercourses and bounded by the distant walls of the Siria escarpment.

From Paul's campsite among the rocks I can look deep into Kenya. At night the lights of Keekorok Safari Lodge glitter in the darkness, some 40 miles away; and next morning, as I watch the hot air balloons rising from Little Governors' Camp, I know that vehicles by the score will be fanning out all over the Mara in search of cats. But on our side of the border we have Africa to ourselves.

Off-track driving is still allowed in the north, and over the next few days Paul and I explore the surrounding maze of nameless valleys. The gift of rain has renewed the land, and wherever we go there is life. Oribi – dainty antelopes with black button noses – browse on green lawns that were dust and stubble a week ago. Sentinel klipspringers frequent the kopjes, and herds of eland with swinging dewlaps trot away at our approach.

There are birds, too; shrikes and orioles, hornbills, wood hoopoes, and a sinister pair of lappet-faced vultures with livid skulls and meat hook beaks. "Nature's can-openers," Oliver calls them.

Elephants are moving solemnly across the plains below, and when we stop above a broad valley to scan the far side with binoculars a lion suddenly swims into focus, picking its way between the rocks. Even from half-a-mile away I can see it is a male, a magnificent beast with a heavy mane.

The abundance of game is indescribable. This is like the Maasai Mara I knew 30 years ago, with animals as far as the eye can see, and huge river crossings when the migration is on the move. One day, out driving from dawn to dusk, the only other vehicle we see is a national park Land Rover full of armed rangers in green combat fatigues.

How could this idyllic corner of the Serengeti have been overlooked for so long? To find out you have only to drive past the Fort Knox-style guard post at Kogatende on the Mara River. Only a few years ago this was bandit country, with heavily armed poaching gangs swarming down from the Isuria escarpment to prey on wildlife and tourists alike. Now the worst of the poachers have fled. Their campfires are cold and the north is safe again for visitors.

From Kogatende it is only a short drive into the Lamai Wedge, a sublime sweep of rolling savannah between the Mara River and the Kenyan border. The contrast with the rock-strewn hillsides and fig tree groves of Kogakuria could not be greater. Here the land is open to the sky, an endless sea of grass in which Thomson's gazelles race this way and that, like shoals of fish, and the wind carries the sounds of the plains, the sad cries of pipits, the shrieks of crowned plovers.

To the north rise Mlima Saba, the hills where Myles Turner's ashes were scattered, and steadily we climb towards them, scouring the grasslands for cheetahs. We find lions aplenty, hiding in the croton thickets and resting on the stony ridges where they can catch the breeze; but the cheetahs Paul had seen a week ago have moved on in the wake of the wildebeest herds, leaving only the slouching shapes of spotted hyenas and the remains of old kills picked clean by vultures.

November 2005: Klein's Camp

I WAS sad to have missed out on the cheetahs but there was still a chance to find them after Paul had dropped me off at Klein's Camp, the private 100,000 hectare concession adjoining the park's northeast boundary.

Al Klein was an American big game hunter who hung out here in the 1920s, and although the name has stuck the ethos has changed completely. These days conservation is the buzzword, and Klein's Camp Safari Lodge, overlooking a hidden valley in the Kuka Hills, is Hemingway's Africa at its best.

Cape buffaloes scowl from its thorny thickets and it had been a long time since I encountered such feisty lions. On one game drive we tracked down a coalition of five young males, fired up with testosterone and looking for trouble. One, a wild-looking tearaway with a rag-tag mane, broke away from his companions and chased us as we drove away.

In the valley bottom, water trickles from pool to pool under a dark canopy of fig trees. This is the Grumeti – the same river that flows out into Lake Victoria through the Western Corridor – and its source is in the hills above. My guide tells me it is a famous place for leopards. But as so often happens in Africa we chance instead upon something quite different, and, in its own way, no less dramatic: a martial eagle, like an emblem from a heraldic banner, glaring at us with mad yellow eyes from its perch in a dead tree.

On we go, climbing in low gear away from the riverbed until finally, in the last hour of daylight with the Kuka Hills already in shadow, we come upon a cheetah on the plains and watch her methodically sniff out a topi fawn in the long grass. For the cheetah and for us, too, it is the perfect end to a perfect East African day.

October 2011: The Crossing

SNUG in my tent in the northern Serengeti, I listen to the strange pulsing cries of a swamp nightjar in the surrounding trees. But later, when the nightjar has fallen silent and dawn seeps through the canvas, a lion begins to roar not far off. I dress hurriedly, step outside and eventually pick him out with my binoculars where he sprawls at full length on a granite kopje, gold mane on fire in the morning sun. What a way to start the day.

Every year, drawn by the presence of some 3,000 lions and above all by the spectacle of the wildebeest migration, more than 90,000 visitors flock to what has become the world's most famous national park. Yet distances are so vast that it is still possible to find space and solitude, especially in the Serengeti's far northern reaches whose horizons are still empty of everything except wildlife.

This is Tanzania's Top End, with nothing but a line of white stones in the grass separating the Serengeti from Kenya's Maasai Mara National Reserve. The migrating wildebeest cross this unfenced border with impunity every year but only recently, after decades of lawlessness, has tourism taken root on these remote savannahs.

Among the safari specialists who have moved in are &Beyond, a Johannesburg-based company whose up-market portfolio of camps and lodges is matched by a long-standing commitment to conservation.

In 2006 they came up with the idea of Serengeti Under Canvas, a seasonal camp with the lightest of footprints that would move to different locations during the year so that guests would never be more than an hour's drive from the migration, and this is where I am staying, in a dappled grove with far-reaching views into Kenya.

Not even Hemingway in his heyday enjoyed such comforts as those provided by its nine spacious walk-in tents, each one a khaki cave of comfort with en-suite loos, hot bucket showers, and polished brass bowls for washing and shaving. Persian rugs complete the picture and nothing is left to chance. There are even brollies for wet days and hot-water bottles for chilly nights. Five-star camping this may be, but it is offered with an elegant simplicity that sits easily in its pristine surroundings.

Around the camp lies a sea of bush, a neglected orchard of small crooked trees lit up by the dazzle of galloping zebras. Through the leafy canopy loom granite whalebacks – including the one where I saw the lion – leading to a wild, broken country of rocky ridges and grassy clefts in which steep-sided *korongos* wind down to the Bologonja River.

In November the camp moves south, following the herds to a new location in the Seronera Valley; and in January it moves again to be on the spot for the season of birth on the short grass plains between Lake Ndutu and the Gol Mountains. But it is here in this far northwest corner of the park that the big river crossings take place, and if you don't want to miss them, this is the place to be.

Delayed by the onset of the rains, the wildebeest had been massing for days in the Lamai Wedge. Now, driven by the urge to return to their calving grounds, there is no stopping them. Regardless of the waiting crocodiles they pour across the fast-flowing Mara River.

With me is Les Carlisle, &Beyond's group conservation manager, who has just flown in from Johannesburg to join me. He is a man who has spent his whole working life in the bush, yet even he is rendered speechless by the drama unfolding around our Land Cruiser. "Unbelievable," is all he can say, over and over again as we watch them plunging headlong into the water.

Mercifully, we witness only one casualty, a yearling wildebeest dragged under by a monster crocodile, and even while the crossing is at its height the other river creatures – hippos, storks and malachite kingfishers – get on with their lives as if nothing is happening. Nearby is a lioness, fast asleep in a thicket, her belly distended by an earlier meal; and at one point an Egyptian goose with a dozen fluffy goslings paddle serenely through the midst of the panic-stricken herds.

An hour later the wildebeest are still storming across in wave after wave of tossing heads, eyes rolling in panic until they stumble clear of the water and thunder past us on either side; and for the next few days the wildebeest are all around camp, filling the air with their sonorous groans as they swarm among the trees, coalescing like molasses on the open hillsides before streaming away in unbroken columns that stretch for miles.

November 2011: Nyamalumbwa

THE area I love best lies to the north of Bologonja Springs, where immense plains roll away to the Nyamalumbwa Hills. This is new country for me – the final piece of the Serengeti jigsaw and every bit as uplifting as the more familiar grasslands in the south of the park. "You'll love it," said my old friend Paul Oliver, who had guided me around the Lamai Wedge in 2005, and he is right.

Apart from the desert dates whose parasol shapes graced every skyline, the plains are virtually treeless. Jackals rise out of the land and trot away at our approach.

Eland run along the horizon and the clear highland air is filled with the guttural cries of sandgrouse.

Late afternoon storms had replenished the plains, greening the hillsides where drifts of white taka-taka flowers now blossom among the scattered bones of old kills.

In this infinity of grass and cloud shadows we drive all day and never see another soul. We search for cheetahs but instead, far out in the all-embracing loneliness of the plains we come upon a pair of mating lions, lying as if half-drugged by the heat and oblivious to the European swallows hawking for insects about their ears.

Back in camp at end of day, I arrive to find that sundowners have been arranged on a nearby kopje. Red Maasai blankets have been laid out on the flat granite rocks, and here I sit in the deepening amber light, cold beer in hand, looking out over what feels like the whole of Africa as thunder rumbles in the hills and curtains of rain trail over the plains.

Chapter Three

Northern Kenya

May 1977: Saving Grevy's Zebra

"KANGANI," says Nyangau, Don Hunt's Turkana tracker, pointing to a speck a mile away on the desert horizon. It is the word Hunt and I have been hoping to hear all morning. It is his name for the animal better known as the Grevy's zebra, and Nyangau assures us this is the stallion whose spoor we found the previous day.

Straight away Hunt slams the truck into gear and we lurch off in hot pursuit. As the distance closes the zebra looks up, big bat ears cocked in our direction, then sets off at a canter that becomes a gallop as we increase our speed. "He's trying to get into the bush," yells Hunt, and we slew round in a swirl of dust to try and head him off.

Chasing zebras is a high-risk business. The plains of Kenya's wild Northern Province are riddled with warthog holes and criss-crossed with *luggas* – the dried-up watercourses that appear unseen as you career through the bush at 60 mph – and it was just such an obstacle that hospitalised two of Hunt's catching team with broken limbs the week before I arrived.

Now all sense of danger is forgotten in the thrill of the chase. Going flat out, we miss an aardvark burrow by inches. Had we not, it would have done for us all. Veering this way and that, we smash through thornbushes, pulverising them into a million fragments that fly overhead in a spattering slipstream.

As we draw closer, clods of red earth kicked up by the zebra's hooves smash against the windscreen, and Ngatia, the Kikuyu catcher, standing braced inside the rubber tyre that protects his ribs, swings the noose of his lasso on its bamboo pole until it is almost within reach of the tossing head. But time and again, like a rugby football three-quarter, the stallion jinks and swerves at the last moment, leaving us floundering in a four-wheel drift.

Time is running out fast. If we don't catch him soon we shall have to abort; otherwise the animal will die from exhaustion and shock. Once more we draw alongside and this time Ngatia makes no mistake. The noose drops over the zebra's head, and we skid to a stop with the stallion plunging on the end of the line like a fighting marlin.

Within minutes the support truck has caught us up and the rest of Hunt's crew leap out to grab the zebra by its ears and tail, hogtie its legs, administer a tranquillising shot, patch up a wound on its flank with a bright purple antibiotic and haul it into a crate. "Dammit," says Hunt, slapping the dust off his hands, "that was the smartest zebra I've ever caught in my life."

Later, back in camp near the great, slab-sided mountain of Ololokwe, Hunt admits he should not have pursued it for so long. But he knew that if he failed its days were numbered, and it would most likely end up being shot by poachers and its skin nailed to the floor of a rich man's penthouse.

🐾   🐾   🐾

Grevy's zebra is the world's biggest and most beautiful wild equid. Once
it roamed in herds hundreds strong from Lake Turkana to the Tana River
and on up into Somalia and Ethiopia. In Kenya alone its numbers were put
at more than 15,000. But that was in the 1960s, since when poaching has
virtually wiped out the Somali and Ethiopian herds and reduced Kenya's
Grevy's to no more than a thousand.

Don Hunt was one of the first to know that all was not well with
the Grevy's, whose elegant coat of slimline stripes had become a prime
target for the *shifta*, the Somali bandit gangs who were making a killing out
of the skin trade. Hunt is a genial, sun-bleached American better known
for running the Mount Kenya Game Ranch in partnership with William
Holden, the movie star. Having thrown up a prosperous television career in
Detroit, he had moved to Kenya and become a hunter until, sickened by the
bloodletting, he had turned trapper instead.

In 1975, following a shock report on the status of the Grevy's zebra
that showed its population in terminal decline, he devised a plan with
Kenya's national park wardens and went to see the government. The
result was Operation Zebra, which gave Hunt permission to catch 140
Grevy's and translocate them from the danger zone to the safety of the
game parks.

It is a controversial scheme and Hunt himself a controversial figure
involved in a business that has raised plenty of hackles among Nairobi's
conservationist circles. But Hunt is unrepentant. "Make no mistake," he
says firmly. The Grevy is doomed outside the parks. If the poachers don't get
them, the lions will. In a couple of years they will all be gone."

According to his reckoning at least 8,000 Grevy's have been poached in
the last three years, sending the price of skins soaring from $150 to $2,000.
"Think about it," he says. "If there are 1,000 Grevy's left, that represents $2
million still running around out there."

By the time I joined him the operation has already cost Hunt $28,000. Or, as he puts it, "nearly $1,000 for every zebra I've saved". But if he is right in moving these gorgeous, jug-headed animals down to Tsavo National Park, then it is worth every last cent.

We catch no more zebras during my stay, but on the last day we come across the totally unexpected sight of a herd of fifty Grevy's to the north of Ololokwe. We find them just as the sun is coming up over the horizon, and as I watch their dazzling pinstriped bodies wheeling and turning as one, kicking up a haze of dust that hangs like gold in the desert air, it dawns on me that I may be witnessing a momentous occasion. Here is a spectacle that soon might never be seen again: a herd of Grevy's zebras running free as the wind across the land that has been their home since the time when man was born.

October 1979: The Night of the Lion

NORTHERN Kenya is a harsh and unforgiving land, yet its beauty is undeniable, its wildness unsurpassed. Here, as soon as you leave the beaten track, disappearing into the fathomless commiphora thickets and heat-hazy mountains, you can feel the years falling away and imagine yourself in the Africa of a century ago when there were no 4WD vehicles to ease your passage through the bush.

This is the age that Julian McKeand has managed to recapture, if only for a week or so at a time, by organising camel safaris into Samburu country from his home in the shadow of Mt Kenya.

McKeand is a former game warden who later became a professional hunter before hitting on the idea of running camel safaris for Kenya's growing numbers of tourists.

Everything is as authentic as McKeand can make it, from the camels themselves to their clanking wooden bells and the ex-British

Army saddles made by Makhanbal & Sons of Bikaner, India, in the last days of the Raj.

Camel trekking, I discover, has one big advantage over horseback riding: no previous experience is required. You simply hoist yourself aboard and then cling on tight as the animal lurches to its feet with an alarming fore-and-aft heave. Each camel is led by a man with a rope and simply ambles along in a tireless soft-shoe shuffle.

Every day on our safari down the Seyia Sand Lugga begins the same: the cold dawn coming alive to a chorus of doves and the sun's red glow igniting the still-sleeping hills – a reverie broken by the bellowing complaints of our camels being harnessed – like someone gargling with a bucket of gravel.

Now it is night. Supper by a huge campfire of dead trees in the lugga is over and I have been guided through the darkness to the trestle bed on which I am to sleep, protected only by a flimsy mosquito net. This is my first taste of fly camping, and as I lie there looking up at the stars I feel for the first time the fear of the preyed-upon.

Suddenly a lion begins to roar, causing the camels hobbled in the lugga some distance away to shift and grumble and rattle their bells. In the silence that follows I can feel my heart beat rising and think to myself, this is how it must be for the zebras whose shrill squeals of alarm now ring out in the black-and-silver night.

Then the lion roars again, much closer this time, its deep voice dying away in a throaty series of rasping grunts. I stare into the shadows, trying to catch the slightest movement, ears straining to pick up the stealthy pad of velvet paws. But the lion did not roar again, and in the end, after what seemed like an eternity, I pulled the blanket over my head and slept soundly until dawn.

January 1980: Adamson of Africa

"A RUSHA, old girl," cried George Adamson, and at the sound of his voice the big lioness left the waterbuck she had killed by the Tana River and padded towards him.

What happened next I could hardly believe as she ran at him, then stood on her hind legs and draped her huge forepaws over the old man's shoulders, grunting with pleasure while he hugged her tawny body and made little moaning lion noises of his own in reply.

I was sitting where Adamson had left me in his decrepit Land Rover, surrounded by the watchful eyes of Arusha's pride. "I shouldn't get out if I were you, old boy," he said casually. I had no intention of doing so, especially as Arusha had now wandered over to inspect me. Her muzzle was still wet with blood and I could smell her warm breath as she panted through the open window only inches from my face.

That was in January 1980, the day after Joy Adamson's funeral in Nairobi. Only two months earlier I had been talking to her at her camp in Kenya's Shaba Game Reserve. Now Joy was dead, murdered by one of her former camp staff. She was nearly 70 when we met and looked nothing like Virginia McKenna, who played her in the *Born Free* movie. One leg was encased in plaster after a fall that had smashed her knee, and long years in the sun had turned her wrinkled skin to leather; but her hair was still blonde and her blue eyes as clear as when they had first bewitched George in 1944.

The event that would transform their lives came twelve years later in 1956 when George had to shoot a stock-raiding lioness and found himself with three orphaned cubs on his hands. The smallest was a female. The Adamsons called her Elsa. So began the poignant story of *Born Free*, which brought fame for Joy but led George down a different road to Kora in northern Kenya, where he devoted the rest of his life to returning lions to the wild.

When news of Joy's murder reached *The Sunday Times* I was sent to Nairobi to cover the story, and it was there I met George for the first time. By then the couple had long since separated, but he had flown in from Kora to attend the funeral, and that was when he had invited me to fly back with him to meet his lions.

When we landed on Kora's dusty airstrip the first thing George did was load up his Land Rover with camel meat and drive down to the river where I witnessed the extraordinary reunion between him and Arusha.

After that we kept in touch and on subsequent visits for *The Sunday Times* I also became friends with Tony Fitzjohn, the tough young Englishman without whose support the grand old Lion Man of Kenya could not have continued.

Fast forward to 19th August, 1989. By now, George was 84 and could only walk with a stick, but after 20 years of struggle he had just learned that Kora was to be made a national park. Only one worry continued to nag him. For months he had seen and heard nothing of his lions. Until that evening when, out of the blue, the entire pride turned up and stayed all night, grunting and roaring as if to salute the old man's achievements.

Next day, he was shot dead by Somali bandits. The world mourned his passing and the eulogies poured in. Adamson was a warrior for conservation, an ambassador for wild Africa. "George Adamson put Kenya on the map," said Richard Leakey.

Fast forward again, to the present day. More than half a century has passed since *Born Free* was published, and what began with an orphaned cub called Elsa has changed the face of Africa. Not only did it breathe new life into Meru and Shaba, but also led to the creation of two new parks, Kora in Kenya and Mkomazi in northeastern Tanzania.

Scientists regularly criticised George Adamson, claiming all he had done was to rescue a handful of lions and return them to the wild. But that was to miss the point. They failed to see that what he discovered through living with them told us more about ourselves. Deep down, he believed in the unassailable dignity of lions, and helped us to believe it, too. And that is the real *Born Free* legacy.

July 2000: To a Wild Land We Came

HIGH above the Great Rift Valley, on a ranch the size of an English county, sits Kuki Gallmann, the blonde enchantress of Laikipia, weaving her stories of Africa. She is the new millennium's Karen Blixen, a blue-eyed Italian whose heart-wrenching autobiography, *I Dreamed of Africa*, was made into a movie starring Kim Basinger.

"To a wild land we came," says Gallmann. "Wild men we married, wild sons we bore." She is talking of the pioneer spirit that arrived in 1896 when Lord Delamere became the first European to settle in what later became known as the White Highlands. Today, more than a century later, Kenya has altered beyond recognition, yet the wildness lingers on this last frontier of the old East Africa, where the descendants of those up-country settlers still live.

The Laikipia Plateau is enormous. It stretches from the Rift Valley walls to the slopes of Mount Kenya and is larger than all of Kenya's protected areas except Tsavo National Park. Although divided into a patchwork of farms and cattle ranches, Laikipia is unique because, unlike anywhere else in the country, wildlife numbers have actually increased over the past two decades. It is one of the last refuges of the critically endangered black rhino and has the largest elephant population outside the parks, and yet until recently it remained relatively unknown.

These days, when chasing the tourist dollar is more profitable than keeping livestock, it makes good sense to transform your ranch into a private game reserve, and Ol Ari Nyiro, the Gallmann ranch, is such a place.

Bounded by the wooded depths of the Mukutan Gorge, it is set in one of the wildest, emptiest landscapes imaginable. Sometimes, says Kuki, when the evening light catches the ribs and folds of Mugungu ya Nguruwe – the Hog's Back – you can see rhinos browsing on the far side.

🐾   🐾   🐾

Born near Venice, Kuki Gallmann first visited Kenya in 1970 and returned to live there in 1972 with her husband Paolo and Emanuele, their son. Tragically, Paolo was killed in a car crash on the Mombasa Road in 1980, and three years later Emanuele also died after being bitten by a puff adder. Both are buried under a beautiful yellow-barked acacia tree whose shade falls across the lawns of Ol Ari Nyiro where she has stayed on with her grief.

Like all Kuki's guests I stay at the Mukutan Retreat, a luxury lodge with a swimming pool and three spacious cottages clinging to the lip of the gorge. Here, solitude is absolute. The air is heavy with the jasmine-sweet scent of carissa bushes. Turacos fly across the void on magenta wings and at night the gorge echoes to the blare of elephants 3,000 feet below. "This place is a cathedral of the spirit," declares Kuki. "Despite everything that has happened it is such a privilege to live here. I love it with a ferocious sense of guardianship and yet nobody owns it. It owns you."

To the people employed on her ranch she is Nyawera – 'the One who Works Hard'. Certainly nobody strives harder than she does to keep Ol Ari Nyiro in good heart; and despite the hardships of living in Laikipia, the droughts, the poaching, the loss of her loved ones, one cannot imagine her living anywhere else.

July 2000: Where God Makes the Wind Blow

EAST of Mukutan, high on a cliff above the Ewaso Ng'iro River, is a lodge called Sabuk, run by a redoubtable lady called Kerry Glen who, just like Julian McKeand (with whom I travelled two decades ago), takes her guests on camel safaris into the great emptiness of the Samburu country.

Together we set off next morning with a string of camels and a posse of Laikipiak Maasai warriors led by Shillingi, a thin man wrapped in a red cotton *shuka*, who once poached elephants for a living.

There are no roads, only well-trodden elephant paths weaving through the tangled commiphora thickets. The elephants have moved on because of the drought, says Kerry, but the ever-present risk of buffaloes causes us to walk warily whenever we cross a patch of thick bush, even though Kerry carries a rifle and Shillingi's sharp eyes miss nothing.

Under the huge African skies in this wild, awesome country I feel absurdly happy and the Maasai are happy, too. Their step is light and they sing as they saunter down the game trails in their thousand-mile sandals made from old car tyres. They sing about the hills thronged about us where the shy kudu roam, and the beauty of their cows, which they value above everything else in the world. In high clear voices they make up the words as they stride along, with each impromptu solo cadenza answered by a stirring, one-two chant, *unhh-hunhhn, unhh-hunhhn*, that makes the hairs stand up on the back of my neck.

As for the camels, they vary in colour from donkey brown to pale creamy suede. At first I thought them ugly cantankerous brutes, but as time goes by I find myself growing inordinately fond of their lugubrious faces, their curious dignity and tireless plodding gait.

By mid-morning it is too hot to walk but by now we have reached camp by the river, in whose crocodile-free pools we swim and cool off until lunch is served under a wide-spreading thorn tree.

Later, when the stone partridges begin to call, we walk into the hills for a sundowner. We sit on a rock and drink cold Tusker beers straight from the can. To the north looms Ol Doinyo Nyiro, the Dark Mountain, and closer to hand soars a bold granite sugarloaf. "The Maasai call it Ngai Susa," says Kerry, "the Place Where God Makes the Wind Blow." A full moon sails up from behind the hills, and as a tawny eagle glides past on its way to roost it is hard to imagine anywhere closer to heaven.

July 2000: Champagne Flight to Cathedral Rock

AT Loisaba, a private lodge not far from Sabuk, I swap my camel for a five-seater, air-conditioned, royal blue helicopter. Loisaba is the former home of an Italian nobleman, Count Ancilotto, who came here to hunt but fell in love with Laikipia and stayed on to become a rancher. When the count died, Peter Sylvester, a professional safari guide, moved in to run Loisaba as a wildlife estate. As Sylvester says over dinner, "Nowadays a dozen tourists are worth more than 2,500 head of cattle."

Among the options available to his guests are helicopter joyrides over the Great Rift Valley, and if you are planning a list of 'Ten Best Things To Do Before You Die', put this near the top.

My pilot is Humphrey Carter, ex Irish Guards, very dapper in his snazzy flying suit. "Let's have some music," he says as the blades start to rotate. Next moment, with Bruce Springsteen in stereo on the headphones, we are swooping out over Losiolo, where the Rift Valley walls drop for 1,800 metres – deeper than the Grand Canyon.

Enclosed in our glass bubble of comfort, we float across inaccessible ravines, above fathomless forests of cedar and euphorbia, over a John Wayne landscape of buttes and badlands, towards range upon range of shark's fin mountains. This part of Kenya is so impossibly remote that a helicopter is the only practical way of seeing it.

On we skim over the Suguta Valley where Turkana tribesmen and their camels eke out a precarious existence on the desert floor. "This is one of the hottest places on earth," cries Captain Carter as we touch down on a black volcanic cone amid a sea of rolling dunes.

It is also a hideout for Turkana cattle rustlers, which is one reason why few visitors ever come to this remote region. Shaped by the cruel land around them, the Turkana are among the toughest people on earth, which is why they are often employed as night watchmen in Nairobi. Their ancestors came from the Karamajong country of Uganda and they have learned to live with very little, sleeping in primitive domed huts made of palm fronds and goatskins.

Among the most prized of their few possessions are the *ekicholong* – wooden footstools carried by the men. Placed under the back of the neck, they lift the head off the ground, so protecting their elaborately plaited hairstyle. Nowadays it is also an increasingly common sight to see Turkana herdsmen toting AK 47s as well as spears.

Stepping outside into the Turkana homeland is like landing on Mars as we sip champagne in the 45°C heat. We watch Cathedral Rock turn deep orange in the setting sun, and when we lift off again, turning for home over the swirling flamingos that come every year to feed in the alkaline shallows of Lake Logipi, I experience one of those pure *Out of Africa* moments that live forever in the memory.

August 2000: In the Land of the Singing Wells

AT Namunyak, on the edge of the Mathews Mountains, where thorn scrub and semi-desert reach out to infinity, Kenya's Northern Frontier Province is enduring its worst drought in living memory. In the bone-dry sand rivers, which flow only during the rains, Samburu herdsmen with pierced earlobes and leaf-bladed spears have dug wells 30 feet deep to find water, filling cans which they pass up in a human chain, chanting as they work.

These are the famous singing wells, without which the pastoralists' scrawny livestock would surely perish. Yet for all their efforts some herders have already lost 90 per cent of their goats and cattle and no rain is due for at least two months.

A sensible time, then, for these tough, proud people to take a hard look at their traditional way of life. After all, even in the longest drought, the wildlife – elephant, oryx and graceful gerenuk – has evolved strategies for survival; and if the Samburu are also to cling on here, they may have to do the same.

Already some have taken the plunge, diversifying into eco-tourism to relieve their dependency on livestock grazing, and at Namunyak, deep in the *porini* – that evocative Swahili word for the bush – a new safari lodge has sprung up.

Called Sarara, it has been helped into being by the descendants of the European settlers who pioneered their way to wealth on the nearby ranches of Lewa Downs and the Laikipia Highlands, and is itself a pioneer, breaking new ground on the frontiers of wildlife conservation in a region with a long history of banditry, blood feuds and ivory poaching.

It was Ian Craig, the visionary founder of the Lewa Wildlife Conservancy, who started the ball rolling after witnessing an elephant massacre with Kinyanjui Lesenderia, his oldest friend.

Kinyanjui was maybe five years older than him, born to a Kikuyu mother and a Mukogodo Maasai father, and when Craig was a boy the two were inseparable. At that time of his life he was obsessed with hunting, and during his school holidays he would take off on foot from Lewa with Kinyanjui as his constant companion.

They would each take a blanket and a few provisions – tea, sugar, rice and *posho* ('mealie maize') – and disappear into the Mukogodo Forest for a week or more, walking for hours through the cedar forests on the trail of the elephants, trying to work out where they might go, sleeping out under the moon on the rocks or by waterholes.

The years passed. The boys grew to manhood and on this particular day they were in the Mathews Range when they heard the all-too-familiar sound of automatic weapons and watched helplessly as a gang of Somali poachers gunned down eight elephants in the valley below.

"Although we were both armed it would have been madness to intervene," he told me on a previous visit to Lewa, "and if ever there was one thing in my life that touched my soul to the core it was this."

It happened in1988 – the year in which the international ivory trade was banned. That was after Richard Leakey set up the Kenya Wildlife Service to take on the bandit gangs that had poached elephants in their thousands and turned much of the north into a no-go area.

Afterwards, returning from that lonely hilltop with the images of slaughter still fresh in his mind, Craig realised the only hope for elephants outside the national parks and reserves was for communities living alongside wildlife to derive a lasting benefit from conservation; and that was when he first had the idea of ending the bandits' reign of terror without direct government help.

"My objective was twofold," he said. "First we would raise the standard of our own security force at Lewa, enabling them to operate throughout the country as Kenyan Police Reservists. Secondly, we would enlist the help of the local communities to win the poaching war, and to do that we had to persuade them that wild animals are more valuable alive than dead."

Namunyak, which came into existence in 1995, was among the first community conservancies to be established, and what happened there has expanded to become the Northern Rangelands Trust, an umbrella organisation of 16 similar conservancies providing benefits for 62,000 people by promoting tourism and conservation. Already it covers nearly two million acres – more than 15 times bigger than Samburu National Reserve – creating a spectacular wildlife haven the size of Tsavo, and it is growing all the time.

Five years on and Sarara Lodge is doing well. Run by the Namunyak Wildlife Conservation Trust, it gives the local Samburu community a 50 per cent stake in the business and is why today there are observation posts on the surrounding hilltops. This is Neighbourhood Watch, Kenyan style, with teams of heavily armed rangers operating round-the-clock patrols to safeguard the Samburu, their guests and the wildlife.

As yet the animals are still wary; but already leopard and elephant come to drink at the waterhole and the poachers are on the back foot. Slowly, after years of lawlessness, Kenya's last great wilderness is being made safe for all and Namunyak is now widely acclaimed as a model of community-run conservation.

August 2000: The Ark of the Desert

FORTY-FIVE miles north of Sarara is another inspirational community-owned lodge. This is Il Ngwesi, an African ark built of dead trees knocked down by elephants, a ship of the desert cast up on a rocky hill at the foot of the Laikipia Plateau.

Il Ngwesi is Maasai country, a land of resounding distance measured by the stark shapes of granite inselbergs that rise like tombstones from the scrub-covered plains. When I arrive I am welcomed by a gathering of Laikipiak Maasai warriors wrapped in blood-red *shukas*, who offer me fresh orange juice and wet towels to wash off the dust before guiding me to my room.

When Il Ngwesi opened in 1996 it became the first lodge in Africa to be 100 per cent owned and run by the local community. Until then its Maasai owners had used their 40,000-acre group ranch exclusively for livestock grazing. Now it is managed primarily as a wildlife resource, bringing in £1 million a year – a sum they could never have earned without tourism.

My room is more like a luxurious private tree house, raised on stilts under a high thatched roof. It has a king-size bed with billowing mosquito nets, solar panels for hot showers under the stars – in fact everything except doors and windows. At Il Ngwesi, everything is open to the wind and yet privacy is absolute.

There is also a spring-fed swimming pool with stunning views and a hide overlooking a waterhole to which a leopard has become a regular nocturnal visitor.

In the evening I speak to Simon ole Kinyaga, the local Maasai chief, who is dressed in European clothes but still carries his ceremonial *rungu* – a wooden club with an elaborate beadwork handle.

He tells me about the visit he had made to London to collect the British Airways 'Tourism for Tomorrow' award that Il Ngwesi won in 1997. What had impressed him most in London, I asked him? "The streets," he said. "So clean. No rubbish. Not at all like Nairobi."

In Maa, Il Ngwesi means 'the Wildlife People' and wildlife is certainly what you get when you stay here. After dinner (roast lamb with mint sauce and assorted vegetables) I sit on the veranda, listening to the rumble of lions on the plains below. Whenever I awake during the night I hear them roaring, sometimes close, sometimes distant; and at first light, while enjoying my early morning tea, I watch entranced as a lioness and her two small cubs emerge from the bush to drink at the waterhole.

December 2008: Among the Elephants

THE Maasai Mara may be Kenya's top tourist destination but its soul lies in the north, in the dry country beyond Mt Kenya, where the green highlands fall away into an arid wilderness the size of Britain. It rests among the proud Samburu pastoralists and with the elephants under the doum palms and all the way from Laikipia to the cedar-clad slopes of the Mathews Mountains. Old Kenya hands still call this region by its former name – the NFD or Northern Frontier District – and it is here that you will find the essence of Africa as you always hoped it would be in the Samburu National Reserve.

Of all the people of northern Kenya none are more colourful than the Samburu. Cousins of the Maasai, this desert tribe of warrior-nomads still cling to their old ways, tending their herds of goats and cattle as they fan out each day across their drought-prone homeland.

Arriving by air from the coolness of Nairobi it comes as a shock to step out into the blowtorch heat of a Samburu morning. The sun glitters on a billion thorns and the grass underfoot is crackling dry. But shade is at hand under the palms and acacia groves that flourish in abundance along the Ewaso Ng'iro, the river whose mud-brown waters divide Samburu from the adjoining Buffalo Springs Reserve.

Here live the beautiful dry-country animals of Northern Kenya that make up Samburu's 'Special Five': gerenuk, oryx, reticulated giraffe, Somali ostrich and Grevy's zebra – that most beautiful of wild horses with its big round ears and pin-striped coat. Leopard and lion leave their tracks in the dust and there is wonderful birding along the river, with vulturine guinea fowls and golden-breasted starlings among the Samburu specials.

But above all Samburu is elephant country. The reserve itself may be one of East Africa's smallest; but combined with the lands over which the NRT holds sway it becomes part of an eco-system the size of Tsavo, in which 7,000 elephants – the second largest population in Kenya – can wander at will.

Arthur Neumann, the renowned Victorian ivory hunter, used to camp right here beside the Ewaso Ng'iro; and in today's more conservation-conscious times this is where Iain Douglas-Hamilton, one of the world's most distinguished biologists, conducts his research for Save the Elephants, the organisation he founded in 1993.

🐾   🐾   🐾

When I first met Iain and Oria, his glamorous Italian-born wife, in 1974 they were already famous, having written *Among the Elephants*, an international best seller which described their adventures while studying elephant behaviour in Tanzania's Lake Manyara National Park. It was the last night of my first visit to Africa, and with typical Kenyan hospitality, although I was simply a young journalist they had never met before, they insisted on driving me to the airport for my flight home and we have remained friends ever since.

When Save The Elephants began in 1993 Iain's principal aim was to assist wildlife departments in their fight against ivory poachers and traders, but he was also intrigued by the choices elephants make, especially when they decide where to go on their long-distance migrations in the rainy season.

"By understanding elephant movements," he says, "we can approach conservation from an elephant's perspective." But in order to do that he first had to identify and catalogue as many elephants as he could by photographing their distinctively different tusks and ear patterns. Some are residents. Others – known as 'sporadics' – come and go with the seasons; but for all of them the Samburu Reserve is their core area in which they feel safe and protected.

From the air (Iain is a hugely experienced bush pilot) he points out the problems tourism can bring as we bank and turn over the reserve in his tiny four-seater Cessna with its distinctive elephant logo painted on the fuselage. Beneath our wings lies a brash new riverside lodge that has effectively deprived the elephants of a favourite crossing-place. But then we turn and fly upstream to where a much smaller camp lies so cleverly hidden under a woodland canopy that I can hardly see it.

This is Elephant Watch Camp, presided over by Oria Douglas-Hamilton. In a small park over-endowed with big noisy lodges this is by far the nicest place to stay. Nowhere leaves a lighter footprint and Oria is the perfect hostess. "We maintain a very low presence here," she says. "Elephants helped us build our camp by knocking down trees whose dead and weathered trunks we have simply re-cycled."

Here, just a few miles downstream from Iain's HQ, nothing separates you from the wild. One night I listen to leopards mating just behind my tent, and where else in the world can you be on first name terms with so many wild elephants? In the course of Iain's research it was necessary to get to know Samburu's elephants as individuals, and uniquely at Oria's camp you can go out and meet them with her marvellous Samburu guides.

Drawn from the local communities and dressed in their traditional tribal finery, they are familiar with all the elephant families – the Virtues and the Royals – and the big breeding bulls such as Rommel, who trashed one of Iain's research vehicles two years ago.

Altogether more than 700 elephants have been named, separated into families, and photographed for identification, as I discover on a game drive with Bernard Lesiren.

Sitting at the wheel of his Toyota Land Cruiser, Bernard wears the beads and robes of a Samburu warrior but is a Silver Standard professional guide whose elephant know-how is second to none. "Those are the Spice Girls," he says, pointing to a group of cow elephants bathing in the river. "And that bull over there – that's Zinedine Zidane."

December 2008: Wings over Samburu

THE early morning sunlight falls like a blessing across the plains, touching everything with gold as red-chested cuckoos call in the riverine forest. Wood doves chant in the trees overhead and the nights echo to the ripsaw grunting of wandering leopards. In such blissfully peaceful surroundings it is impossible not to unwind. Overlooking a wide bend of the Ewaso Ng'iro just beyond Samburu's West Gate entrance is Sasaab Lodge on the Ngutuk Ongiron Group Ranch – another example of what the NRT has helped to create in association with the local community. It is run by Mikey and Tanya Carr-Hartley, a well-known Kenyan family who have been at the forefront of the safari business for almost a century.

Named after a local species of morning glory (*ipomea*), whose white flowers bloom beside the airstrip, Sasaab has already acquired a reputation for being one of East Africa's most exclusive holiday addresses. Beyond the main dining area with its brass lanterns and Moorish arches are nine spacious thatch-and-canvas rooms, each one set apart from the rest, with its own plunge pool and view of the river.

"From July to September," says Mikey, "elephants gather below the lodge to drink and wallow and cross the river; and one of the nicest things to do is to take your glass of Pimms down to our infinity pool and watch them."

The alternative is sundowners atop a granite monolith with stupendous views of Laikipia, the cedar-clad Mathews Range and the perfect pair of breast-shaped hills known locally as Sweet Sixteen.

But of all the activities on offer the best by far is an early morning flight with Will Craig and his Waco Classic, a bright yellow bi-plane designed in the 1930s for the likes of Beryl Markham and Denys Finch-Hatton, and rebuilt in 2007 for joyrides over Samburuland.

Kitted out in goggles, helmet and leather flying jacket, I shoehorn myself into the open cockpit for what has to be the most exhilarating of all game drives. Craig, an experienced bush pilot with more than 6,000 flying hours under his belt, clambers into the seat behind me and we're off with a cloud of red dust in our wake. "Wonderful, isn't it?" he shouts above the engine's roar. "She's the Cadillac of aviation."

To complete my Karen Blixen moment, the theme music from *Out of Africa* fills the headphones as we soar like an eagle towards Koitogorr, the broken hill that dominates the Samburu Reserve. Below us our shadow skims across a yawning infinity of sand rivers and acacia bush. This is some of the most savage country I've ever seen, accessible only on foot or by camel.

We surprise a herd of waterbuck, startle a flock of European storks on a sand bar and spot a bull elephant under a thorn tree. Then we bank over Romot, where the Ewaso Ng'iro snakes through a spectacular gorge, and fly home past the steep folds of the Laikipia Plateau.

After 45 minutes it was all over but I wished it would never end. Joyride it may have been, but it also demonstrated the key role elephants have played in creating the unique landscapes of northern Kenya. "Thirty years ago when elephants were still widespread," Craig said to me, "much of those plains we flew over were grassland."

"Then the poachers moved in. The elephant population crashed and the acacias took over, shutting out the grass and creating a closed canopy in places. So the local people actually need elephants to open up the bush for the benefit of grazing animals; but of course that's a very difficult message to put across."

Now, with security better than it has ever been, their numbers are increasing again, and with luck they may yet re-discover the tolerance that existed once before when people and elephants lived side-by-side in Kenya's last great wilderness.

July 2012: The Sandgrouse of Kisima Hamsini

"WATCH out for Russell and Bromley," warns Alex Hunter, the owner of Ol Pejeta bush camp. "Russell is usually OK but Bromley has a mean glint in his eye."

It turns out that Russell and Bromley are two grumpy old buffalo bulls that have taken up residence around the camp, but all I ever see of them are their footprints outside my tent.

Alex is the grandson of J.A. Hunter, the legendary big game hunter who arrived in East Africa in 1908 as a 21-year-old greenhorn with no worldly goods except his rifle. He was a crack shot, a skill passed on to Alex's father and one that Alex himself has also inherited, although he was never bitten by the hunting bug.

"I did some game control work," he says, "shot one or two bad lions and was very nearly nailed by a bull buffalo which has left me with a profound respect for those dangerous old boys."

Instead, in 2004 he set up his own safari company, Insiders Africa, operating first in the Maasai Mara and now in the Ol Pejeta Wildlife Conservancy on the Laikipia Plateau. His latest venture involves walking safaris in the newly established Sera Wildlife Conservancy, roughly midway between Archer's Post and Marsabit.

Next morning it is time to move on. A cold wind is blowing across the plains as we leave camp, but as the sky begins to clear and sun breaks through we come upon a cheetah and her five small cubs, and watch them romping through the grass, tails held aloft like meerkats.

First stop is Nanyuki to pick up supplies. Then we drive north on the new blacktop highway built by the Chinese, through Isiolo and the sprawling Somali suburb known to Kenya's expats as Little Mogadishu.

Beyond Archer's Post looms the flat topped massif of Ololokwe, its soaring cliffs spattered with vulture droppings, and on the opposite side of the road stand the twin rock steeples called the Cat and Mouse, marking the gateway to what used to be called the NFD – the lawless Northern Frontier District that extends all the way to Ethiopia.

Here until recently came the *shifta* – wild men armed with AK 47s and hell-bent on poaching. Over the years they finished off the rhinos and decimated the elephant herds before the area was made secure.

An hour later we leave the tarmac and go bumping down a red murram track into a desolation of commiphora scrub. "Welcome to Sera," says Alex, who has been given exclusive rights to operate walking safaris in this roughest, toughest and most remote of all the NRT's conservancies.

At last we reach the Kauro Lugga, a sand river as wide as the Thames at Richmond. In 2006 the BBC's *Mission Africa* team built two *bandas* ('guesthouses') here in the deep shade of a palm grove, and this is to be my home for the next four days.

My banda stands open to the elements with bare stone floors under a high thatched roof, but it comes with all essential creature comforts: a huge bed with pristine white sheets and mosquito nets, an en-suite loo and open-air bathroom for showering under the stars. I awake every morning to the powerful dynamo hum of wild bees in the palms above the roof. Then, after a quick coffee beside the embers of last night's campfire, we set off on foot while the air is cool.

❀   ❀   ❀

Sera, I discover, is a place where you can drop out of the 21st century and disappear into 300,000 acres of nothing but thorn trees, lizards and an echoing silence broken only by the insane clucking of yellow-billed hornbills.

The landscape is mostly low-lying, rising in places to form long lava ridges known as *merti*, veined with sand luggas and scattered with red rocky kopjes in which leopards have their lairs.

In every direction distant mountains float on the horizon, presiding over a sea of thorns. One by one I learn the names of these enigmatic summits: Longtopi, Ol Kanjau, Ol Doinyo Lenkiyo and Warges, the highest peak in the Mathews Range. On our daily walks they are the signposts we steer by.

Laetato, a Laikipiak Ndorobo with beanpole legs and pierced earlobes, leads the way. Then comes Hunter, cradling his rifle, then me. "I never walk without my rifle," he says. "It's when you haven't got it that you're going to need it most."

The paths we follow are elephant trails – the oldest roads in Africa – flushing coveys of quails as we cross blond meadows of crows' foot grass. Sightings of animals are few: mostly dik-dik and gerenuk, another dry-country antelope with a long thin neck and lustrous brown Audrey Hepburn eyes.

But tracks in the sand tell a different story. Here we see where lions and leopards have been prowling during the night, their pugmarks mingled with fresh signs of giraffe and the dustbin-lid footprints of elephants.

By mid-morning it is too hot to walk. The horizon dissolves in a heat-hazy dazzle of fierce wind and equatorial sunlight, painting the land in the parched desert colours of the wild north: ochre, terracotta and burning bronze, and we return to camp to shower and relax until the golden hour before sundown when all time is distilled into one pure moment of euphoric beauty.

On our second day I walk down the Lenkoli Lugga – "the first visitor to do so," Alex tells me – past tumbledown piles of granite boulders and rushy pools that echo to the rattle of frogs. Elsewhere are deep pits where elephants have tusked in the sand for water. Their dung is everywhere among the mingled hoof prints of kudu antelopes and Grevy's zebras.

In these harsh semi-deserts water is the key to life, and the most precious oasis for miles around is a place called Kisima Hamsini. Its Swahili name means 'Fifty Wells' and here the local pastoralists have dug deep holes through the surface rock to reach the natural reservoir beneath.

When the dry season peaks, Samburu, Rendille and Boran tribesmen co-exist here in an uneasy equilibrium with the wildlife. By day the herdsmen bring their cows to water, but the nights belong to the elephants.

For as long as anyone can remember Kisima Hamsini has also been home to one of the great unsung spectacles of the bird world, when upwards of 40,000 sandgrouse fly in from the surrounding deserts to drink.

Alex is keen to show me this miraculous gathering, which happens every morning during the long dry season. So off we go to spend the night fly camping in what Hunter calls his 'meat safe'– a flimsy rectangle of mosquito net with a sewn-in groundsheet and enough room inside for a bed and a few personal belongings.

The first thing we see on arrival is a large male lion that bursts out of a thicket and trots off down the lugga, leaving me with the thought that perhaps I am to be the meat in the safe.

I turn in early and lie on my back looking up at the stars that shine overhead with unbelievable brilliance in the pure desert air. But the night passes uneventfully and in the morning I wake early and climb the granite whaleback in whose shelter I have slept, to see Sera's mysterious Gong Rock: a boulder pitted with cup-shaped depressions. When struck with a rock it bongs like a bell and may be one of the world's oldest instruments.

An hour after sunrise the first sandgrouse appear. Most are black-faced sandgrouse with strange, guttural cries, like someone muttering "six o'clock, six o'clock". Soon their numbers begin to swell as they hurtle in from all directions, a thousand a minute, pouring overhead like an arrow storm.

Imagine an airborne version of the Serengeti wildebeest migration and you get some idea of what it is like, complete with attendant predators – not lions and hyenas but goshawks, peregrines and scavenging ravens.

Each bird remains for no more than seven seconds in which time the males, their breast feathers more absorbent than a sponge, soak up the water and fly back with it to their thirsty chicks in the desert.

Forty-five minutes later the show is over. The wells are silent and the birds won't drink again until the same time tomorrow.

Chapter Four

Kenya's Deep South
(Tsavo, Amboseli, Shompole and the Chyulu Hills)

November 1996: Return to the Killing Fields

FINCH HATTON'S, overlooking a clearwater spring in Tsavo National Park, is arguably the most luxurious safari camp in Kenya. At dinner, attentive waiters clad in white *kanzus*, like those who once served at Karen Blixen's table, pad silently among the guests, pouring wine into crystal goblets. Snatches of Mozart from the *Out of Africa* soundtrack compete with the choirs of frogs outside, and I wonder what Denys Finch Hatton himself would have made of it, Blixen's Old Etonian hunter-lover who died when his plane crashed at Voi in 1931.

It is all so different to the last time I was in Tsavo. That was in 1988 when I had come to Kenya for *The Sunday Times* to report on the poaching war that had turned East Africa's biggest national park into an elephants' graveyard.

Wherever I travelled, dead elephants outnumbered the living. Once, deep in bandit country, I found six carcasses huddled together, an entire elephant family gunned down on their way to drink at the Galana River. I could see where the poachers' bullets had struck and where their *pangas* had hacked out the tusks, leaving everything else to the vultures.

No wonder the Wakamba people had named this place Tsavo, 'the Place of Slaughter'. Its beauty and wildness were undiminished but the threat of further violence hung about the plains like the taint of an old kill, and as I drove away, a wind blew over the park, drawing curtains of rain across the Sagala Hills as if God was trying to obliterate the obscenity I had witnessed in the Garden of Eden.

It was a bad time for Kenya. Morale within the national parks was at rock bottom and *magendo* – the Swahili word for corruption – ran deep in Tsavo. Park rangers worked in cahoots with the poachers, and worse still for Kenya's image abroad, the bandit gangs – Kalashnikov-toting desperados from neighbouring Somalia – had taken to shooting tourists, with disastrous effects on the safari trade.

Now I am back, and the transformation could hardly be more dramatic. The air holds the wonderful smell of earth after rain. The skies are alive with golden pipits and herds of oryx gallop off through the bush as if running for the sheer joy of being alive.

There are elephants everywhere and no longer do they run in panic at the sight of a vehicle. The camps and lodges are full again and tourist minibuses cruise through the park, pausing to photograph buffalo herds and prides of Tsavo's feisty lions.

Staff morale is higher than ever now that the Kenya Wildlife Service (KWS), a squeaky-clean fighting force led by Richard Leakey, has taken over the running of the parks. Corrupt rangers have been sacked and replaced by tough new recruits armed with modern semi-automatic weapons.

❁   ❁   ❁

It was primarily to save the elephants that Tsavo became Kenya's second national park in 1948. Here, it was hoped, the herds might wander across a wilderness the size of Wales. At least, that was the dream. But in the 15 years leading up to 1988, the country's parks and reserves lost 83 per cent of their elephants and almost all their black rhinos to the Somali poaching gangs.

Since then, Leakey and the KWS have managed to regain control. International trade in ivory has been banned. The poachers have been pushed back and Tsavo's elephant population is increasing by five per cent a year.

"The Somalis are still out there," says Stephen Gichangi, the park's senior warden.

"They're waiting beyond the Tana River and if ever the ivory ban is lifted they'll be back. So we keep our forces ready and armed to the teeth. It's a war we are fighting here."

In Gichangi's spartan office at the park headquarters at Voi is a roll of honour listing the names of Tsavo's previous wardens, including the legendary David Sheldrick whose widow, Daphne, now runs the elephant orphanage in Nairobi.

"I live with David's ghost," says Gichangi. "He is still my mentor. He had 44,000 elephants to look after. I have only 8,000 but today they represent one third of all the elephants left in Kenya."

In spite of everything that has happened, if the elephant has a future anywhere in East Africa, one feels, it will be here in the vast emptiness of what Gichangi calls 'the mother of all parks'.

"Tsavo is no good for farming," he says. "It's too hot, too dry. Maize withers. Cattle perish. But elephants thrive and tourists will always pay good money to see them."

September 1999: In the Shadow of Kilimanjaro

ACROSS the plains of Amboseli comes a lone bull elephant. He strides towards us with a sailor's roll, huge ears swinging to keep himself cool. Even in a park renowned as the home of a thousand elephants, he is a colossus. "I know this bull," whispers Letaloi, my safari guide. "We call him Goliath."

Still he approaches, growing bigger all the time until at last, when he is only an elephant's length away from our open-topped Land Cruiser, he stops, a grey shadow towering over us, with tusks so long they almost touch the ground.

Out of the corner of my eye I notice Letaloi reaching for the ignition key, ready to switch on and gun the engine in case of trouble, but there is no need. After staring down at us for a minute, Goliath dismisses us with a contemptuous flap of his dusty ears and continues on his way.

By East African standards Amboseli National Park is small. It covers a mere 150 square miles and yet it is a land of giants. For this is where Kenya's mightiest tuskers wander freely against the stunning backdrop of Kilimanjaro, the world's highest free- standing mountain. The Maasai people who live in its shadow call it Ol Doinyo Oibor – 'the White Mountain' – a reference to the eternal snows that crown its 19,000-ft summit, and it is so big that you could drop the whole of Yorkshire into its outermost contour and still have room to spare.

Although it lies across the border in neighbouring Tanzania the meltwaters from its lofty glaciers bubble up in Amboseli, feeding the lush green swamps without which the park and its wildlife could not survive. Most of Amboseli is flat and dry, littered by the bleached trunks of fallen acacias felled by elephants in times of drought. But miraculously, in the midst of these unforgiving thirstlands, the swamps with their tall reeds and cool waters provide a permanent refuge for the park's resident pachyderms.

To aid the scientific studies conducted in Amboseli for more than twenty years by Cynthia Moss and others, each elephant has been given a name and an index card complete with photographs for identification purposes.

"That's Joyce," says Letaloi, pointing out a knuckle-headed matriarch with long thin tusks. Yet even without his ID cards Letaloi can recognise all the key players. A little deeper in the reeds we spot a bull elephant called Chris, with a broken left tusk, and another matriarch known as Qualida, with a tiny calf in tow.

All have been in the swamps, their bodies marked with a distinct Plimsoll line – pale grey above and black below – where they have sloshed belly deep through the mud.

The babies are adorable. With their Mickey Mouse ears and floppy trunks they run around at the water's edge while their older siblings spar and play-fight, going head-to-head with a clash of tusks.

For such large and potentially dangerous animals they are surprisingly easy to approach, having been habituated over the years to the presence of tourist vehicles.

"They are so docile," says Letaloi. "Sometimes they stand so close I could reach out and touch them."

These close encounters are what draw visitors back to Amboseli time and again, and yet the time I enjoy most is when we head slowly back to camp in the hour before dusk, when the light turns to gold and the air is filled with a grey fog of dust in which solemn processions of elephants appear as ghostly silhouettes.

By now Kilimanjaro's base has turned mauve although the sun still gleams on its ice-bound summit. Marsh owls flit through the evening sky and far off across the plains the mountain called Longido rises from the haze like the upturned face of a Maasai warrior.

December 2008: A Short Walk in the Chyulus

SUNDOWNERS don't come any better than this. I am sitting in the heart of Maasailand on a rock the size of St Paul's Cathedral, looking for cheetahs on the plains below.

This is a widescreen Africa I have never seen before. Far to the northwest, across endless vistas of grass and thornbush, lies the elephant country of Amboseli. Turning around I can make out the distant summits of Tsavo National Park receding over the horizon. Ahead, backlit by the setting sun, looms the unearthly vision of Mt Kilimanjaro; and behind, drenched in golden light, are the Chyulus, a voluptuous backdrop of volcanic hills smothered in dense cloud forest.

The Chyulus are the youngest hills in Africa. Their slopes and folds – emerald green after the November rains – look as if they have stood here forever, yet they were flung up around the time Columbus was discovering America. Only the black lava flows dribbling down their steep flanks bear out the truth of their cataclysmic birth.

Hemingway had them in mind when he wrote *The Green Hills of Africa*, and no wonder. This is landscape on an epic scale, and Luca Belpietro, who has brought me here, wanted to show me why of all places on earth he and Antonella, his wife, chose to make it their home.

With his close-cropped hair and faded blue eyes, Luca has the patrician profile of a Caesar "I was born too late," he laments as we sit on a Maasai blanket, drinking wine from Antonella's Italian vineyard, scanning the crags for sure-footed klipspringers as shadows lengthen and a rind of moon appears above us.

He grew up in Italy but his father, a doctor, had a passion for big game hunting and was a regular visitor to East Africa. "He took me for the first time when I was 10," says Luca. "I was totally bewitched and knew straight away I would live there one day."

In 1995 he left his management consultancy company and flew out to Kenya for good. There, on the 400 square miles of the Kuku Ranch he and Antonella built Campi ya Kanzi, a luxury safari lodge. The ranch is communally owned by 7,000 Maasai pastoralists, and money raised from tourism helps to maintain their traditional way of life.

"We sank every last lira into this crazy venture," he says, "but profit is not the final goal. The investment is in seeing that the Maasai and their culture survive along with the landscape and the animals that live here."

The local Maasai call him Saruni – 'the One who helps' – because of the Maasai Wilderness Conservation Trust he founded in order to realise his dream.

One of the Trust's must urgent objectives has been to persuade the Maasai to stop killing the lions that prey on their cattle.

Until the turn of the century lions were quite common in this part of Maasailand. But between 2001 and 2006 more than a hundred were speared or poisoned in a deliberate attempt to get rid of them once and for all. At this rate the local lion population would be gone in a couple of years. So, in a last-ditch bid to prevent their extinction, Luca and the ranch-owners hammered out an agreement under which they are paid compensation for stock lost to lions – provided that they do not kill them in revenge.

Last year alone, Luca paid out more than £20,000 in livestock compensation, since when only two lions have been killed. "It sounds like a lot of money," he says. "But that's what it costs to help 57 lions stay alive in an area two-thirds the size of the Maasai Mara. After all, that's only about £1.50 per day to keep a lion alive – no more than the price of a cup of coffee."

With a maximum of only 12 guests, staying here is like being invited to an exotic private house party. In the colonial-style dining room with its coffee-table books and bowls of fresh-cut flowers, everyone eats *en famille* at a long table presided over by Luca and Antonella, and although the conversation is mostly in English the cuisine is triumphantly Italian. The pasta dishes, focaccia and ice creams are all home made and the salads come from the camp's organic garden.

Outside on the terrace there's a hammock in the shade and it would be tempting to loll here all day, listening to the red-chested cuckoos crying 'it-will-rain' despite the cloudless sky above. But the temptation to explore is too strong to ignore. So next morning, accompanied by Pashiet, one of Luca's Maasai guides, I set off for a walk in the Chyulu Hills.

We drive to the starting-point, toiling up bottom-gear slopes where taka-taka flowers bloom like discarded confetti and mountain reedbuck keep watch on the skyline. The sun gleams on a million points of dew, on the electric blue wings of swallowtail butterflies and on the sleek flanks of hartebeest as they canter away through the grass.

In the aftermath of the December rains the hills are an impossible shade of green. Bracken grows on their upper slopes, and flights of European swallows go dipping past, beginning their great northbound migration. It all feels comfortingly familiar, not so different from the hills around my West Dorset home, until I catch sight of a red-robed Maasai herdsman and his brindled cows as we make for the cloud forest up ahead.

Once in the forest Africa re-asserts itself. The tall trees close in, giant greenhearts and strangler figs, their branches bearded with hanging moss, their buttressed flanks scarred by leopards' claws.

Pashiet and I walk warily now, for the soft mud between the outstretched roots is pitted with the cloven hoof prints of buffaloes. The air is scented with the moon-white flowers of wild magnolia. Mist hangs about the summits, lowering the temperature, and out of its coolness float the woodwind calls of forest orioles.

When at last we reach the top the view is completely hidden by cloud. But as we retrace our steps, picking our way back down the hill's steep flanks, the mist rolls back to reveal the sunlit plains below, stretching for 25 miles all the way to Kilimanjaro.

The sense of space and distance is overwhelming. The Kuku Ranch and the adjoining Mbirikani rangelands cover an area greater than the Maasai Mara National Reserve, and I recall something Luca told me. "The Mara may have more lions than we do, but we have more room," he said. "In the Mara, wilderness works out at about 80 acres for every visitor. At Campi ya Kanzi every guest has 33,000 acres in which to be alone."

January 2008: Last Chance for the Lion King

EARLY morning in Maasailand. Kilimanjaro on the horizon and the sound of cowbells in the air as red-robed herdsmen drive their cattle to water across the dusty plains.

The Mbirikani Group Ranch, a quarter of a million acres of unfenced savannah, is home to 10,000 Maasai pastoralists and I have come to meet one of them, a young *moran* whose name is Koikai and whose job is to protect the lions that live here in an uneasy symbiosis with his fellow tribesmen.

With me is Stephanie Dolreny, an American wildlife biologist working for the Kilimanjaro Lion Conservation Project, and together we are waiting at the entrance to the boma where Koikai lives with his wife and newborn son behind a lion-proof barricade of acacia thornbush.

When at last he appears it comes as something of a shock to see that instead of a spear he is carrying an aerial for tracking radio-collared lions.

Today's Maasai warrior, it seems, still braids his hair into ochre ringlets and wears 'thousand-miler' sandals cut from old car tyres. But, like Koikai, he is also just as likely to be sporting a state-of-the-art digital watch and have a cell phone tucked under his robe.

We jump in Stephanie's Land Rover and head out into the bush to search for a radio-collared lioness known as Nemasi. When last seen she was heavily pregnant, says Stephanie, and is believed to be hiding not far off.

For a mile we bash through thickets of whistling thorn, stopping now and again while Koikai stands up and rotates his aerial, trying to pick up Nemasi's signal. For me this is a novel adventure but for him and his eight fellow lion guardians it is just part of the job, something they do three times every week.

Eventually we pick up a steady pulse on the aerial and locate the lioness lying on a rocky outcrop. When she stands up to stare at us it is clear that she is lactating – a sure sign she has given birth – and Koikai is overjoyed. "When I was 14 I took my spear and went lion hunting to prove my courage and impress the girls," he says. "Now I cannot imagine killing a lion."

What triggered this Damascene change in thinking is a deal that now gives the Maasai a financial alternative to killing the carnivores that prey on their livestock. Every two months the herdsmen of Mbirikani receive compensation at full market value for any animals taken by lions.

"That is the carrot," says Richard Bonham, the driving force behind the scheme to resolve the conflict between people and predators. "The stick is that they also face collective penalties if anyone breaks the rules. That means if a lion is killed in retaliation for loss of livestock, nobody gets paid."

Bonham, a Kenyan-born safari guide and honorary game warden, has lived on the Mbirikani Ranch since the 1980s, and Ol Donyo Wuas, the lodge he built here at the foot of the Chyulu Hills, has become one of Africa's most exclusive hideaways.

Lying as it does between Amboseli and Tsavo national parks, this is classic big game country. Cheetahs are regularly seen on the plains, and from the lodge swimming pool you can watch some of the biggest elephant bulls in Kenya drinking at the waterhole in the acacia forest below.

But lions have become much harder to find, which is why Bonham founded the Ol Donyo Wuas Trust in the early 1990s. Then, faced with their imminent local extinction in 2003, he and fellow trustee Tom Hill created the Mbirikani Predator Conservation Fund, and the following year attracted the support of the USA-funded Kilimanjaro Lion Conservation Project to halt the big cats' decline.

Twenty years ago Africa's lion population stood at around 200,000. Ten years ago that number had halved and since then it has plummeted to as few as 20,000. "When I first came to Ol Donyo Wuas there were 50 lions on the ranch," says Bonham. "Now we're lucky if we have 15. What we have here is a snapshot of a major conservation crisis that has scarcely touched the outside world. The king of beasts is striding to oblivion and no one is listening."

Part of the reason the world doesn't appreciate the situation is because visitors see lions in tourist hotspots such as the Maasai Mara and think they are plentiful everywhere. The truth is that lions need vast areas in which to roam and only a few parks can satisfy their need for space and prey and full protection. Outside the parks, conflict with pastoralists such as the Maasai is inevitable.

In the old days the Maasai tolerated the lions' presence. They respected the power of the big carnivores and measured their own courage by killing them in ritual lion hunts. But then, in the space of a few years, their attitude changed.

❧   ❧   ❧

At Mbirikani it all began one hot afternoon in 2001 when a group of

Maasai elders met under a tree to debate the fate of the lions on their ranch. The prevailing mood did not bode well for the big cats. "I think we should get rid of them once and for all," said one of their leaders. "We'll be far better off without them."

Their chosen method was not the spear but carbofuran, an agricultural pesticide widely available in Africa. A carcass laced with this chemical cocktail becomes a lethal weapon. "It's cheap, too," says Tom Hill, the Texan entrepreneur and philanthropist who is Bonham's business partner and fellow trustee. "For a couple of dollars you can buy enough to poison every lion in Maasailand. It's a horrible death and the stuff remains active for weeks, killing not only lions but vultures and other scavengers."

Why would a people who once revered the lion as part of their culture come to regard these magnificent cats as vermin? The answer, Hill says, lies in the exposure to Western culture that is hauling these traditional pastoralists out of their dung-plastered huts into the world's cash economy. "Nowadays, instead of regarding their cattle as mere status symbols they have begun to see them in terms of hard cash," he says.

Understandably, they want bicycles, cell phones, money for school fees and medical care; and the wealthiest – the Maasai cattle barons – want television sets, cars and Western-style houses.

Over the next two years the Maasai set about ruthlessly exterminating every lion they could find, and by 2003 the last great pride of the Chyulu Hills was gone. "This was the scale of the problem we were up against," says Tom Hill. "All we had left were a dozen lions in what experts believe is the very epicentre of the lion's world."

It was then that the Predator Compensation Fund kicked in. "If we hadn't got the scheme off the ground when we did," says Hill, "we would have lost our lions for good. Instead, so far as Mbirikani is concerned, the killing virtually stopped."

Then in December last year came a major setback when two lions were poisoned. One was the local pride male, a magnificent specimen known as Sangale ('the Clever One'). The other was a pregnant lioness that was found to be carrying five cubs when she died.

Tom Hill was distraught. "For the sake of a $200 cow," he says "this man killed two lions, each one of which was worth hundreds of thousands of dollars to the Kenyan tourist trade."

Yet even this tragedy had a silver lining. In the old days the Maasai might have closed ranks to protect the culprit, but not this time. He was quickly identified and is now languishing in jail in Nairobi, leaving the local community to mourn the death of their favourite lion. "We miss Sangale," one old man told me, brushing the flies from his face. "To us it was like losing a prize bull."

Now at last the project seems to be paying off and Tom Hill is quietly optimistic. "The first thing to say about our economics-based strategy to save lions is that it is working," he says. "Secondly, the idea came from the Maasai themselves. At the end of the day we ignored conventional wisdom and listened to what they had to say."

There is no doubt that the compensation scheme has proved crucial in persuading the Maasai to spare the lions and it has brought about all kinds of benefits. For a start, to remove lions from the ecosystem is to set in motion the law of unintended consequences – including an increase in the number of hyenas that kill three times as many livestock. At the same time wildebeest numbers also expand, bringing with them diseases that can devastate Maasai cattle herds in a way that a few lions can never do.

In addition, besides employing 38 people as game scouts and lion guardians, the scheme is funding new schools and medical aid. "At present we're paying out compensation at the rate of two livestock a day but it's a mistake to think we are just saving lions," says Hill. "The lion is just the totem at the top of the food chain. Protect the lion, we figure, and you'll save the whole habitat and the Maasai culture as well."

If proof was needed that the Maasai have been won over you need only talk to Kiyok Mamai, chief of the 800-strong Mbirikani *morans*. "I would hate it if there were no more lions," he told me. "They are part of our life and our culture. Without them we cannot truly be Maasai."

Two years ago, entirely on his own initiative, he set up the Mbirikani Conservation Society to help save the big cats and asked Richard Bonham to be the patron. "You can imagine our surprise and great joy when this happened," says Bonham. His reward was a trip last year to San Diego, where he told reporters: "We have laid down our spears to save the lion."

"The key to our breakthrough was listening to the local Maasai community," says Tom Hill. "Pay us for our livestock losses and we'll stop killing lions. That is what they were saying and that has been the catalyst for change. The next step is to expand the programme, to roll it out across the rest of the unprotected areas between Tsavo and Amboseli. Otherwise we will have won the battle but lost the war."

May 2010: The Lions of Shompole

WHAT an extraordinary lodge is Shompole. As you fly in from Nairobi the first thing you notice are its rooftops, be-wigged with thatch, like an African ark come to rest on the Nguruman escarpment. From here it presides over a vast private wildlife fiefdom on the floor of the Great Rift Valley, with stunning views deep down into Tanzania.

Its designer is Anthony Russell, the maverick son of a white Kenyan hunter, an engaging and multi-faceted character, an artist, rock musician and mad-keen conservationist whose passion for lions and Maasai culture is overshadowed only by his success at building exotic safari lodges.

Straight lines and right angles are anathema to him. Instead at Shompole you live among curving, icing sugar walls that reflect the rolling Rift Valley contours, in palatial rooms without doors or windows, each with its own plunge pool and water flowing along shallow runnels, as in the Gardens of the Alhambra, creating the perfect counterpoint to the blinding heat of the Rift.

The pillars supporting the high-peaked roofs are simply the bleached and polished trunks of dead sycamore figs, and its bare decks are fashioned from the same pale timber. Decoration comes in the form of riverbed pebbles, arranged here and there with Zen-like simplicity, and in the centre of each room stands a king-size bed which, draped at night in its filmy mosquito net, becomes a bug-free zone within a house that is always open to the wind.

It is an idyllic place. Wood doves call in the depths below, giving the heat a voice in harmony with Shompole's mood of seductive indolence, and in the evenings with the night breeze blowing in under the thatch, it induces in me a feeling akin to standing in the bows of an old-time clipper ship, as if at any moment we might cast off and sail out into the dark void of the Rift beyond.

The lodge is named after Shompole Mountain, whose furrowed flanks rise steeply from the Rift Valley floor near the border with Tanzania. Beyond it lie the soda flats of Lake Natron, coloured candy pink in places by clouds of lesser flamingos, and the smoking cone of Ol Doinyo Lengai, the holy mountain of the Maasai.

The Maasai are very much in evidence at Shompole, whose 40,000-acre concession is part of a much bigger group ranch owned by the local community and provides them with a handsome income while allowing their pastoral way of life to continue. At the same time, as in other private game conservancies elsewhere in Kenya, it has encouraged the Maasai to preserve wildlife rather than seeing it as a threat to be disposed of by fair means or foul.

When Russell first came here in 1999 there were only five lions left alive. "Today there are 68," he says. "Along with at least eight leopards and a dozen cheetahs. So we must be doing something right."

A self-confessed lion junkie, he is eager to show me the hunting grounds of the Shompole prides. It is the beginning of the *kiangazi*, the dry season, and as we bump down the steep track to the Rift Valley floor we disturb thousands of doves that have flown in to feed on the ripening grass seeds. Coveys of quail shoot away from beneath our wheels and the skies are alive with migrating bee-eaters.

By mid-morning the Rift will become a furnace, its sandy surface tormented by dust devils; but at this early hour the air is still cool and crisp as we scan the plains for cats. Their prey is everywhere: zebra, wildebeest, giraffe, impala; and so is their sign. Between the swamps and the gallery forests of flat-topped acacias we cross open ground littered with horns and bones – a charnel house of old lion kills.

Accompanying us is Russell's best guide. Ngatia Sempeta is a Loita Maasai with a profile like Keith Richard, traditionally dressed in a brightly coloured *shuka* and bead earrings. Ngatia, says Russell, is a classic case of poacher-turned gamekeeper. "He speared thirteen lions and nine rhinos before he saw the light."

As we drive along they talked with the easy banter of lifelong chums. "If you don't find us a lion," says Russell, "I may have to cut off your left testicle." Ngatia just grins, and ten minutes later his manhood is made safe when he spots two male lions with tobacco brown manes resting in the shade. "Beautiful, aren't they," says Russell admiringly as one of them treats us to a prodigious yawn. "These guys are brothers; four years old and just coming into their prime."

In the afternoon, as a change from game driving, Russell takes me to meet the Maasai. By the simple expedient of buying a goat for a meat-feast, he has persuaded the local warriors and their girlfriends to put on a dance.

So here we sit in a forest of fig trees, in canvas-backed chairs on the banks of a sand river as the young men and girls emerge from the trees in two swaying lines, chanting and stamping as they approach.

This is *Strictly Come Dancing*, Kenyan style, and while the girls bob in time to the rhythm, making their bead necklaces bounce up and down, the warriors in their ostrich plumes and lion-mane headdresses take it in turns to advance with hands held stiffly by their sides as they compete to see who can leap the highest.

Maybe it is just a show put on for my benefit but it is as authentic as anything I have ever seen, and as much a part of Africa as the big cats we found earlier, whose survival is increasingly dependent upon the Maasai and their new understanding of the need for conservation.

Chapter Five

Southern Tanzania

July 2004: Sand Rivers

EVER since I first read *Sand Rivers*, Peter Matthiessen's classic account of a Selous safari undertaken in 1979, I had dreamed of visiting Africa's biggest game reserve.

Now here I am, crammed in the back of a six-seater Cessna, flying from Dar es Salaam over a sea of *miombo* – the crackling dry deciduous woodlands that seem to stretch forever across southern Tanzania.

For mile after mile I can see no settlement. No villages. No maize fields. Not so much as a dirt road to break the monotony of the bush as we lurch from thermal to thermal through the hot African sky, until at last I can make out the gleam of a huge river up ahead, coiling between sandbars the size of Blackpool beach.

"The Rufiji," shouts the pilot over his shoulder, and suddenly we are banking in a 45-degree turn that brings us low enough to see pods of hippos in the coffee-brown water, the glimpse of a safari camp hidden in the trees, and a big bull elephant with .yellow tusks shaking his ears in displeasure at his peace being disturbed.

The first thing that strikes you about the Selous – apart from the bludgeoning heat – is the sheer size of it. This is wilderness on an epic scale. Think of a game reserve larger than Wales, three times the size of Tsavo and almost four times bigger than the Serengeti, with not so much as a square metre of tarmac and no habitation of any kind except for a handful of safari lodges.

Its most defining feature is the Rufiji itself. For 30 miles, fed by the Great Ruaha and a host of lesser tributaries (Luwegu, Mbarangandu, Kilombero), Tanzania's mightiest river flows through the reserve, breathing life into the riverine forests and creating a lush maze of lakes and bird-haunted channels before sweeping on down to the Indian Ocean.

The presence of so much water in a thirsty land is one reason why the Selous is able to support such a high density of game. In the dry season when many tributaries are reduced to sand rivers, the Rufiji still flows, helping upwards of 100,000 Cape buffalo and 60,000 hippo to stay alive, not to mention the numerous leopards, lion prides and packs of highly endangered wild dogs, whose last true stronghold this is.

Tourism is largely confined to the 12 per cent of the reserve that lies north of the Rufiji. The rest, mostly tsetse-infested *miombo* woodland, is given over to trophy hunting. But that still leaves more than 2,000 square miles of pristine big game country for photo safaris.

At the Selous Safari Camp (since re-named Siwandu) you'll see why Prince Charles brought William and Harry here in 1997. With a dozen palatial tents overlooking Lake Nzelakela, this really is a hideaway fit for princes. Behind the camp, impalas flit through endless glades of terminalia woodlands, but most of the game is concentrated closer to the lakeshore where lions often lie in ambush.

For a closer look at the local wildlife I embark on a cruise in an aluminium boat.

Borassus palms rise from the water like the temple columns of a lost city – a defining image of the Selous – and the scent of wild jasmine hangs in the air. Buffaloes glower from the banks; elephants crash away through the trees; and, as we drift deeper into the labyrinth of narrow channels that flow between the lake and the river, the skies fill with white-fronted bee-eaters as they swoop and shrill above their burrows.

🐾   🐾   🐾

After three blissful days I move on to Sand Rivers, the luxury lodge set up by veteran guide Richard Bonham in 1984, the year he kick-started the concept of old-fashioned foot safaris using fly camps and long lines of porters – as the early explorers had done a century beforehand.

The location is hard to beat, with eight open-fronted cottages looking out over a wide, sunset-facing bend in the Rufiji. From here I have planned to go fly camping, forgoing the lodge's five-star comforts to explore the surrounding maze of sand rivers on foot.

But first I want to see something of the Rufiji itself, and by far the most enjoyable way to do this is to cruise upstream for a picnic breakfast at Stiegler's Gorge. Stiegler was a Swiss adventurer, killed here by an elephant in 1907, but hippos present a greater hazard. Hippos are the 'Jaws' of Africa, and bumping into a territorial Rufiji bull – one ton of pure testosterone with cavernous mouth and curving tusks – is an experience well worth avoiding.

That is why, as we putter between sand bars where skimmers preen and crocodiles bask with jaws agape, we steer a cautious slalom course around the hippos whose pools we have invaded.

At last we arrive at the mouth of the gorge where the river emerges after its four-mile journey through the hills. Here we haul the boat ashore in a sandy cove with fresh leopard prints all around, and picnic on a rocky ledge while trumpeter hornbills call in the hanging woods and a crowned eagle sails past on outstretched wings.

Sadly, the integrity of this special place is once again at risk for, although the Selous is a UNESCO World Heritage Site, the Tanzanian Government has revived controversial plans to build a hydroelectric dam and power plant in Stiegler's Gorge – a scheme that could alter the life of the Rufiji forever.

Back at the lodge it will soon be time to put on my walking boots and explore the Selous on foot as Matthiessen did three decades ago with a group that included Richard Bonham, the wildlife film-maker Hugo van Lawick and a young Zambian called Robin Pope who is now one of his country's most distinguished safari guides. Led by Brian Nicholson, who had served there for many years as a game warden, Matthiessen and his colleagues could not have been in better hands, and his book, *Sand Rivers*, brings the Selous vividly to life, together with the characters who have become a part of its history, including the taciturn, hard-as-nails Nicholson himself.

Their intention was to undertake an expedition deep into the southernmost reaches of the park where the Mbarangandu River meanders through a sun-scorched world of endless thornbush, tsetse flies, swampy valleys and impenetrable *miombo*. In the words of Tom Arnold MP, who had dreamed up the idea, it was to be "the last safari into the last wilderness." But whereas they had a month to pursue their dream, I have only two days in which to get a taste of the hardships and pleasures they encountered.

At last I switch off the light, put *Sand Rivers* aside and lie in the darkness beneath my mosquito net listening to the staccato barking of baboons in the riverine forest. Somewhere out there a predator is moving, probably a leopard, and the big, dog-faced males are giving voice to their fears: *waah-hu, waah-hu*, echoing down the moonlit Rufiji.

The baboons are still shouting from their treetop roosts when I set out next morning with Sandor Carter, a pony-tailed ex-British army officer carrying a heavy rifle, and Emmanuel Senkoro, a hawk-eyed tracker from Kilimanjaro.

The two of them are ideal companions for a walk in thick bush where anything could be lurking – especially as Sandor's plan is to intercept a herd of elephants on their return from the woodlands where they feed every night. Sure enough, we come upon a group of eight. "Let's get a bit closer," Sandor whispers, and we creep to within 25 metres of them, holding our breath as they pass slowly by without ever knowing we are there.

Towards evening we make camp in the middle of a sand river and after a hearty fireside supper I turn in. My tent consists of nothing more than a groundsheet and a mosquito net propped up on four beanpoles; but the bed is comfortable and I lie for a while, looking up at the stars seething overhead with unbelievable brilliance. Somewhere not far off a lion begins to grunt, the most thrilling sound in Africa, and I find it oddly satisfying to know that nothing lies between me and the big cats but a flimsy sheet of gauze.

September 2007: The Dogs of Beho Beho

THREE years have passed since my last visit to the Selous, but stepping out again into its heat-stunned wilderness it feels as if I were here only yesterday.

The first thing I see are the words Beho Beho, spelt out in bleached white hippo bones at the edge of the landing strip. Beho Beho is the most comfortable safari lodge in southern Tanzania. It takes its name from a local dialect word, meaning breeze; and while the rest of the Selous swelters in the lowland heat, Beho Beho keeps its cool in the encircling hills.

It began life in 1972 as a hunting camp set up by Brian Nicholson, the reserve's famed warden, and was run by Ker & Downey, the East African safari operators. Later it became the private home of a local businessman who died in 2002, but not before transforming it into the oasis of comfort that is Beho Beho today, complete with swimming pool, cocktail bar and a full-size billiard table.

Luxury is all very well, but what Beho Beho offers above all is wilderness on an epic scale. The Selous is the largest animal sanctuary on the continent – big enough to swallow up the whole of Wales or Maryland and still have room to spare. It was named after Frederick Courteney Selous, the 19th century naturalist, elephant hunter and soldier who died here in 1917 during a fierce skirmish with the Germans. His grave lies only a couple of miles from camp.

Born in 1852, he became the greatest white hunter ever to set foot in the African bush and the prototype for Allan Quatermain, H. Rider Haggard's hero in *King Solomon's Mines*. Credited with extraordinary powers of endurance, he shot elephants on horseback, met the Matabele king Lobengula, was mauled by a lion and became a close friend of President Roosevelt.

When the First World War broke out he was living quietly in Surrey but immediately volunteered for active service and returned to East Africa in 1915 to take on General von Lettow Vorbeck's formidable *Schutztruppe* in what was then called Tanganyika. Here he was awarded a DSO for conspicuous gallantry, but a year later, at the age of 66, his luck ran out at Beho Beho when he was shot in the head by a German sniper.

Today it is hard to imagine a more peaceful setting than the battleground where Selous met his end. "The rarest sight around here is another tourist vehicle," says Sean Lues as we set out on my first game drive. Lues is a professional safari guide, one of the best in the business, who learned his trade in Zimbabwe but moved on when President Mugabe's excesses made life impossible. Now happily settled in Tanzania, he loves the remoteness of the Selous, its wildness and untrammelled horizons.

We drive slowly, eyes peeled for the carnivores whose presence adds a frisson of excitement to every moment spent in big game territory. But although the Selous is renowned for its big cats – its prowling leopards and prides of lions – our hearts are set on tracking down an altogether more elusive predator.

Wild dogs are what scientists call *Lycaon pictus* – the painted wolves – a perfect description for these lean and rangy creatures with their brindled coats and big bat ears. Like the timber wolves of North America they roam in packs and are among the most endangered hunting animals on earth, living everywhere in the shadow of extinction except in the thorny vastness of the Selous, their last great refuge.

In the whole of Africa maybe fewer than 3,000 wild dogs survive. And of those, perhaps half of them live in the Selous. Their Swahili nickname is *chaka-chaka* – 'the ones that trot' – referring to the loping gait they maintain for miles, wearing down their prey in a single-minded chase to the death.

We stop to scan the surrounding hills, and as I raise my binoculars a sudden movement catches my eye – it's a herd of panic-stricken impala dashing headlong across a distant hillside. My first thought is a leopard hidden in the rocks. But then we hear an eerie hooting. "Know what that is?" asks Lues. I do. It's the contact call of wild dogs.

Moments later we see a spiral of vultures dropping out of the sky. Maybe they know something we don't? So we head towards them, crashing through the bush in a cloud of dust.

No wonder the *chaka-chaka* are hot to trot. By the time we find them they have made their kill – a full-grown impala ram. There are only two dogs – both adult males – but they dispose of the carcass in double quick time, putting away a good 18 kilograms of meat between them. Then, after slaking their thirst at a nearby spring, they melt away into the fathomless thickets with not so much as a backward glance.

No matter what excitement each morning brings it is always a joy to return to camp. Most days there is time for a swim before lunch, and the food is outstanding, with lobster and other seafood treats flown in fresh from the coast.

Afterwards there is time for *pumzika* – the wonderful Swahili word for 'a snooze'. But when I reach my thatched chalet with its polished stone floors and Turkish rugs I find it impossible to ignore the view. There is a telescope on the veranda and the plains below are alive with game: elephant, buffalo, giraffe and eland.

On my last day in the Selous I go walking with Sean, who now carries a rifle as we follow well-trodden game trails beside a dried-up watercourse. We walk in silence and in a little while, half hidden in a forest of leaning palms, we come upon a solitary elephant, a giant bull with ears like barn doors and tusks that almost touch the ground. He has not heard us. He is too busy scooping up the fallen palm fruit with his trunk and the wind is in our favour. So, step by cautious step, we approach even closer.

"It's Majembe," whispers Sean. "He's at least 50 years old and is the biggest elephant for miles around." Somehow I feel sure he knows we are there, yet still he continues to feed peacefully as the light deepens to melted gold and the calls of the doves ring on and on.

In the evening, instead of returning to the lodge we make our way to a small bush camp on the banks of the Beho Beho Sand River. Set in a grove of sheltering palms, this is fly-camping deluxe, in a candle-lit tent with a proper double bed, silk wall hangings and an en-suite shower.

Dinner is served in the middle of the riverbed. There are lanterns around the table but the moon is so bright they are scarcely needed. Later, after turning in, I look out through the mosquito net window at the black-and-silver riverbed and listen to the Scops owls' repetitive chirruping calls and the far-off groan of lions, and wonder where the dogs will be sleeping tonight.

October 2007: The Park that Time Forgot

BOUNCING through the mid-day thermals, I watch the shadow of our 12-seater bush plane flitting over the hot dry heart of Tanzania. As we draw closer to Msembe airstrip the landscape changes. Our final approach reveals a range of broken hills and a herd of zebra beneath our wingtips, stampeding across a yellow plain. Beyond it I can see a mighty sand river bordered by flat-topped acacias, and still further off, solemn giraffes standing like markers, measuring the yawning distance.

This is my first sight of Ruaha and already one question is running through my head. Why did I wait so long? There is a rawness here I have never seen before. Here at last is the real thing, the unexpurgated Africa of long ago, and the moment to explore it has arrived.

Waiting to greet me is Chris Fox, a barefoot figure in faded khaki shirt and shorts. Chris is the owner of Mwagusi, the best lodge in the park. "Straight to camp or the scenic route?" he enquires. "I choose the second option and off we go in his open Land Cruiser, heading for Kilimamatonge Hill, a soon-to-be familiar landmark.

It is late September, deep in the dry season. The blue skies are hazy with the smoke of bush fires. The combretum thickets are in flower and kudu antelope – the males with handsome corkscrew horns – are nibbling at the flame-red blossoms.

Eventually we reach camp: eight spacious bandas on the banks of the bone-dry Mwagusi River. Each one has a high-peaked roof of makuti thatch, giving them the air of Noah's arks left stranded among the rocks, although Noah never lived in such comfort.

At lunch I meet a fellow guest, an American called Ed who tells me he has been all over Africa but doesn't bother to go anywhere else now because nowhere is better than Ruaha. "I've been here only two days and already I have seen three cheetahs, two leopards and God knows how many lions," he says.

Over much of Africa lions are declining, but not in Ruaha. Chris Fox knows of 185 within 30 kilometres of camp and he's not joking. I know this because one night five nomadic males pay us a visit. They are hell-bent on a pride take-over and for the next two hours they roar and roar. Their message to the resident males is unambiguous, and in the morning I find their tracks outside my door – each paw print as big as my outstretched hand.

Ed is right. There is nowhere better, and with each passing day, following its red ochre game trails among the smouldering purple hills, I can feel the Ruaha getting under my skin. There is nothing gentle about it like the Serengeti. Its beauty is of an altogether harsher kind. Its parched plains are littered with granite boulders and wherever one looks there are grotesque baobabs as old as London, bare branches outstretched against the sky as if begging for rain.

By chance my visit had coincided with the arrival of John 'Steve' Stephenson, the Ruaha's first game warden. Now in his eighties and living in Dorset, he has come back to see how the park has fared since he helped to establish it in 1962.

Together with Chris we visit the palm grove beside the Mwagusi where he had arrived in his beaten-up old Land Rover to set up the park's first HQ. We poke around in the grass, but apart from an overgrown slab of concrete no trace of the original buildings remains. "It's as if those days had never been," he says. But later he is overjoyed when we find a lioness suckling two small cubs where he used to stroll when the world was young.

I ask Steve if the park has changed. "There was lots more water in the Ruaha River," he says. "But once you get into the bush it's as wild as ever."

Back at camp a bush dinner has been prepared with tables set out in the sandy riverbed. As we eat under the stars our meal is interrupted by a line of chanting figures coming out of the darkness, each one carrying a lantern that swings in time to the rhythm of their song. Without any prompting Chris's camp staff have decided to put on a show to welcome Steve back to the park he helped to create half a century ago.

Next morning we set off on a game drive before the sun has risen. Elephants cross the road in front of us, led by a matriarch with ragged ears, and as we pass through a grove of baobabs Chris points out a tree with pegs hammered into its bloated trunk by past generations of honey-hunters.

On we go, looking for lions along the sand rivers, and with every mile I find myself slipping deeper under Ruaha's spell. In September the landscape is everywhere painted in the muted colours of the dry season, but towards evening it glows like amber; and it is now, in the golden hour before sundown that we spot three cats in the grass: a mother cheetah and her two cubs.

Over so much of Africa our covenant with the wild has been broken beyond repair; but not here. Not yet. These Ruaha cheetahs no longer run at the sight of a vehicle. The youngsters are almost full-grown and lie apart from their mother, calling to her with un-cat-like chirrups. When at last she rejoins them they rub against each other in an orgy of affection, then jump down into the riverbed to pose for us on a fallen tree trunk.

By now I have realised how lucky I am to have Chris Fox as my guide. Like so many men who grow up in the wild he oozes charisma. Over a bush breakfast on the banks of the Mwagusi he tells me about the female leopard that sometimes sleeps on his bedroom floor and I have no reason to disbelieve him. Apart from schooldays spent in Devon, he has known the Ruaha all his life and his passion for it shines through in everything he says.

As a boy he and his family were often the only visitors. He remembers how, as an eight-year-old, he would go hunting on foot with his father in this secret, unheard-of paradise.

"Those were the days when a character known as Old Man Scotty used to hunt crocodiles in the Great Ruaha River," he recalls. "Scotty used an aluminium boat he'd converted from the fuselage of a crashed light aircraft and hunted at night by torchlight, shooting the crocs between the eyes with the same .22 rifle he eventually turned on himself when hunting was banned."

Even after Ruaha was given national park status in 1964 it continued to be overlooked, and in the mid-1970s its very survival was put at risk by a rice-growing scheme on the Usangu plains – the main catchment area for the Great Ruaha River.

Today the river is so starved of water that it ceases to flow for four months of the year, with disastrous effects for the vast buffalo herds that were the main prey for Ruaha's lions. "What a sight it was," says Chris, "to see a thousand buffaloes, a wall of horns confronting a determined pride. Often they would bring down four or five in a single raid. Then the river dried up. The buffaloes crashed, from 32,000 to 2,000, and those ancient confrontations are history."

Then came the 1980s, the dark decade when the ivory poachers moved in and the elephant population fell from 40,000 to just 9,000. Every dry season the park went up in smoke as the poachers set their bush fires, and on moonlit nights the woodlands echoed to the sound of gunfire and the whooping of hyenas drawn to the carcasses. At its peak, ivory poaching was accounting for 1,500 elephants every year and rumour has it that the great TAZARA railway, built by the Chinese, was paid for with the blood of Ruaha's elephants.

"I thought I would never see an end to the killing," Fox confesses. But end it did. In 1987 a new warden arrived, vowing he would stop the poaching. "I listened politely but didn't believe him," said Fox. "After all, Ruaha was the punishment posting, Tanzania's most neglected park. But he was true to his word. As the year progressed he drove out the poachers and in 1988 the ivory trade ban brought the killing to a standstill."

Now, nearly two decades on, things are looking up. Ruaha's elephant population has risen to 30,000 – the biggest in East Africa – and now that the adjoining Usangu Game Reserve has been added, Ruaha is bigger than the Serengeti and second only to Kafue in Zambia as the biggest national park in Africa.

Visitors, too, are increasing. Twenty years ago Ruaha attracted little more than 350 tourists a year. Today that number has risen to 6,000 – still a drop in the ocean compared to the Serengeti – but not enough to satisfy the Tanzanians.

Tanzania's new national tourism policy contains radical proposals that could change the face of Ruaha forever. These plans would double the size of the park's four existing camps and encourage new ones, bringing mass tourism to what has hitherto been a pristine wilderness.

You might wonder how such an increase could possibly spoil a park twice the size of Belgium. But while the Ruaha looks big on a map its prime game-viewing circuits are confined to little more than a hundred kilometres of tracks beside the Mwagusi and Ruaha rivers. Beyond this stunningly beautiful core area, much of the park consists of monotonous sun-scorched *miombo* – where game is sparse and tsetse flies can make life a misery. Far better, urge conservationists, to establish new low volume, high yield camps in the Usangu wetlands for the lucrative top-end tourist market.

If ever a park depended upon responsible tourism it is Ruaha. Until now, remoteness has proved its salvation. To fly there from Dar es Salaam still takes the best part of three hours, so it can never hope to compete with easy-to-reach destinations like the Serengeti or Maasai Mara.

Such thoughts cast a shadow across my stay, but are set aside next morning when we go out early to look for leopards.

When your eyes have been away from Africa for a long time, they hunger for the sight of a leopard. Why this should be so is hard to describe, but big cat fanatics will know the feeling. It is not just that exquisitely dappled coat, or the leopard's secretive lifestyle. There is something else; and that is why even the unseen presence of this elegant carnivore injects every game drive with an extra pulse of excitement.

So picture the scene at dawn: the baobabs casting long shadows across the road and a big male leopard stalking guinea fowl in the backlit grass. Chris recognises him at once. "He's the son of the mother that visits my bedroom," he whispers.

At our approach the hunt is aborted. Exit guinea fowl in a clatter of wings, and now, tail held in a graceful curve, the leopard strolls nonchalantly towards us. As he walks past our vehicle I can barely resist an insane desire to reach out and stroke him. Then, with not so much as a backward glance he is gone, melting into the boundless thickets of the park that time forgot.

Chapter Six
Zambia

July 1978: Confrontation in Kafue

WHEN I was still new to Africa I went into Zambia's Kafue National Park on a walking safari with a veteran guide called Cecil Evans. The bush was dense in places and I was relieved to see that he carried a rifle. Suddenly, without warning a very aggressive bull elephant exploded from the trees and came straight for us, head high and screaming like an express train.

I can still recall that moment as if it happened yesterday. "Stay where you are and don't run," says Evans, a singularly worthless piece of advice since my legs have already turned to jelly, rendering the option of running impossible. He steps forward, slapping the butt of his gun and shouting obscenities at the angry tusker, which skids to a halt just a few metres in front of us, shaking its huge ragged ears as it towers over us.

There follows a nail-biting stand-off which ends only when Evans takes off his bush hat and hurls it at the elephant, screaming "Bugger off" at the top of his voice, after which the big bull spins around and lumbers off into the bush, ripping a sapling out of the ground as it does so.

Had we been subjected to a mock charge or faced down the real thing? "Could have gone either way," says Evans afterwards, "but I sure didn't want to shoot unless I had to."

July 2003: Eyeball to Eyeball with the Kutandala Pride

WALKING in lion country is a good way to increase your attention span, and when it comes to foot safaris there is nowhere better than Zambia. After all, this is the country where the old-fashioned, Dr Livingstone-style safari was reinvented.

How fast the world has moved on since Livingstone died at Chitambo in the Bangweulu Wetlands in 1873. Today's travellers come prepared for everything Africa can throw at them. They pop anti-malaria pills, zoom in by plane, hit the bush in padded Toyota Land Cruisers and relax in five-star luxury lodges.

Yet there are still those who hanker for a more down-to-earth safari experience – one that brings you face to face with nature on level terms – showering under the stars, travelling on foot, the way it used to be. And that is what North Luangwa National Park offers.

When Rod Tether meets me at the dusty airstrip we drive for an hour down a rutted track, then park on the banks of the Mwaleshi River. "It's boots-off time," he says. "The camp is on the other side. We won't need the vehicle again until you leave."

Unlike the Luangwa River, the Mwaleshi flows crystal clear and is, Rod assures me as we wade across, virtually free of crocs and hippos. "Although we did have a rogue hippo last week," he adds. "It demolished one of the deck chairs we had left by the bank. Then it defecated on it for good measure, just to make its feelings known."

North Luangwa is serious wilderness. Imagine a park the size of Mallorca with no roads, no permanent buildings and no people except for the likes of Rod, who started guiding in 1989 at the age of 18, and Guz, his wife, a kitchen wizard who learned how to cook at Ballymaloe in Ireland and conjures up Cordon Bleu miracles on beds of hot wood ash.

Their small camp, Kutandala, is one of only three in the entire park and accommodates no more than six lucky guests at a time. At its heart stands a giant Natal mahogany tree whose generous shade and low-slung branches serve as dining room, bar and library. In short, it's a place for safari purists.

"I'm a Luddite when it comes to bush camps," Rod confesses. Not for him the glitzy lodges of other parks with their safari-chic furnishings. Instead, my home for the next few nights is a rustic affair of reeds and thatch, with rush mats on a bare earth floor and a shower open to the sky.

At dawn a tea tray is brought to my bedside. The bamboo blinds – lowered at night to deter lions and hyenas – are rolled up, and there, beyond the waist-high wall at the end of my bed, is Africa: a wide-screen vision of a red dawn sky, the river flowing, and an endless frieze of woods beyond.

Rod has news for me when I meet up with him again by the campfire. A buffalo bull was killed in the night not far from where I slept. Now only the horned head and a black bag of bones remain at the scene of the crime; but the butchers, the Kutandala lion pride, can't be too far away. By now they will probably be resting, Rod says, sleeping off the effects of their meal somewhere in the uncombed tangles of combretum bush down by the river.

So we go looking for them, walking quietly between the thickets, talking in whispers. In front is Tryson Nkhoma, our armed ranger in his green uniform; then comes Rod, then me.

Suddenly Tryson freezes. Rod points. And there are the lions – an adult lioness and three young males with rag-tag manes, resting on the far side of a clearing. We move closer, more slowly now, approaching obliquely until no more than a hundred feet of open ground lies between us, and it occurs to me that a lion could cover that distance in about four seconds flat.

For maybe five minutes we stand there. We watch them and the lions watch us, until eventually the three youngsters switch off. One by one their heads drop and they begin to doze, panting in the windless heat; but not so the lioness. Her whole body language says: "Don't mess with me," and even when we back away I can still feel her pale eyes upon me, as if she is looking deep into my soul.

September 2004: Night Hunters of the Busanga Plains

I AM back again in Kafue, the oldest and biggest national park in Zambia, more than twice the size of South Luangwa, and Busanga Bush Camp lies in its northern sector in the heart of the Busanga Plains. If there is a more remote camp in Zambia I have yet to find it. To reach it I have driven for three hours from Lunga River Camp through the tsetse-infested *miombo* followed by a canoe trip through the Lufupa swamps.

With room for no more than six guests at a time, the camp is simplicity itself, set in an island of fig trees with mind-blowing views across the encircling plains – and what an extraordinary place this is. For much of the year the plains are flooded, and the famous Busanga lions become semi-aquatic, splashing across its drowning landscapes in search of lechwe. But for a few precious months, when the rainy season ends in May and the floodwaters recede, it becomes a Zambian Serengeti of zebras and antelopes and bugling cranes reaching out as far as the eye can see.

Days at Busanga begin just after five when the pre-dawn light seeps over the plains and the bees begin to hum in the tree above my tent. There is coffee and toast by the campfire, and then it is time for my first game drive with Lexxon Munana, who knows this land like his own garden.

Inevitably it is Lexxon who first spots the local lion pride at rest under a massive fig tree whose iron-grey boughs are scarred with claw marks. In the heat of October, he tells me, the lions climb this tree to seek the breeze. Now, they sprawl in its shade: six lionesses and an 11-year-old male known as Earl.

Resplendent in his heavy mane, Earl is a magnificent specimen, and we meet him again at the end of the day. We are driving back to camp with the spotlight on, and pick out his lionesses as they fan across the plain. A herd of lechwe is not far off, so we kill the light and settle down to wait.

We sit in silence. The Milky Way glitters overhead and the smell of the grass is all around us. Then, out in the darkness comes a sudden rush of bodies. Lexxon snaps on the light to reveal a lechwe with a lioness on its heels. She grabs and misses and the antelope jinks away to freedom – only to be pulled down by a second lioness lying unseen in the grass.

It happens so fast. Even while the lechwe is still kicking in its death throes, the rest of the pride emerge from the shadows and fall on the kill, only to be shouldered aside by Earl as he muscles in for his share.

Ten minutes later – ten minutes of ill-tempered snarling and crunching of sinews – nothing is left but the horned head, which Earl picks up in his jaws and carries off into the night.

September 2004: In Search of the African Tiger

SUNRISE in the Zambezi Valley and the low light pours across the plains, igniting the tops of the winterthorn glades. Among the trees is the dark outline of an elephant bull. Its ears swing slowly as it feeds on the fallen seedpods, delicately searching for them with its trunk.

Grant Cumings, my companion, is just the kind of guide you need when walking in elephant country; confident, capable, thoroughly bush-wise. Elephants are his favourite animals, he tells me, and there is nowhere else he would rather be than here on the Lower Zambezi. "This is real, in-your-face Africa," he says. "Big skies, big trees, big elephants."

Much of Zambia is like this. One third of it is national parkland, and the accent is on small, owner-run camps offering the opportunity to explore some of Africa's most pristine wildlife areas with the best guides in the business.

Twenty years ago, when Grant and his dad used to come here to fish, the Lower Zambezi National Park didn't exist. They were the ones who put it on the tourist map, chased out the poachers, cut the first vehicle tracks and built the first camp.

Chiawa, where I am staying, should be on everybody's list of Top Ten Camps. It is set right beside the river in a mahogany grove and there are no fences to keep out the animals, as I discover at supper when an elephant looms up out of the dark, lured by the winterthorn seedpods that lie scattered around.

He stands behind us as we dine, close enough to touch, and the thought occurs that with one sweep of his trunk he could send us all to kingdom come: candles, wine glasses, cutlery and all. But, like all the bulls I encounter in this land of giants, he turns out to be a thoroughly well-behaved old gentleman, and eventually wanders back into the night from whence he has come.

At Chiawa the Zambezi is over a mile wide, and the next day I get a closer look at it on a fishing trip. Our quarry is the tiger fish. Its Latin name is *Hydrocynus vittatus*, the striped water dog – an apt name for a predator with Alsatian teeth and the disposition of an angry pit bull. Cumings describes it as a cross between an Atlantic salmon and a piranha. "Pound for pound it's probably the feistiest freshwater sport fish in the world," he says.

We anchor in midstream and bait up with chunks of fresh ox heart. Out flies the line and I sit down to wait – but almost at once I feel a hit. It's a tiger – nine pounds of fighting fury. Until this moment I have never been an angler. Now I'm hooked.

Despite the late September heat there is always coolness on the water, and when we stop fishing, we drift downriver to watch the wildlife. By now, the sun is sinking into the haze of bushfire smoke that hangs over Zambia in this season of burning; and behind us, outlined against the glowing sky like participants in a shadow play, two young bull elephants wade out into the river and begin to spar. I grab my camera, hoping to capture the moment, but I know that nothing will compare with being here, hearing their tusks click-clack as they thrust and grapple in the dying light.

June 2007: Walking with a Legend

"IF you're looking for wild, uncharted Africa," says Robin Pope, "Zambia is one of the few countries left where you can still find it." To be more specific he is talking about the Luangwa Valley, an immense offshoot of the Great Rift Valley.

Through it runs the mighty Luangwa, a vital tributary of the Lower Zambezi, coiling for 500 miles past sand bars as big as Cornish beaches and riparian forests of great blowsy trees. During the rains it bursts its banks, replenishing the ox-bow lagoons that are the ghosts of its former meanderings; but even in the dry season when it is shallow enough to wade across, it is the valley's lifeblood, sustaining the extraordinary cavalcade of wildlife to be found in the South Luangwa National Park.

It was Norman Carr, the legendary ex-warden and visionary conservationist, who re-invented the walking safari. That was back in the 1970s when ecotourism was in its infancy and the Luangwa was an unknown wilderness. Today, led by Carr's disciples, of whom Robin Pope is by far the best known, the Luangwa sets the benchmark for walking safaris.

It was Carr himself, the grand old man of the valley, who gave me my baptism in bush bashing, tracking black rhino from his camp at Chibembe. "I want visitors to touch the earth and smell the air," he declared, "and feel what it is like to be in the bush without being shut up in a vehicle."

That was where I had first met Robin, who was then a young protégé learning his trade. Now, 30 years on, the rhino are no more, every last one slaughtered by poachers, and Robin, who has since become a legend himself, has invited me to join him on a walking safari down the Mushilashi River into what he calls "wild and desperate country."

To reach it we are taken by road and dropped off deep in the park, an hour's drive from the well-used trails that hug the Luangwa River and its lagoon systems, on a hilltop called Kapiri Mfumu – 'the Hill of the Chief'. From here we follow a ridge walk through glades of autumn-coloured terminalia trees before dropping down into the fathomless *miombo* woodlands that run north for hundreds of miles all the way to Tanzania.

It is now two months since the last rain fell but the land is still green. Not until August will it acquire the tawny lion colour of the dry season as heat and drought intensify, and only then will the faultless blue sky turn hazy with the smoke of bush fires.

Walking releases you from the tyranny of roads and awakens senses you never knew you possessed. Only on foot are you free to interpret the maze of tracks in the dust, hear every sound and catch the scent of sun-dried grass.

Across the valley and beyond the trees I can see the dim blue outline of the Muchinga Escarpment, part of the Great Rift Valley wall that marks the western borders of the park. Then the long grass closes in around us, tall enough to hide an elephant. It's what Zambians call suicide grass – for obvious reasons – and is why Robin carries a heavy rifle.

Quiet and unassuming to a fault, he could pass for a librarian if you met him in London; but in Zambia, in his faded shorts, calf-length 'hot-pursuit boots' and beaten-up, wide-brimmed bush hat he is the consummate safari guide.

Like all true professionals he appears totally relaxed, yet he never drops his guard. He is like a leopard; he never completely switches off, and even in mid-conversation he will suddenly break off to point out a bird he has spotted. "Look, a Dickinson's kestrel!"

I ask him about the dangers posed by walking in big-game country, and which animals he most respects. "Elephant and hippo," he says without hesitation. "They're the ones you have to watch: elephants because of their size and unpredictability; hippos because they have this habit of hiding in the thick stuff." In all his years in the valley, he tells me, he has only had to drop two animals. Both were hippos.

"Don't expect to see a lot of animals," warns Robin. "This is a wilderness experience rather than a big game spectacular. It's a walk for those who want to see what Africa looked like in the long ago." Even so, no sooner do we reach the Mushilashi than we find fresh tracks of lion, leopard, elephant and buffalo together with those of hartebeest, zebra, giraffe and kudu.

The Mushilashi is a seasonal tributary of the Luangwa, prone to flash floods in the wet season; but now it has become a sand river, its flow reduced to the shallowest trickle, although elephants need only to dig down a foot or so to find water. We follow it for about ten kilometres until we reach a grove of borassus and hyphaene palms in which Robin has established a simple bush camp.

☙　　☙　　☙

He found the site on an anti-poaching patrol in 1991. Robin, who is also an honorary park ranger, stumbled across it when he and his team were on the track of a poaching gang. He had dreamed of building a camp there ever since, but not until last year did he obtain permission to go ahead.

Robin's first clients – a Swiss couple – had arrived only a month before me, yet it was still a thrill to be told I was the first British visitor to come here. Robin clearly loves it, too. "Wild country; no people," he says. "The kind of place I like best."

We take a shower, then sit in the shade with a hydraulic sandwich – Luangwa slang for a cold beer – with the wind sighing and the palm fronds cracking and flapping above our heads like the canvas sails of an old-time schooner as Robin tells me how he and his wife Jo were married in the park under a giant fig tree to the crying of fish eagles instead of church bells. (Later, back in Lusaka, Jo described coming to Luangwa and meeting Robin as 'finding the glove that fits'.)

Next morning the lyrical serenade of palm thrushes serve as a wake-up call, and at breakfast Robin demonstrates the bush-wise skills he learned when camping with his father by cooking eggs-and-bacon on a shovel over a mopane log fire. "Mopane is the best firewood in Africa," says Robin. "It burns with an intense heat but gives out little smoke."

Setting out at sun-up there's a coolness in the air that is scarcely believable by mid-morning when the valley becomes a furnace. We walk among fallen palm fronds with serrated edges like swordfish bills, then drop down into the riverbed and find fresh lion tracks.

"See how the front paws are bigger than the back ones," says Robin, "because they have to support the lion's head and shoulders." Older tracks show where buffalo have sunk up to their hocks in the damp sand beside the last meagre rivulets, and Robin explains that the animals can still find water here until the rains come in November.

Africa always seems bigger when you are on foot, and although Robin is never without his rifle I feel the tingle of heightened awareness that comes with walking in big game country. This is not just a stroll in the park and, as if to emphasise the point, a line of elephants emerge ahead of us, crossing the riverbed as if on a mission, leaving their wild-beast whiff of dung in the air.

We walk on to the squeal of brown parrots and drop down into a lugga, a dried-up watercourse overhung by figs and marula trees where we surprise a diminutive antelope. It is a common duiker and its black button nose twitches as we draw closer but it does not run. "It's probably never seen a human before," whispers Robin.

I am not surprised. So dense are the woodlands, so tall the grass in this pristine, back-of-beyond bush country that it would be virtually impenetrable but for the maze of trails beaten down by elephant and buffalo.

By the end of the day we have crossed the Luangwa and are back where my safari had begun, in the heart of the park with its well-used roads and luxury lodges. At the time, despite the hum of tourist vehicles, it had seemed like the wildest place on earth.

But now, after the total solitude of the Mushilashi, returning from the valley's outermost limits is almost as much of a culture shock as flying back to Lusaka.

June 2007: The Elephant House

THE big lioness came barrelling out of the thorn thicket and launched herself at the vultures that were stealing her kill. She came so fast that the birds were caught unawares. One moment they were squabbling and feeding and the next she was among them, lashing out as they departed in a panic-stricken explosion of flapping wings and falling feathers.

Earlier I had seen her gentler side as she lay with her sister while her three small cubs romped in the shade, tumbling over her tawny flanks and biting her tail in play. The two adults had killed a warthog that morning and it was the pig's half-eaten carcass that had attracted the scavengers.

Such encounters are commonplace when you rent Luangwa Safari House on the edge of Zambia's most famous national park. The house belongs to Robin Pope, with whom I had just walked down the Mushilashi, and is set in a private game concession area adjoining the Luangwa River. Robin's own home is just down the road, sharing the same idyllic views of the Chindeni Hills framed by dark groves of ebony trees.

Designed by Neil Rocher, the architect who created Kenya's stylish Shompole Lodge, Luangwa Safari House brings penthouse chic to the Zambian bush. From the outside, with its thatched roof propped up on six-ton leadwood trunks, it looks like a medieval tithe barn; but inside all is coolness and elegance, open to the wind and overhung by high rafters where fruit bats snooze in baronial splendour, suspended like ripe fruit among the crossbeams.

The house sleeps eight in four spacious rooms, and comes with its own chef and housekeeper. Meals are usually served outside, either beside the plunge pool or on a raised wooden deck in the shade of an ebony grove, and it is not uncommon to wake up after a lunchtime snooze to find one's self surrounded by elephants drinking and wallowing under the trees.

If renting a house in the bush is a novelty, so is the luxury of having your own safari vehicle to go with it, and an experienced Zambian guide to take you on game drives. Jacob Shawa is a big man in every sense, with a baritone voice and beaming smile. His people, the Ngoni, were famous warriors and his surname means 'spear-thrower', he tells me proudly as we cross the bridge over the Luangwa River.

Enclosed by green walls of riverine forest, the Luangwa is one of Africa's last untamed rivers. For much of its length it is as wide as the Thames at Westminster and alive from end to end with hippos – 40 for every muddy mile.

Soon we are deep in the park, eyes peeled for animals. South Luangwa is classic big game country and the dirt road ahead is criss-crossed with signs that Jacob's expert eyes translate: the cloven hoof prints of kudu and buffalo, and the thrilling sight of fresh lion spoor imprinted in the dust.

We drive on, stopping to photograph herds of impala mirrored in a dambo – an ox-bow lagoon enclosed between dark colonnades of water-loving ebony trees whose shady presence underlies the fact that the Luangwa is above all a woodland park.

Here, too, grow lofty marulas with mottled trunks, mighty tamarinds and strangler figs, grand old winterthorns, indestructible leadwoods, wide-spreading kigelias with fruit like outsize salamis, and centuries-old baobabs as fat as gasometers.

Under the trees, in the dappled aisles and grassy glades, parties of zebra seek the shade, and after a while you become aware of the horizontal browse line 18 feet above the ground, clipped by generations of giraffes, creating a natural sense of order amidst the bewildering chaos of nature.

Wherever I look there are birds: bee-eaters and spoonbills; guinea fowls with polka-dot plumage; metallic blue starlings; pied kingfishers hovering above the river, and emerald showers of Lilian's lovebirds hurtling through the woodland canopy.

From its perch overlooking the Mfuwe Lagoon, a fish eagle flings back its head and yelps at the sky and its cry echoes on and on. In the silence that follows, a sudden, urgent barking of baboons pinpoints the presence of a predator on the move. "Maybe it is the magnificent spotted one," says Jacob mysteriously.

But I know what he means and eventually we find him. A leafy pattern of light and shadow miraculously re-arranges itself to become a leopard sprawled full length at the water's edge. The Luangwa is famous for its leopards and this one is a full-grown male, his lustrous coat splashed with sooty rosettes. He returns our stare, cold eyes unblinking, then treats us to a prodigious yawn that exposes his fearsome canines.

He has a kill hidden in the thickets behind him – I can just make out a glint of horns through the leaves, and a telltale splash of blood. But when we try to drive closer he gets to his feet, picks up what is left of the dead antelope in his jaws and swaggers off with it. Then, as only leopards can, he vanishes.

But not all the excitement revolves around the big cat families and their secret lives. One evening we enjoy sundowners on a pontoon moored in the middle of the river, with hippos surfacing all around us with huge watery sighs and the western sky on fire. Suddenly, out of the gathering dusk a black silhouette appears, as silently as a stealth bomber, and goes scything over our heads on switchblade wings. It's a bat hawk – a twilight hunter – a species to make any keen birder jump for joy.

Next morning Jacob has another surprise in store. He takes me to see the yellow-billed stork colony at Chipela Lagoon, where a thousand pairs nest every year. In June their woolly grey chicks are just fledging, making this one of the great wildlife sights of Africa. The noise is deafening, the air is thick with their henhouse reek and the islands of ebony trees in which the storks build their nests are whitewashed from top to bottom with guano.

At the end of the day we drive home in the golden hour when the light deepens to melted honey, transforming the browsing herds of puku into antelopes carved in amber, and on the way we encounter a family group of elephants marching slowly across a plain. Their bodies are still wet and shiny, showing they have just crossed the river, and among them is a baby no more than a few months old, trundling along beside its mother.

Soundlessly they stride past, barely acknowledging our presence: four giant ebony shadows with swinging trunks and flapping ears, and one little one. There goes the future of Africa, I say to myself, and wish the youngster well.

Chapter Seven

Zimbabwe

July 1982: Horn of the Elephant

THE Super Cub bucks viciously in the hot African sky. To the east, from my place in the co-pilot's seat, I can see the immense horizons of Mozambique. To the south lies South Africa's Kruger National Park. But our concentration is centred on the ground beneath, where our shadow flits over the autumn-coloured treetops of Gonarezhou, the wildest national park in Zimbabwe. Somewhere down there, hidden among the baobabs and mopane glades, is an elephant called Kabakwe, and my mission is to find him.

Gonarezhou – 'Horn of the Elephant' – is a fitting name for the home of Zimbabwe's most famous tusker. In a country of big elephants, the park has always been renowned for its giant bulls, and the veteran Kabakwe is the king of them all.

Although he must have roamed the lowveld for at least half a century his existence was not confirmed until 1979, when stories of an old bull with colossal tusks began to circulate among the local Shangaan tribesmen. It was they who called him Kabakwe: 'the Big One'. That same year he was seen and photographed for the first time, and almost overnight he became a legend, a kind of living national monument. But it was not just his bulk that distinguished him.

Even in Gonarezhou there are bigger bulls than Kabakwe. What sets him apart are his tusks: six-foot scimitars of dull yellow ivory, thick as telegraph poles and perfectly matched. Weighing perhaps 120 pounds a side, they must be two of the heaviest teeth on earth, worth at least £20,000 to the ivory traders of Hong Kong.

"Gonarezhou elephants have the longest tusks and the shortest tempers," says Dennis Van Eyssen, the park's senior ranger, sitting next to me in the pilot's seat, and it comes as no surprise in a part of Africa with a long history of poaching. In more recent times guerrilla warfare and the never-ending trade in illegal ivory have done little to soothe the extreme edginess of Gonarezhou's 6,000 elephants.

Many were blown up by land mines during Zimbabwe's war of independence, and others, including Kabakwe, have lost the tips of their trunks, agonisingly severed by poachers' snares.

Only the week before my arrival a gang armed with semi-automatic weapons had moved in from Mozambique and gunned down 14 elephants. This is why Kabakwe has to wear a radio collar, so that the park rangers can keep track of him. Now, however, as we swoop low over the treetops, there are no signals to guide us.

The batteries in his collar have been run down for weeks and nothing has been seen of Kabakwe – until Van Eyssen spotted him from the air on a routine patrol.

Below us, vultures come boiling up from a dead kudu caught in a poacher's snare, and we slide away to avoid them. Then, as we resume our course, Van Eyssen jabs a finger at the ground to our right. "Kabakwe," he shouts above the engine's roar.

And there he is, together with two *askaris*, or young guard bulls, instantly recognisable by his massive tusks. He flaps his huge ears as we pass overhead, then all three animals turn and run headlong into the scrub.

Back at the park HQ we set out again, this time by Land Rover, jolting down the park's dusty game trails to the spot where we saw him disappear. From here on it has to be on foot, following close behind Van Eyssen as he searches for Kabakwe's spoor.

In one hand he carries a heavy calibre rifle; in the other a small cloth bag filled with wood ash. He shakes the bag and a puff of ash drifts away on the air. "Good," he whispers, "I hope the wind stays in our favour because I would rather shoot you than have to kill Kabakwe."

With Van Eyssen's words echoing in my head we find him half a mile away, feeding peacefully with his companions. Again Van Eyssen shakes the bag. The wind is still carrying our scent away from the elephants, so we creep closer.

Only 30 yards away now. Surely he can see us? He is standing broadside on, idly plucking leaves from the scrub mopane whose leaves fold like butterflies and turn to face the sun, reducing transpiration. Then slowly, so slowly, he turns to face us, foursquare and formidable. His two young companions are unhappy, raising their trunks to sniff the breeze as if they can sense trouble; but Kabakwe himself is still oblivious to our presence, and I am aware of a sudden dryness in my throat as I try to hold my camera steady.

Afterwards, driving back through the deepening light of late afternoon with the Chilojo Cliffs glowing red across the golden woodlands, the image of Kabakwe still burns in my mind. The wise-seeming eyes set in the great wrinkled head; the shrunken temples that spoke his age; the ragged ears swinging to keep him cool; and above all those monstrous tusks. "Man," sighs Van Eyssen, "I've seen some tuskers in my time; but after Kabakwe the rest are just warthogs."

July 1993: Conan the Barbarian

JULY is Africa's midwinter. At night, frost forms on Hwange's plains and the soft Kalahari sands shine like fresh fallen snow when the moon is full. On dawn game drives it's essential to wear a couple of sweaters and a padded jacket, and a pair of gloves don't go amiss; but by mid-morning the temperature is back in the high seventies under a cloudless blue sky.

This is the season when the ordeal trees turn to gold and the buffalo herds come marching out of the bush, thousands strong, heading for the nearest waterhole under a banner of dust.

There is no permanent water in Hwange, only the pans, shallow pools topped up by ramshackle pumping stations to keep the game alive through the lean winter months, and at one of them, an amphitheatre of open grassland, is Makalolo, the camp Alan Elliott built around the fallen wreck of a massive, 300-years-old acacia.

Elliott has the good fortune to have the exclusive right to operate safaris here in what is one of the most remote and beautiful areas of the park: a million acres of private wilderness where the boundless spirit of an older Africa still breathes among the golden grasslands and lofty anthills.

For my money Makalolo is the best camp in Hwange, and Elliott, a tough, fourth-generation hunter-turned conservationist, is the best man to reveal its wonders. After growing up in the bush with the local Ndebele children he now runs one of Zimbabwe's most successful safari companies, called, appropriately, Touch the Wild.

His success derives in part from his extraordinary affinity with elephants. "Zimbabwe's unpaid ambassadors," he calls them. "It's their presence that helps bring in the tourist dollars."

One of his tricks is to pick up a handful of acacia seedpods – elephants find them irresistible – and invite them to extend their trunks and pluck them from his outstretched fingers. These are, of course, elephants that have become totally habituated to Elliott's presence; yet watching him it is hard to believe they are truly wild.

"It's dry now," he says, gesturing with a chicken drumstick as we enjoy an early breakfast in the bush, "but in summer these pans are covered with water. You'd never recognise it. Blue water lilies everywhere. Storks in the thousands, and wild ducks swimming across the roads."

Breakfast over, we head in the direction of Ngamo Plain, a miniature Serengeti whose San bushman name means 'the Place that Glitters from Afar'. On the way there we drive past shady umtshibi trees and squat baobabs like temple columns holding up the sky, and then cut the tracks of a big male lion. His spoor is plain to see, a line of deep paw prints filled with shadow, blooming like flowers in the Kalahari sand. "They're so fresh," says Elliott, "only minutes old. Let's see if we can find him. He can't be far away."

He parks the Land Rover and grabs his rifle. "Always carry insurance," he says. We tread quietly, following the lion's spoor down an elephant path through tall yellow grass and autumnal thickets that look like an English hazel coppice. Twice Elliott stops and raises his hand in warning. Twice we freeze and stare into the tangled scrub ahead, ears straining for the faintest sound. But all I can hear is the insane braying of hornbills and the far-off blare of an elephant.

Soon the bush grows even thicker, reducing vision to a few metres. Elliott stops. "Time to turn back," he whispers. "No point in going in there. We could walk right into him."

Surely, I think to myself on the drive back to Makalolo, not even Elliott can come up with anything to match the adrenaline rush of tracking lions on foot. But I am wrong.

Next morning we move on to a wide, shallow valley at the edge of the park, called Dete Vlei. Here, sable antelopes with magnificent swept-back horns are among the star attractions; but this is also the place to see what have become known as the President's Elephants.

For 20 years Alan Elliott has been following these wild elephants of the Hwange lowveld. In the beginning there were little more than a score of very frightened animals. Now there are around 300, all protected by a special decree issued by President Robert Mugabe, and the remarkable change in their behaviour demonstrates the measure of Elliott's achievements.

We have not driven far when out of the teak forests at the edge of the valley comes a giant shadow. Sunlight gleams on two heavy tusks as he advances towards us. "It's the bull we call Conan the Barbarian," says Elliott.

Moments later, Conan is looming over our Land Rover, close enough to touch. When he flaps his ears he covers me with fine grey dust. "Hello, old fellow," says Elliott quietly, and dips his hand into a bag of acacia seedpods. He scatters a few on the ground and immediately Conan begins to pick them up one by one with the tip of his trunk and transfer them to his mouth. Then he picks another pod from the bag and shakes it, causing the dried seeds inside to rattle – and without hesitation Conan extends his trunk and delicately takes it from Elliott's fingers.

In the old days, conditioned by decades of persecution, Conan and his companions would have responded very differently, either charging on sight or high-tailing it into the trees. Now Elliott has them eating out of his hand.

"For me, one of the saddest sights in Africa is to see an elephant running away because it is terrified of people," says Elliott. "So I was determined that this would be one place where they could lose their fear and live their lives without stress."

When at last Conan the Barbarian wanders off we resume our journey. Wheels slewing in the soft Kalahari sand, we drive on at a leisurely pace, stopping to admire a crimson-breasted bush shrike and a family of kudu, grey ghosts of the teak forests, drifting among the dappled trees.

Around a bend in the track we run into more elephants; this time a whole breeding herd, maybe 50-strong. "See how they are all feeding on the ground, trunks hanging?" says Elliott. "It's because the leaves on the trees have all been frosted, so they're digging up roots with their feet."

"See that bull with the crescent-shaped nick in his ear? I call him Moon." Buthelezi, Dillinger, Catullus, Whinger – he knows them all by name. To him they are as familiar as old friends. "Come on, Moon," he calls softly, shaking another seedpod.

"He'll sometimes feed from my hand, too."

Soon we are completely surrounded by a grey wall of elephants; adults and calves, all feeding quietly. In the mid-day heat the forest is hushed, with only the occasional crack of a breaking branch to disturb the silence. Elliott breathes a deep sigh of contentment. "It's strange," he muses, "when I first came here I followed the elephant paths. Now they follow the roads I've made."

July 1994: Stargazing in the Matobo Hills

MALINDIDZIMU is its Matabele name – 'the Place of Spirits'. Cecil John Rhodes, the founder of Rhodesia, whose body still lies buried on its barren summits, called it 'the World's View', and both names are fitting for what is now the Matobo Hills National Park.

At Rhodes's grave I am standing on the roof of a tumbledown landscape that was cast in stone 2,000 million years ago. In every direction, weather-stained pinnacles and rock castles stretch to the horizon, as if God had gathered up all the odd lumps of granite left over when the world was complete and scattered them across a thousand square miles of Matabeleland.

Many of these extraordinary hills are nothing but colossal whalebacks of rock. Others resemble the ruins of lost cities, with boulders balanced precariously on top of each other like children's bricks. One shove, you feel, could send the whole lot crashing.

It was here that Lord Baden-Powell had the inspiration to form the Boy Scout movement; but the whole area with its sacred caves and prehistoric rock paintings has a far greater significance.

These strange, brooding hills are a holy place, still held in awe by the Matabele people (now also known as the Ndebele). Mzilikazi, their first leader, is buried here.

Mzilikazi fled across the Limpopo River in 1822 to escape from King Shaka Zulu, who called this place of granite domes Matobo, meaning 'Bald Heads'.

British soldiers fought and died here in a series of bloody skirmishes with King Lobengula's warriors. Lobengula, who was Mzilikazi's son, had made a treaty with Rhodes. Too late, he discovered that Rhodes and his settler cronies had been economical with the truth. By 1873 the British flag was flying over Bulawayo, the Matabele capital, and Lobengula's army retreated into the Matobos where they hid in caves, waging guerrilla war until their king's death in 1894.

Now the Matobos are at peace again, with nothing but the cry of a black eagle to disturb their silence, and the land belongs to the leopards and klipspringers that share these haunted hills with the ghosts of Lobengula's warriors.

🐾　　🐾　　🐾

Ian MacDonald, who runs the Matobo Hills Lodge, has known the area all his life and has promised to show me some of the cave paintings for which the park is renowned.

The rains ended in early January – a month earlier than normal – leaving the bush parched, the grass yellow. Now it is July – the African winter – and although the days are hot and the skies a perfect cloudless blue, the nights are as sharp as a driven nail, bringing five degrees of frost by dawn.

Together we scramble over a pile of boulders to reach an overhanging cliff whose smooth granite surface had been used as a canvas by the long-vanished San bushmen.

Here, captured in red ochre pigment is a whole cavalcade of running animals: warthog, zebras, the horned head of a tsessebe, a man spearing a scrub hare, and a big cat – perhaps a lion – attacking a hunter.

The pictures look so fresh, as if the unknown artists had only just left. It is the strangest sensation. Here I am, sitting on the same ledge they had sat on, warmed by the same sun while the sounds they, too, had known float up to me on the windless air: the purring of doves, the cackle of guinea-fowl. Ten thousand years have passed and nothing has changed.

For a long time I stare at the painted frieze, and when I turn around there are more animals, but these are real – a herd of sable antelope with high curving horns – moving through the golden grass in the valley below.

Above the cliff face is a cave, its upper chamber lit by a long shaft of light from somewhere even higher. On the floor stands a row of rough, red clay bins, each big enough to hide a man. Empty now, except for the dried droppings of bats, wild cats and porcupines, they had stored Matabele grain when Lobengula's spearmen hid out in the hills. And who knows – maybe the great king himself once sought shelter here?

It is an impressive spot but MacDonald knows of an even better one, he says; a much bigger cave with marvellous paintings in the Tongwe Wilderness Area.

We set off early next day, leaving our Land Rover at the Toghwana dam and continuing on foot. Lost in a lonely world of granite, we climb over boulders as big as bungalows, following a dry watercourse through the dead grey husks of the resurrection bush, which bursts into life when the rains return.

Farther on, MacDonald points out a black eagle's eyrie on a dizzy cliff ledge. The black eagle (also sometimes known as Verreaux's eagle) is one of Africa's most spectacular raptors and the Matobos are its greatest stronghold.

Later we see the eagles themselves: a pair of them, with golden beaks and glittering eyes, their twin shadows sailing along the lip of the crags high above us. They are hunting dassies – squat, furry mammals that look like guinea pigs and live in crevices in the rocks – and we watch them until they drift out of sight.

Underfoot, the rough granite feels wonderfully secure, yet I can see where the rock has peeled and cracked under the endless cycle of sun and frost. "When the sun is hot the whole mountain expands," says MacDonald. "At night, when it cools, it contracts and cracks."

At last we reach our destination: a great hollow in the side of a cliff, like one half of an inverted dome, a Sistine Chapel of Stone Age art, covered with the now familiar outlines of matchstick men with bows and arrows pursuing giraffe, zebra, kudu and eland, each one as vivid as on the day it was painted.

As we leave the cave we pass the track of a large snake leading down into a dark crevice. "It's very fresh," says MacDonald. "Probably a mamba," he adds casually. "Must have gone in as we approached. There are plenty in these hills. The locals would tell you it's the guardian of the cave."

By the time we got back to the lodge it was dark and the African sky was hung with stars. This was the night when the planet Jupiter was about to be struck by a giant comet.

When the predicted time approached I went outside and lay on my back and stared up into deep space through my binoculars. There was Jupiter, bigger than the surrounding stars, and the air was so clear that for the first time in my life I could even see its moons.

Was it simply my imagination, or did the planet really grow brighter when the comet struck? I cannot say. What I do know is that, with uncanny precision, at the very moment of impact, all the jackals of the Matobos began to cry, their eerie voices rising and falling among the echoing hills.

Chapter Eight

Okavango

October 1994: Adrift on the River of No Return

FIRST light at Delta Camp, deep in the Okavango. Mist on the water and the cry of a fish eagle echoing over this vast African fen. Around six-thirty, as soon as the sun is up and the hippos have retreated into the reeds, we set off by *mokoro* – the traditional Delta dugout canoe.

My mokoro is a precarious-looking craft. Hacked into shape from a sausage tree's solid trunk, its low-slung gunwales rise only a few inches above the water. One sideways lurch, you feel, and the whole thing will overturn. But Ishmael, my boatman for the day, could handle a mokoro almost before he could walk. Now, pole in hand, he stands in the stern, an African gondolier, guiding us down the Delta's reed canyons on a slow boat through paradise.

If you have ever gone punting along the Cambridge Backs you will understand something of the joys of travel by mokoro. But there the resemblance ends. For this is wildest Africa, with hippos guffawing in the big lagoons and the cry of the coucal – the water-bottle bird – bubbling out of the papyrus.

What an extraordinary river is the Okavango. It rises in the mountains of Angola less than 200 miles from the Atlantic. Then, perversely, it strikes out in the opposite direction, heading for the Indian Ocean on the other side of Africa.

For nearly 1,000 miles it flows strongly until, in the endless flatness of northern Botswana, its waters falter. In vain they fan out, trying to find a way through the papyrus swamps, only to meet the Kalahari thirstlands on the other side, one of the driest places on earth where the rate of evaporation exceeds rainfall by five to one.

But before it dies, this river of no return spreads out to create one of the most hallowed places on earth. The Okavango Delta is Africa's biggest oasis: 10,000 square miles of reed-choked lagoons and golden floodplains braided by a maze of channels. Marooned among the water lilies are a million islands. Some are little more than a termite mound with a single palm tree. Others, like Chief's Island in the Moremi Game Reserve, are the size of Greater London.

The islands are a refuge for some of Africa's most elusive creatures – leopards and wild dogs have their home here. An aquatic antelope called the sitatunga clings on like a legend in the depths of the papyrus beds. When night comes, rare fishing owls emerge from their roosts in the darkest ebony groves to fly across the water like giant orange moths. And at the heart of it all is Delta Camp.

The camp hides away on its own small island in the reeds, and to reach it I have flown in a six-seater Cessna from Maun, the dusty little town on the edge of the desert that has become the safari capital of the Okavango.

Only when you fly over these immense African everglades does the sheer size of the Delta begin to sink in. Below, as you leave the Kalahari behind and the land beneath your wings turns from brown to green, you see your first animals. Elephants feeding under the palm trees; a herd of lechwe – foxy red antelopes with elegant horns – plunging through the shallows in a welter of spray and the glitter of water all the way to the horizon.

There is more wildlife waiting for me when I drive into camp. In front of the reception desk lies a large warthog, fast asleep. "Don't mind him," says the camp manager. "That's Cecil. He's extremely good-natured."

My home for the night is a house of reeds with a giant knobthorn acacia growing through the roof. From my bed, piled high with cushions and cocooned with mosquito netting, I can see elephants feeding on the other side of the river, and later when I fall asleep it is to the sound of a million reed frogs clinking like ice in a glass.

Now it is morning and I am out with Ishmael and his mokoro. Soundlessly and with scarcely a ripple we glide on down the Boro River, drifting over submerged sandbars, spotting pygmy geese and malachite kingfishers and surprising a family of otters playing tag among the water lilies.

Later, before the sun is too high, we step ashore on a palm-fringed island. Nobody lives here and its sandy trails are mapped with animal footprints: zebra, impala, giraffe and kudu. I clamber onto an anthill steeple and stare into the long grass ahead. Only yesterday, says Ishmael, a pride of five lions was seen here. But all I spot is a sharp-eyed reedbuck, bouncing away with a whistle of alarm.

Too soon it is time to pole back to camp for breakfast. I trail my fingers in the water that is deliciously cool and clear. Ishmael makes an impromptu goblet from a lily-pad and drinks from it with immense satisfaction to demonstrate how pure it is.

A week ago, sweating in the burning heat as we crossed the Mababe Depression, I had longed for this moment. Now it has come and I can hardly bear for it to end.

July 1997: Wild dogs at Chitabe

CHITABE, on the fringes of the Moremi Reserve between the Gomoti Channel and the Santandibe River, has the reputation of being one of the best places in Africa for seeing wild dogs. Encircled by golden grassy flood plains, the camp is set on a classic Okavango Delta island of ebony trees and ilala palms, and its owners, Dave Hamman and Helen Heldring, are generous supporters of the Wild Dog Conservation Fund. For every guest who stays here, a percentage of the accommodation charge is given to the fund.

Wild dogs are Africa's most efficient predators. Their heads are broad, their muzzles short. When they yawn they reveal a fearsome array of teeth including their carnassials, whose jagged edges have evolved to shear through flesh and sinew.

There is strength in the neck, stamina in the chest, endurance in the long slim legs. They are not built like cheetahs to produce a blistering turn of speed. Rather, they are the brindled coursers of the woods and flood plains, who seldom raise their hunting pace above 30 mph but wear down their prey by a remorseless and single-minded chase to the death.

As for the Chitabe dogs, they have denned an hour's drive from camp in a sandy tract of mopane woodland that has been coppiced by generations of browsing elephants. This is where Twinspot's pack – three adult females and four males including Twinspot the alpha male – produced its first litter a month before my arrival.

Rob Matthews, one of Botswana's top guides, knows where they are and we reach the den in late afternoon to find a bateleur eagle watching the entrance from a nearby tree. There is no other sign of life, so we settle down to wait for the adult dogs to return from their regular five o'clock foray.

Suddenly the eagle flies off and moments later the dogs are back, snuffling eagerly at the mouth of their burrow. Somewhere out on the flood plain they have made a kill, probably an impala or perhaps a lechwe. Now it is time to feed the family and within seconds of their return they are greeted by an eruption of puppies – 16 in all – a twittering scrum of tiny black bundles fighting over the regurgitated meat the adults have brought back for them.

Fifteen minutes later the show is over. One by one the puppies retreat to the safety of the den and the adults lie down to sleep.

It is time to leave. We retrace our tracks under blue skies softened by a pale haze of smoke from distant bushfires burning somewhere upcountry.

A pair of barn owls – twin feathered gargoyles with almond eyes – stare down at us from a marula tree. Their nest hole is nearby, says Rob, but had been found by a leopard that had hooked out their fluffy white owlets and eaten them one by one.

These minor dramas – the small print of everyday life in the bush – are meat and drink to Rob, who is scathing about some of the safari guides employed elsewhere in southern Africa. "Gucci rangers," he calls them. "They think they're so macho. You know; two testicles and a rifle."

Yet he, too, can display nerves of steel when the occasion demands. Driving home in the dusk, we encounter six elephants, a small breeding family led by a splendid old matriarch. While the rest huddle defensively around the two babies, she marches out towards us. Rob switches off the engine. "Just keep still and trust me," he says quietly.

Three times she comes for us, screaming and growling, and each time she comes closer. At the third charge she halts less than a vehicle's length away, a towering, dark, angry colossus, shaking her huge ears and kicking dust right over us. Nobody speaks. Rob turns the key in the ignition and the engine purrs into life, but still we do not move away. "She's OK," he whispers.

And so she is. Having made her point she hurries off to rejoin her family and together they melt away into the swiftly falling darkness, leaving me to ponder the worlds of Iain Douglas-Hamilton, one of the world's leading authorities on elephant behaviour.

"An elephant's threat display is meant to impress; it has taken millions of years to perfect it."

July 1998: Lions in Winter

FROM the air Savuti seems as dead as Mars. As we fly in over the great Chobe National Park the land below resembles a threadbare lion pelt, furred with grasses, veined with game trails. Yet from the moment we touch down and I step out into the oven-dry air, the African book of life falls open.

Flocks of queleas – small finch-like weaver birds with coral-red bills – take wing like puffs of smoke. Impalas bound across the roads and elephants stand under the camelthorn trees, swinging their huge ears to keep cool.

Beyond the trees a level plain reaches to the horizon. In the wet season it is a marsh where thousands of migratory zebras feed and fatten, where the grass is as green as Ireland and tall enough to hide a stalking lion. But that was three months ago. Now it is an emptiness of yellow stubble, a subdued winter landscape of elephant-grey termite mounds and blackened tree stumps.

Without animals, Savuti is like an arena when the players have departed. An indefinable air of sadness hangs over it, as if this is how Africa will be one day when the game is gone. In the distance a handful of tsessebe – Africa's swiftest antelopes – are moving along the horizon; but most of the herds have trekked north into the Linyanti Swamps.

It was not always so. Until the 1980s, winter floods from the Linyanti dribbled down the Savuti Channel, providing enough water to see the game through the dry season. Then tremors deep under the Kalahari caused a shift on the surface, cutting Savuti's lifeline.

When the channel finally dried up in 1982 the Savuti hippos walked for nearly 40 miles to seek refuge in the Linyanti Swamps. Two crocodiles wandered off and hid in a cave, where one is said to have survived for two-and-a-half years before being killed by a leopard. Now, when winter comes and drought grips the land, the animals that remain in Savuti gather around Pump Pan, whose waters are piped from a nearby borehole.

We drive there one evening to see the show. Already, more than 50 elephants are standing quietly around the pan and others are trekking in all the time. Big bulls mostly, with heavy tusks, they crowd around the water's edge as flights of sandgrouse whirr in to drink between a forest of legs. One bull, bigger than the rest, passes within an elephant's length of our vehicle: six tons of silence, leaving a set of prints the size of dustbin lids.

Back in camp beside the waterless Savuti Channel, I discover why Gametrackers, the owners, have named it Elephant Camp. After dinner, with everyone comfortably seated around the campfire, there comes a sudden crash, followed by the giant silhouette of a fully-grown bull elephant advancing through the hole he has just made in the camp fence. With scarcely a glance in our direction he strides past in the flickering firelight and begins to shake down showers of seedpods from the overhanging camelthorns.

"We get elephants turning up every night," says Rowan Vickery, the camp manager. "We employ seven men here who do nothing but repair our fencing. Every day they put it back up; and every night the elephants return and knock it down again."

Even as he speaks, three more elephants wander in. Among them is a ragged-eared bull with broken tusks. "That one can be a bit cheeky," says Rowan, whose laid-back attitude conceals a profound respect for his nocturnal visitors. "If you shout at him he may give you a mock charge; but if you just talk nicely to him he will usually move off."

Later, after everyone has turned in, I lie in my bed listening to the symphony of shaking branches and contented belly rumbles as the ragged-eared bull and his companions continue their midnight feast only metres from my tent. The last thing I hear before falling asleep is the dull roar of a lion, signing off with a deep, grunting coda.

Savuti is renowned for its lions. Many scientists have studied them, intrigued by their extraordinary ability to survive for long periods without water; and for the past 20 years, the lives of the Savuti prides have been lovingly chronicled by Dereck and Beverly Joubert, two of South Africa's finest wildlife filmmakers.

Closest to the Jouberts' hearts was Maome's pride, a savage sisterhood led by Maome herself and watched over by two magnificent pride males, Mandevu and his brother Ntchwaidumela – 'He Who Greets with Fire'.

But lions lead brief lives. In 1991 Mandevu and his brother were shot when they strayed outside the park. Maome, too, is long gone, leaving new prides to rule the Savuti, and I am eager to see them.

Maome's successors include a pride of 26 lions with exceptional hunting prowess. A few months earlier they had even managed to kill an elephant, grabbing it by the trunk and suffocating it. Since then, I was told, the pride had split. Most have gone north with the migrating plains game, preferring to skirmish with the Linyanti prides rather than starve in Savuti. But a few have stayed behind.

So, rugged up against the near-zero chill of an African winter dawn, we set out to look for these elusive survivors. There is no wind to stir the dry leaves of the Kalahari apple thornbushes, no sound except the chanting of doves in the rain trees. Long reefs of light lie above the eastern horizon as the sun rises, throwing into sharp relief the maze of prints on the trail. Almost at once we find fresh lion tracks in the soft Kalahari sand and follow them for over an hour, crossing and re-crossing the Savuti Channel – until a sudden movement catches my eye.

Out of the backlit bushman grass two lionesses come padding. In the morning light the plain is grey, and grey the dust that hangs in their wake as they make their way through the leadwoods.

At first, although they must have been long used to the presence of tourist vehicles, they seem ill at ease and slink away to hide in a thicket. But after a while they began to relax, rubbing heads and grooming each other with pale pink tongues before flopping down to rest. They are sisters, ten years old, and are Maome's sole surviving daughters.

July 1998: A Dream of Water in a Thirsty Land

FOR the Savuti lions, the African winter brings hunger and hardship; but in the Moremi Game Reserve only 25 miles away the rules are reversed. At the height of the drought, while Savuti is gasping for water, the miraculous arrival of the Okavango floods heralds a dramatic change of fortune for the big cats that hunt along the Khwai River.

The Khwai is the outermost finger of the Okavango Delta and is fed by the summer rains that fall on Angola. But Botswana is so flat that the floods do not reach it until four months into the dry season.

For a few weeks more, the river flows before the floods recede. In vain it tries to push up into the Mababe Depression, only to exhaust itself and evaporate under the hot African sun. But on its journey it creates a thin green line of reed beds and hippo pools, attracting animals for miles around.

Gametrackers have a lodge here on the edge of the floodplains. Its scattered rustic chalets are soon due to be replaced by spacious new tents of the kind installed at Savuti Elephant Camp. But everything else will stay the same; the sweeping views across the river and the sheer numbers of game around the lodge.

How beautiful is this dream of water in a thirsty land. Every hippo pool is adorned with lilies, and every day a procession of animals marches out of the woods to drink – giraffe and buffalo, proud kudu bulls with spiral horns, herds of lechwe and troops of zebras – all risking death in the tall reeds where the Khwai lions lie in ambush.

When the river runs and game is plentiful, the pride grows fat on a glut of kills. In all, says Mothupi, my guide at Khwai, there are nine lionesses and four awesome males known as Bafana-Bafana – 'Our Boys' – the South Africans' name for their national football team. "The lodge is the core of their territory," says Mothupi. "They often wander through at night."

Sure enough, after supper, a lioness walks towards us as we sit around the campfire. She roars as she comes, padding through the firelight on her big soft paws. But she is a cat on a mission and she strides on past us with barely a glance in our direction until the darkness swallows her up.

Mothupi is an ideal companion. His family were Bayei, or water bushmen, and he has spent all his life in the Delta. "When I was a boy I lived by hunting and fishing," he tells me. "Life was simple. I had no clothes. We dressed in skins. The floor was our table and we ate with our hands. We ate lots of fish and every kind of animal. We ate bullfrogs, pythons, even leopards." He turns and gives me a huge African grin. "That's why it is so hard to see leopards today," he says. "Because I ate them all!"

But times change. When the Moremi Reserve was created in 1962, Mothupi got a job at a safari lodge, taking visitors for rides in his mokoro, and eventually became one of the Moremi's most respected guides. "So you could say I have had two lives, one old and one new," he says. "Yet even now I cannot say which life I have enjoyed the most."

Next morning we drive into the Moremi, crossing the Khwai River on a rickety bridge of mopane poles that creak alarmingly under the weight of our vehicle; and no sooner have we reached the other side than we find three lionesses lying beside the remains of a zebra. "They must have killed early this morning," says Mothupi. "See how full their bellies are."

How different they look, these fat cats of the Moremi, compared with the lions of the Savuti thirstlands. But their day will come. Three months from now when the drought breaks, when Savuti marsh is green again and the game returns from their dry-season wanderings, Maome's daughters will have 5,000 zebras to choose from.

April 2000: Abu the Elephant

E LEPHANTS love the Delta's woodlands. Even when you cannot see them you know they are there, tearing down the mopane trees with cracks like gunshots. Their presence is everywhere. Their stable-yard smell hangs in the air; their giant footprints flatten the dust. And sometimes, from the depths of the forests, their strident trumpeting splits the silence.

In the midst of this timeless kingdom of elephants, on an island deep in the heart of the flood plains, is Abu's Camp, springboard for the ultimate safari. Abu is the name of its most distinguished resident, a magnificent, ten-foot-tall African elephant bull on whose broad back I am sloshing belly-deep across a lily-covered lagoon.

There is a long-held belief that African elephants, unlike their Asian cousins, are treacherous, unpredictable and impossible to train. But Randall Jay Moore, a cigar-smoking American biologist, Vietnam War protester and animal trainer, has turned conventional wisdom on its head by offering elephant-riding safaris in the Okavango where he arrived in 1990.

Now, ten years on, he is a legend in Botswana. In his own way he has become the George Adamson of the Delta, doing for elephants what Adamson did to raise the profile of lions in the 1980s.

"They're a lot smarter than a lot of people I've met," he says. "I can say I generally prefer elephants to people. Elephants never lie or let you down. Their social structure is so like ours in so many ways. They love their young, become teenagers just like we do, grow old at the same age as us and grieve for their dead. All the best qualities we have as humans I see every day in my elephants."

His three adult riding elephants, Abu, Benny and Cathy, were reintroduced to Africa from zoos and circuses in America, where they had originally been sent as orphans. Together this trio formed the nucleus of Abu's herd, which expanded in Botswana with the arrival of seven baby elephants – the brat pack, as Randall likes to call them – survivors of a cull in South Africa's Kruger National Park.

Abu, Randall's pride and joy, is probably the most famous elephant in the world, having starred in several films including *White Hunter, Black Heart*, in which he appeared alongside Clint Eastwood; but it is as a riding elephant that he excels, a wise and gentle giant who can respond to seventy commands.

He was born in the wild in 1960, but then captured and transported to the USA where he grew up in a Texas safari park. That was where Randall found him, chained in a barn, smothered in his own dung and sleeping on a bare concrete floor. Abu's handler told Randall he was uncontrollable. "But all I saw," he says, "was a sad, mistreated animal."

On an impulse, Randall offered to buy Abu for $10,000. "It was the best deal I ever made," he says. It was also the beginning of an extraordinary partnership that would ultimately lead them both to a new life in the Okavango.

The camp itself is in a pristine wilderness concession of 2,000 square kilometres overlooking a permanent lagoon whose Setswana name translates as 'the Place where the Women come to Gather Reeds', and is designed in a style Randall likes to describe as 'Afro-Bedouin'. Lots of celebrities have stayed here, and in 2000 Prince Harry and Prince William came out and rode on Abu and swam in Randall's private pool on the other side of the lagoon where he has a house adorned with African artefacts and coffee-table books on big game.

Out in the drowning seas of grass Abu's family becomes a flotilla, ears flapping like the sails of old-time barges as we roll on towards the wide horizon. From time to time the elephants pause to snatch up a trunk-full of palm fronds – a takeaway snack to be munched *en route*. "Get it and go," cry the mahouts, and on we ride, with Abu rumbling a message to flop-eared Benny and the babies trundling along in the rear with their fat little bodies outlined in a halo of ginger hairs.

One day, riding behind Big Joe, Randall's senior mahout, I discover just how intelligent an elephant can be when I drop the lens cap from my camera and it sinks into a foot of water. First, Big Joe orders Abu to back up. Then, "Pick it up, Abu; pick it up," he urges. And a moment later, Abu lifts his trunk triumphantly aloft and hands Big Joe my lens cap.

Every ride follows a different route, exploring islands marooned in the flood plains, padding silently over the Kalahari sandveld, following hippo trails through tasselled reeds even taller than ourselves. As for Abu, he is in his element, a perfect six-ton, all-purpose safari vehicle of awesome power and, apart from a few cavernous rumblings at the rear, entirely pollution-free.

Sometimes, instead of riding, I walk with Randall at my side; and it is then, as we follow in Abu's giant footsteps through a backlit haze of golden grass-heads amid a forest of pillared legs and flapping ears, that I sense what it might feel like to be an elephant, a member of a close-knit family bound by kinship ties as complex as our own. Looking up into Abu's benign brown eyes with their long dark lashes, I feel humbled by their tolerance. There is something almost spiritual about being accepted into the company of elephants, and to walk with them is to come tantalisingly close to bridging the gulf that separates us from the rest of the animal world.

That is why I find it hard to say goodbye at the end of my stay. Tears are not far off when I shake hands with the mahouts, Big Joe and David and Sumanadasa, and they are closer still when I make my farewells with the elephants. I think of the babies splashing through the floods, kicking up water like kids in a paddling pool, and little orphan Kitimetse plucking a water-lily and carrying it in the curled tip of her trunk; and of course, Abu, my big grey friend, eating up the ground with his massive swinging stride. Even now I miss them more than I can say.

September 2002: High Drama at Duba Plains

CAPE buffaloes are formidable animals, especially the cantankerous old bulls that end their days living apart from the herd. In southern Africa these are known as 'Dagga Boys', and they are buffaloes with attitude, lowbrow thugs tooled up for trouble, with sweeping horns and mud-caked flanks, and a way of looking at you as if they would love nothing better than to fling you over the nearest bush.

But to see buffaloes *en masse* you must stay at Duba Plains, the Delta's most remote bush camp. Beyond its seasonal flood plains lies nothing but the impenetrable papyrus, and the only way to get there is to fly in.

At Duba Plains it is quite common to see a thousand head of buffalo in a single herd, and with so much meat on the hoof it comes as no surprise to learn that Duba also has the highest concentration of lions in Africa.

These Duba lions have become specialist killers. Not only are they perfectly at home splashing around in the Delta's floodwaters. They have also become adept at the art of killing buffaloes and are so confident of their abilities that they hunt regularly in daylight, sometimes pulling down four or five victims in a morning. "In the past month," says James Rawdon, the camp manager, "our lions have killed 25 buffaloes, one lechwe and a warthog."

Rawdon, a self-confessed lion fanatic, keeps a map in the bar on which he marks every lion sighting with a coloured pin. He points to a spot called Python Pan. "Drive out there this afternoon and you're bound to run into the Tsaro pride," he says.

A couple of days earlier, two bull hippos had fought to the death for the ownership of the Pan's shallow waters. Now the vanquished hippo lies dead in the middle of the lagoon, and its half-eaten wreck of ribs has become the cause of a turf war between the Tsaro lions and the local hyenas.

First it is the turn of the lionesses to chase the hyenas off the carcass. But within minutes, reinforcements arrive, and the hyenas, emboldened by their greater numbers, advance with tails erect and fur bristling in a show of force that drives back the lionesses.

All this time the Tsaro pride males have been watching at a distance, but this is too much to take. One by one they rise and stretch and swagger down to the water's edge, then charge across the pool, scattering the hyenas before settling down to feed.

The sun passes down, its deepening glow throwing the big cats and their reflections into stark silhouettes. By now their faces are smothered in mud and blood, so that whenever they lift their huge, shaggy heads to stare at us, their pale eyes burn through masks of black and red. In all my years in Africa I have never witnessed such a scene of raw, primeval savagery.

Such is the drama that we had quite forgotten about the other hippo. We are still watching the lions when a dust storm comes racing towards us across the dried-out flood plain. The sky changes colour, first yellow, then to a dull orange in whose baleful light the phantom shapes of hyenas flit like figures in a bad dream.

As the storm intensifies the wind throws wild waves across the water, and it is now that the hippo decides to remind us of his presence by charging our vehicle with open jaws. Only in Botswana, I think to myself: big game, big skies, big country.

September 2006: Where the Lion Roars

WE are out on a game drive when the call comes. Lion in camp says the radio message. Brent Reed, our safari guide, guns the engine and we drive back through the knobthorn woodlands to the swish of our tyres in the Kalahari sand.

By the time we return the lion has moved off but we soon pick up his tracks in the sand and find him not far off, slumped at the foot of a termite mount. We recognise him at once. It is the same lion we had seen earlier, before the sun was up, one of two resident males that rule the Dead Tree Island pride.

In his prime he must have been magnificent. Now he dozes with his head on his paws. His glory days are ending and his thin grey haunches are mapped with scars. Soon the nomads will come, the young challengers who will seek to drive him out and steal his pride. But when he roars I can feel the air vibrate around me and sense his reign is not yet over.

Such are the rewards of mobile camping safaris in the Moremi Game Reserve. For without the freedom to plan our day, to be awake at five and out before dawn, we might never have found that tragic old warrior.

The Letaka Brothers (*letaka* is the Setswana word for 'reed') belong to the new generation of safari guides. Both still in their early 30s, they grew up in South Africa's Magaliesberg Mountains, watching birds and catching snakes, but always longing to see the Okavango.

"When we finally got here in the mid 1990s it was everything we'd ever dreamed of," says Brent, who has just renounced his South African citizenship and become a full-time Botswana resident. Now there is no going back, and I can see why.

Fed by the third largest river in southern Africa, the Okavango Delta is a labyrinth of forests, reed-beds, lagoons and floodplains; and at its heart, protecting a quarter of this miraculous oasis, is the Moremi Game Reserve. Established in the 1960s at the behest of Chief Moremi III's widow, it contains the Delta's heaviest concentrations of game and some of its most exclusive campsites.

Our first camp is set in a feverberry grove beside a lagoon where hippos rest, half-submerged, and crocodiles bask with jaws agape. "Not a good idea to go too near the shore," advises Brent. "Don't want you ending up inside a Gucci handbag."

The site is called Bodumatau – 'Where the Lion Roars'. An apt name as it turns out, for at suppertime we are just sitting down to Frank's first course of chilled gazpacho when a lion begins to call, stopping all conversation. (Frank, incidentally, a big, jolly Zimbabwean, spent ten years refining his skills at an Italian restaurant in Bulawayo, and if there is a better bush chef in Botswana I haven't found him.)

Next morning, after tea and toast around the campfire, we are off before sun-up. Lesson one: mobile camping safaris spell freedom. Released from the curse of rigid mealtimes, with my own guide and my own vehicle, I am at liberty to do what I want – to look for the lion I heard at suppertime.

In the crisp, clear light of a Botswana dawn his overnight tracks are plain to see; a line of blue shadows in the sand, each one as big as my outstretched hand.

An hour later and there he is – a full-grown male with a wind-blown mane. Utterly unconcerned by our presence, he lies on top of a termite mound where, head raised against the cloudless sky, he stares imperiously across the floodplain. "Look at him," whispers Brent admiringly. "What a poser."

Later that day Brent decides to take us south towards the Gomoti River, where he saw a young female leopard a week ago. We pull up at the edge of the plains and wait, and as is the way with leopards, she materialises out of nowhere. One moment there is nothing but grass and leaves. A second later, there she stands with the sunlight shining on her black rosettes.

Afterwards, when the leopard has gone and the shadows are lengthening, we stop for sundowners beside a lagoon. This is the Delta's witching hour, when everything is suffused with gold: the reeds, the spear grass, the air itself. Brent opens the cool-box and we stand around, sipping chilled Cape Sauvignon and nibbling at leathery strips of biltong while flock after flock of red-billed queleas pour overhead on their way to roost.

It is one of those magical, unscripted moments that happen so often in the bush. The sky is filled with the rush of birds. Like locusts they come in such vast numbers that a haze of dust drifts up from the reeds in which they settle, and between the dust and the setting sun I can see columns of spray slowly rising and falling as hippos exhale like breaching whales in the open water beyond.

Our next campsite lies north of the Khwai River, whose reed beds and hippo pools are the last gasp of the Delta's floodwaters before they expire in the Mababe Depression; and now, having rattled over a makeshift bridge of mopane logs, we follow the river's faltering course to find our tents waiting under a canopy of flowering camelthorns.

Here, being outside the reserve, we can go on bush walks; and what joy it is to wander at first light in the camelthorn woodlands with the smell of wild sage in the air and the soft voices of doves all around.

Mostly though, we drive, idling along in Brent's open-sided Land Cruiser through a landscape that constantly re-arranges itself, from sagebrush flats to rain-tree glades, following the silver-grey sand trails across yellow floodplains to look for owls in the jackalberry (African ebony) groves and watch lechwe antelope herds plunging across the lagoons.

Every game drive dissolves into an endless series of vivid snapshots: a pair of pygmy geese framed by water lilies; a green-backed heron swallowing a frog. We photograph the River Club, as the local lion pride are called, sleeping it off after a heavy night's hunting, and watch a bull elephant cross the river, trailing its penis like a fifth leg. "Can you imagine?" says Brent. "It weights 54 pounds."

On our way back to camp I sit beside Brent while he talks about snakes – his passion since childhood – and how safari holidays have been driven up-market by rich Americans who prefer the comforts of luxury lodges. "It's getting to the point where you might as well stay in your New York apartment and watch wildlife on TV," he says.

Back in the Moremi for our third and final campsite, we arrive to find our tents arranged around a giant moporoto (sausage tree) whose flowers – deep crimson trumpets filled with nectar – had been shaken down by the dry-weather wind to form a carpet in the dust.

In late afternoon we drive to Dead Tree Island for sundowners in a skeletal landscape of stricken leadwoods. The trees were killed off in the early 1980s by abnormal floods, yet still they stand, seemingly indestructible.

Around us, all is silence, deep as a well, punctuated only by the cries of fish eagles and the piping lament of red-billed hornbills; and as the sun passes down, beating a molten path across the lagoon, elephants come ghosting out of the woods to drink.

In minutes we are completely surrounded by slowly swinging trunks and legs as scores of mothers – several gaunt old matriarchs among them – lead their babies to the water's edge. One cow bolder than the rest turns and advances towards us, shaking her huge ears in displeasure until Brent claps his hands and shoos her away.

Our last day begins with an early start, the sun not yet up and a full moon still hanging over the trees. In a little while we come to a marshy clearing, a green arena in which we stop to watch a gaggle of spur-winged geese at the water's edge.

Suddenly, from beyond the clearing comes a clamour of francolins, and out of the woods steps the most perfect leopard I have ever seen. It's a male, broad-muzzled and heavy-shouldered, his coat as dark as African honey, strolling towards us through grass. Dismissing us with barely a glance he strides deeper into the marsh until he is up to his belly in water, standing over a perfect mirror image of himself.

Spellbound we watch as with consummate stealth he slinks through the reeds and launches himself at the spur-winged geese; but the water slows his charge and the geese are aloft before he can reach them. For a moment he stares up at them with water dripping from his whiskers. Then, tail curved in an elegant question mark, he walks on across the drowning marsh and vanishes on the other side.

March 2009: Cruising in the Realm of the Fishing Owl

THROUGH my mosquito net on the *Kubu Queen*'s upper deck I am watching the dawn break over the Okavango just as Prince Harry did when celebrating his 25th birthday. I had been awakened by the sound of hippos harrumphing in the river. Now, as the coucals cry from the reed beds, I look over our stern to a horizon so flat and so wide I can sense the curve of the earth as it rolls through space to meet the rising sun.

No wonder Harry is so fond of this wild African river. And no wonder he loves to explore it aboard the *Kubu Queen*, a double-decker houseboat based at the waterside village of Shakawe in northern Botswana.

From here at a stately seven knots she embarks on leisurely cruises up and down the Panhandle, the northern reaches of the Okavango River near the Namibian border. In all but name she is a floating safari lodge, 12 metres long, moving every night from one idyllic mooring to the next, with an outboard-powered skiff in tow for birding and fishing expeditions.

Built 25 years ago, she has enjoyed a chequered career. She started life as a ferry but subsequently sank in the late 1990s and there she lay until five years ago when Greg Thompson, her present owner, bought her for a song and lovingly restored her, complete with shower, flush toilet and an array of brass signs, one of which reads: 'Ship's bar – open from 09.00 to 08.59'.

In truth she is a slightly raddled old matriarch. Her paintwork is faded, her varnish blistered by too much time in the African sun. Never mind. What she offers for her six lucky passengers is simple comfort, sumptuous meals and bags of character; and if that is good enough for Harry it is good enough for me.

As we cast off, a late afternoon storm trails curtains of rain across Namibia, which is only just across the border; but where we are the sun shines warmly and we go with the flow, cold beers in hand on a slow boat to paradise.

Downstream we drift on the swirling current, over amber depths so crystal clear I can see the bottom four metres below. Although the riverbanks at Shakawe are three kilometres apart, the main channel is no wider than the Thames at Richmond, unwinding in sinuous coils through floating beds of papyrus. We pass a cluster of bee-eaters balancing on a swaying reed stem and then spot a fish eagle in a dead treetop. As we chug by, it flings back its head and utters its wild yelping cry – the authentic voice of the Okavango.

Parts of the Panhandle remind me of the Norfolk Broads – all thatched wooden houses and neat waterside lawns – but there the resemblance ends. There are parrots in the treetops, and instead of motor cruisers lining its banks you are more likely to see crocodiles basking with mouths agape.

One morning Thompson takes us ashore for a stroll in the forest. We cross riverside glades lit by swarms of glittering dragonflies and find the two-toed tracks of a sitatunga, a shy, swamp-dwelling antelope that moves through the papyrus by using its cleft hooves like pincers to clasp the reed stems. "If it is hunted," says Thompson, "it will hide underwater with only its nose above the surface."

In his time Thompson has been a professional hunter and a safari guide but his greatest passion is angling. That is why he came to live here, and if you are a fisherman there is no better time to be here than during the barbel run.

This is one of nature's great events and it happens every year from August to October when thousands of barbel pour down the river, hunting the smaller fry that breed in the shallows. Birds and animals join the feast: otters, fish eagles, herons and pelicans. Flocks of egrets smother the reeds like falling snow. "Sometimes there are so many fish that the water seems to be boiling," says Thompson. "And among them are the tiger fish – voracious predators that have made this one of the world's top sport fishing hotspots."

Every day towards sundown when the painted reed frogs begin to call like ice cubes clinking in a glass, we moor up for the night under the jackalberry trees. A campfire is soon glowing on the riverbank and in no time we are tucking into a supper of grilled eland steaks obtained from a local game farm.

Now is the time to listen for the fishing owl, a local rarity that attracts birders from all over the world. By day it hides in the darkest treetops, seeking refuge from the fish eagles that are its sworn enemies. But at night it emerges to feed on fish and frogs – even small crocodiles – and it is then you may hear the gruff voice of the adults or the eerie cry of the young that Thompson describes as sounding "like that of a lost soul falling into a bottomless pit".

Next morning, skimming in the skiff down a quiet backwater, we encounter another Panhandle special, a rare white-backed night heron skulking in a thicket. Along with pygmy geese, goliath herons and giant kingfishers the size of chickens, it is just one of the 350 bird species to be seen here.

On we go, ever deeper into the secret world of the papyrus. Like paintings from a pharaoh's tomb its tasselled tops close in around us. Pied kingfishers hover in the blue, and farther downstream we surprise a family of spotted-necked otters playing follow-my-leader.

Then suddenly we emerge to see the open floodplains spread out before us. As if in a dream we putter for miles across this strange, drowned land, forging a path through drifts of water lilies. It is so inexpressibly beautiful that when at last the sun goes down we can hardly bear to turn for home.

Back on board it's time to scribble in the visitors' book. Among its pages (made of recycled elephant dung), I look in vain for Harry's comments. But I wouldn't mind betting that he, too, had a right royal time in the realm of the fishing owl.

April 2009: Safari Life in the Comfort Zone

"HERE'S the evidence," says Solomon Kanyeto, my keen-eyed guide, pointing to fresh tracks on the road. "But where is the criminal?"

For two days we have been searching for leopards, in particular a female known as Amber, scanning every likely tree, chasing shadows in the grass. Now, against the early morning light they stand out sharply, like blue flowers in the Kalahari sand.

Somewhere nearby a red-billed francolin begins to shriek its alarm call. But if Amber is hiding there she remains true to her kind – the shyest and most elusive of Africa's big cats.

For once I do not mind. It is a pleasure just to be back in the bush again, and returning to the Selinda Game Reserve, one of the blessed places of Botswana, is reward enough.

In some parts of Africa it is hard to avoid the tourist convoys that set out each day in search of cats. But in Botswana they do things differently. Here, much of the bush is parcelled up in private concessions the size of small countries, each with no more than a couple of camps designed to appeal to the kind of visitors who are willing to pay premium prices for exclusivity.

Such a place is Selinda; 300,000 acres of pristine wilderness between the Okavango and the Linyanti Swamp near the western end of the Savuti Channel. The only way to get there is a 45-minute flight by light aircraft from Maun, and once you have arrived you will never want to leave.

The area is used by upwards of 9,000 elephants and is also a famous hotspot for predators. Until a couple of years ago, there was a small, six-bed bush camp here called Zibadianja. Its regulars called it Zib and loved its feeling of exclusivity and closeness to nature. They came to look for leopards in its fathomless woodlands, search for the wild dogs that hunt on its plains, and photograph the famous Selinda lions – a pride that had become notorious for their habit of killing hippos.

Then the reserve changed hands. The new owners were Colin Bell, founder of Wilderness Safaris, and the celebrated wildlife photographers

Dereck and Beverly Joubert, and their dream was to transform Selinda into one of Botswana's most sought-after destinations.

Space and privacy, the abundance of game; everything else was there. All it needed was a beautiful new lodge to match its surroundings. So down came the old camp and up went Zarafa in a location to die for, looking out over Zibadianja Lagoon to the palm groves and golden plains beyond.

Zarafa – its name comes from the Arabic word for giraffe, meaning 'the Lovely One' – is designed for life in the comfort zone. For the price of three nights here you could buy a whole week elsewhere in Africa with flights from London thrown in; but the views alone are worth the money and the camp's arrival on the scene is a direct response to the kind of visitors who now demand the same kind of luxuries under canvas as they might expect in a five-star hotel back home. And that is what Zarafa provides – at a price.

No noisy generators disturb its soothing tranquillity. The entire camp runs on solar power, creating the lightest of carbon footprints among the towering leadwood trees whose branches form a natural canopy.

Its four guest tents are as big as tithe barns, raised off the ground on decks built of South African railway sleepers that have been buffed and burnished until they glow like the richest mahogany. From inside comes the gleam of old-fashioned copper bathtubs and brass bound chests that recall an earlier era of safari travel. There are leather sofas, Persian rugs, king-size beds with overhead fans – not to mention a choice of indoor and outdoor showers and your own personal plunge pool.

Breakfast on the dining tent deck is a sumptuous affair, as is dinner under the stars, and with every meal comes the view across the lagoon, stippled with lilies and thronged with waterbirds; a giant theatre-in-the round in which elephants have walk-on parts and lechwe antelopes plunge through the shallows in a welter of spray.

Even the game drives offer something you won't find anywhere else: a professional quality Canon 40D camera with a 400mm lens for your own personal use.

I try mine out when we meet a bull elephant on the road one morning. Ears spread like barn doors flung open, the big tusker swings around to stand head-on, then moves menacingly towards us. Closer he comes and closer still until he fills the camera frame. Snap! The perfect shot of a brief encounter with the scariest of Africa's Big Five.

But Zarafa's greatest luxury is its privacy. I stay for three days, exploring the reserve from end to end, and never see another vehicle. In early April the grass is tall and there is water everywhere – even in the mopane woodlands. Giraffes watch us cruising across the floodplains and bateleur eagles rise on the thermals, describing immense parabolas across the sky. At one point we surprise a serval cat and soon after encounter a herd of roan antelope led by a bull with trophy horns.

In mid-morning we stop for tea beside waterholes where kudu and elephant come to drink and the sad piping cries of grey hornbills fall from the rain trees; and at the day's end after sundowners we drive back to camp with the spotlight on and nightjars fluttering like ghosts in its beam.

At the end of my stay I am handed the guest book, in which Dereck Joubert has summed up the ethos of Selinda in a welcoming message. "The reserve," he has written, "is designed to be a sanctuary for wildlife, space, that spirit of wildness – and for you. Please make it your own and enjoy your safari."

He is right about the space and the wildness because that is what you buy into when you come here; a mind-blowing distance of woodlands and floodplains dotted with grazing animals, creating the beautiful illusion of an Africa that is yours and yours alone for as long as you stay.

Chapter Nine

Kalahari

March 1998: The Whole Lion

BACKLIT by the Kalahari dawn a black-maned lion comes walking. He moves unhurriedly, shaggy head bowed down as if by the weight of years; but his yellow eyes miss nothing as he crosses the bone-dry Nossob River and flops down under a camelthorn tree.

Where has he come from, this desert lion? From Botswana or South Africa? Because the Nossob, which flows perhaps once in a hundred years, forms the border between these two countries. The border itself, a line of white stones in the middle of the Nossob, is all that divides South Africa's Kalahari Gemsbok National Park from Botswana's Gemsbok Park, and there are ambitious plans afoot to knit the two together.

Inspired by the vision of the South African-based Peace Parks Commission, it will become the Kgalagadi Transfrontier Park – the first natural refuge in this vast continent where conservation will take precedence over sovereign borders. But lions know nothing of international frontiers. Like other wanderers of these lonely thirstlands – red hartebeest, blue wildebeest, Kalahari gemsbok – they will continue to come and go as they please.

Despite its huge size it will occupy just one small corner of the greater Kalahari, which covers an area ten times the size of Britain. Sandy soils and an almost total lack of surface water have made this one of the harshest places on earth. True, much of it is covered with a scrawny pelt of grass. In places, camelthorns and shepherd trees cast welcome pools of shade, and tsamma melons are both food and drink for the drought-proof gemsbok antelope. But desert this is, racked by cold winter dawns and summer days when the temperature regularly hits 40°C.

That is why everything that lives here must follow one unbending rule: adapt or die.

That is why desert beetles draw breath only once every 20 minutes to prevent water loss. It's why sandgrouse withstand the long waterless sieges by flying 40 miles to drink; why ground squirrels use their tails as sunshades, and the gemsbok – the classic symbol of the Kalahari – can survive without drinking for a month.

Yet the Kalahari can also be a place of spectacular beauty, a red-and-gold world of rolling dunes and desert flowers. The March rains have made the desert bloom, and all along the lower reaches of the Auob River valley the sands are carpeted with the yellow flowers of devil thorns.

It is now, between December and April, that the Kalahari Gemsbok Park receives its entire annual rainfall, usually in the form of a dozen furious thunderstorms whose coming unleashes a frenzy of activity. Almost overnight, exquisite pink-and-white vlei lilies spring up and goshawks keep watch in the camelthorns, waiting to ambush the flurries of delicate Namaqua sandgrouse on their way to the newly replenished waterholes.

Finch larks swarm over the dune flowers, and tshongololos – giant millipedes the size of frankfurters – emerge from their burrows to trundle across the rain-washed sands.

At this time of year these desert skies are never empty. The air is filled with the cries of plovers and Cape turtledoves; and birds of prey are never far away, from pygmy falcons tinier than a thrush to martial eagles big enough to kill a small antelope. But animal predators – cheetah, leopard and lion above all – are what most visitors hope to find.

"We have about 116 lions on our side of the Nossob," says Dries Engelbrecht, the park's head warden, "and there's a good chance you'll see them because they frequent the river beds so much. They are not especially big, but they are totally wild and when you find them the habitat is so open that you see the whole lion."

He is right. The whole lion is exactly what I saw this morning beside the Nossob. I had come a long way to see him but it was worth it. He was an old lion with a grey pelt and a scarred muzzle, and when he panted, slack-jawed in the heat, I could see his blunted yellow canines, the size of my thumbs. But until the nomads move in to drive him out and take his pride, this is still his kingdom of the dunes.

March 1998: Meerkats United

THE Kalahari Gemsbok Park is home to many animals. Not just the famous black-maned lions but also eland, springbok, jackals and Cape fox. Last year, miraculously, an elephant turned up – the first to be seen for decades. It had trekked south all the way across the Kalahari from the Okavango Delta, only to be shot by a farmer on its return journey.

But the most famous animal residents are those adorable stars of the BBC television wildlife documentary, *Meerkats United*. These diminutive members of the mongoose tribe live in close-knit social groups and are amongst the most fascinating of all African mammals.

For the past four years the Kalahari Gemsbok meerkats have been the subject of a scientific study that has been unravelling their most intimate family secrets. "Co-operative breeding systems are a very popular issue with animal behaviourists," says Justin O'Riain, the South African researcher in charge.

"We have been flat out getting data 365 days a year. Now we know every meerkat along 40 miles of the Nossob Valley: their sex, age, genetics – everything." Each meerkat has been tagged with a microchip and the main study group are weighed twice a day. "It was remarkable how quickly they accepted us," says O'Riain. "They have become so used to the weighing-in routine that they jump unbidden on to the scales. To them, I'm just another piece of Kalahari furniture."

Five meerkat families share the Nossob Valley study area, with each group occupying a linear territory of about two-and-a-half miles. Their main requirement, apart from food, is lots of safe, deep boltholes in which to sleep or hide from their enemies. Usually they requisition ground squirrel burrows, taking them over whether the owners are at home or not. "As far as meerkats are concerned," says O'Riain, "ground squirrels are second-class citizens."

Yet for meerkats, too, life in the desert is a daily struggle for survival. A year ago the main study group was 29-strong, but a prolonged drought reduced their number to 15 adults and four pups, and one third of all meerkats in the park were lost, most to predators.

Martial eagles, tawny eagles and jackals are the main killers, and meerkats are always on the lookout. "Their eyesight is uncanny," says O'Riain. "They can tell if a dot in the sky at a height of one mile or more is a martial or a tawny eagle, and they have a different alarm call for each predator."

After survival, the meerkats' most urgent imperative is reproduction. "The BBC film showed how endearing they can be, but we have been watching a new scenario – meerkats at war. It was all about sex and it ended up with a major punch-up between two of our study groups. These fights are serious. They start with a war dance, but when the fighting begins it can get really nasty, and they sometimes die from the bites inflicted."

On my last day in the park I set out with O'Riain to meet one of his study groups. We park by the roadside and walk across the riverbed in the bright desert dawn. Quietly we stand by the burrows where the meerkats live but there is no sign of them. "They're being lazy this morning," says O'Riain cheerfully. "There's a constant temperature inside and it's still quite cool out here."

But eventually they emerge one by one, churring and muttering to each other as they stand upright, eyes peeled for predators, their gingery fur backlit by soft haloes of sunshine. Forepaws folded demurely on their soft grey tummies, they turn to face the sun.

"Soon, the adults will be away foraging for scorpions and other meerkat delicacies," says O'Riain. "But they always leave one or two baby-sitters behind to keep an eye on the youngsters."

Even in repose, their black button eyes and eager pointing snouts are never still, and their alert features convey such a sense of high intelligence that it is hard to think of them as meerkats. To me they are more like little people, aliens from another world that I have been privileged to enter.

January 2006: The Emerald Desert

A T Deception Valley Lodge in the heart of the Kalahari the chest-high grass is a dazzling green. The terminalia trees are heavy with seedpods that glow deep burgundy in the sun. Among the trees stands a group of hartebeest, sleek and fat in their foxy coats; and massed flocks of queleas – seed-eating finches with blood red masks – erupt with a sudden rush of wings as the sun goes in and the rain belts down. Not your average desert, then.

Scorching temperatures and a total absence of permanent water define this as one of the harshest spots on earth. Then the rains come. They arrive at the turn of the year, when thunderheads build in the afternoon heat and storms roam along the immense horizons, ushering in a miraculous season of renewal.

Jacobus Slabbert, my safari guide at Deception Valley, had just driven up from Port Elizabeth, 800 miles away in South Africa. "It's raining everywhere," he says, "but nowhere is as green as this."

Jacobus is the son of the lodge's Afrikaner owner, Gerard Slabbert, a retired pharmacist who fell in love with the desert and bought a 15,000-hectare chunk of bush adjoining the Central Kalahari Game Reserve, a wilderness the size of New Mexico. The lodge opened six years ago and has eight twin-bedded, thatched cottages plus – a novelty for the Central Kalahari – a swimming pool.

Every night I hear lions roaring, but they are hard to see in the long grass. Instead we look for greater kudu – 'the grey ghosts of the African bush' as Jacobus calls them – and go spotlighting at night to find porcupines and eagle owls.

Next day Jacobus wants to take me to Deception Pan in the heart of the reserve. It's a two-hour drive and we set off early, skirting the veterinary fence built to stop wildlife spreading bovine TB among Botswana's beef herds. Goshawks glare at us from the fence posts and we drive for miles through clouds of butterflies.

At last we cross a sandy ridge and there lies the Pan, a shallow valley in which isolated acacia groves stand out like islands in a sea of grass. Wherever we look there are herds of animals: oryx and springbok, and flocks of wintering European storks.

We picnic under a shady tree – kudu kebabs and beers from the cool-box – and I remember the last time I was here. But that was in July, and the dustbowl I saw then bears no relation to the ephemeral paradise of Deception Pan in the rains.

Back at the lodge, Jacobus has arranged another outing. This time we are on foot, accompanied by Chota and Xhase, two Naru bushmen who have swapped their everyday working clothes and turn up in nothing but kudu-skin loincloths to lead us on a morning walk.

The transformation is extraordinary. Around the lodge they were shy and diffident. Now, with bows and spears slung over bare brown shoulders, they are confident and at ease as they demonstrate their bush-wise skills.

Eagerly they translate the calligraphy of animal tracks left in the sand and explain how the Kalahari is at once a natural pharmacy and a food-for-free larder if you know where to look. They demonstrate how to trap guinea fowl and go through the mime of luring a warthog from its lair. They make a fire, using nothing but two rubbing sticks and a handful of tinder, and dig for tubers that provide water in the dry season.

It could have been cheesy, a tired charade played out for tourists. Instead it turns out to be totally absorbing, an illuminating glimpse of a way of life that has almost vanished, demonstrated with such pride and dignity that I am moved close to tears.

❖   ❖   ❖

I want to stay longer but it's time to meet Dave Dugmore, who drives me to Meno a Kwena – 'Crocodile Tooth' – his camp on the Boteti River, three hours away by road.

The Boteti was a vital water source for the animals of the Makgadikgadi Pans National Park, but it hasn't flowed for years. Now they have to rely on

Meno a Kwena's man-made waterhole, which attracts upwards of 5,000 zebras every day in the dry season.

"There's no need for game drives," says Dugmore. "You just grab a beer and watch it happen right in front of you." But now the rains have come and the animals have dispersed, leaving only a couple of elephants in view.

With its faded green tents and bucket showers Meno a Kwena must be the only genuine, no-frills bush camp left in Botswana, where up-market, safari chic lodges are the norm. The swimming pool is full of tadpoles, although that didn't stop the Royal Princes, William and Harry, from having a good time here.

My tent stands inside a stone walled compound with wooden poles across the doorway. "It's important to put them back once you're inside," says Dugmore casually. "It keeps the lions out."

Apparently the lions are used to nosing around the nearby village in the hope of finding a cow for supper, and I soon understand what he means. I'm just about to fall asleep when a lion begins to roar. It sounds as if it is just outside, but when I look around next morning its footprints are 30 metres away.

Meno a Kwena is the springboard for day trips to Nxai Pan National Park, where herds of zebras are munching their way across endless vistas of emerald grass. There are springbok, too, but no sight of the cheetahs that prey on them.

In the afternoon we move on to Baines' Baobabs, a sacred grove of ancient trees marooned among the flooded pans. In this vast, flat land their swollen trunks are visible for miles, an enigmatic landmark that draws the eye. Except for a few tyre tracks, nothing has changed here since Thomas Baines, the Victorian artist and explorer who was a contemporary of Livingstone, painted this scene in 1862.

And so to Jack's Camp, my last port of call on this desert safari, and one that should be on everyone's list of the Ten Best Places to stay in

Africa. Not just for its stunning location, in a palm grove on the edge of the Makgadikgadi Pans, but for its style and sheer romanticism.

The camp was founded in the 1960s by Jack Bousfield, a former hunter credited with having killed 53,000 crocodiles, and is now run by Ralph, his son. Impossibly good-looking with his shoulder-length hair and thousand-mile stare, Ralph Bousfield is an articulate conservationist whose knowledge of the Kalahari and its wildlife is second to none. He is a deep thinker, too. His safari company, Uncharted Africa, has the motto: 'Give them what they never knew they wanted'.

On a previous visit Ralph had taken me to see another famous Kalahari landmark. Chapman's Baobab, named after James Chapman, another Victorian explorer who came here in the 1850s, is a living colossus as old as Stonehenge. By day the desert winds rush among its seven spires with a sound like distant surf. Lanner falcons nest among its branches and Chapman's initials are still there – together with the scars left by Stone Age hunters who stripped its bark to make rope for traps.

By the time we had reached it the sun was down but the tree still glowed like a kitchen stove and we sat for a long time in its comforting shadow, warming our backs against its trunk while Ralph reminisced about his father.

"He was never cut out for a quiet life," said Ralph. "During the Second World War he fought in North Africa with the Long Range Desert Group, and when the war ended he couldn't settle down. So he became a hunter, first in the Congo, then in Tanzania and finally in Botswana where he became disenchanted with the hunting business and turned instead to photo-safaris."

Yet even in Botswana, true wilderness as measured in Jack Bousfield's terms was becoming harder to find. Then one day someone mentioned the Makgadikgadi. Jack asked what was out there. "Nothing – only idiots go there," came the reply. "Fine," thought Jack, "that's the place for me."

Jack found it harsh, wild and empty and he loved it from the moment he saw it. With Ralph's help he set up camp and was soon attracting a stream of visitors. But in 1992, tragedy struck when their plane crashed in the desert. "I was badly burned," said Ralph, staring out into the gathering dusk, "but Jack was killed."

Earlier on that same trip I had driven out with Ralph on quad bikes into the searing heart of Ntwetwe Pan. The bikes enabled us to go where ordinary vehicles might break through the pan's crusty surface and become bogged down, and an hour later, far out in that great white emptiness, we stopped to watch the sun go down, and saw the earth's shadow flung out against the eastern sky. Then the moon rose – a huge, distended bubble that floated free like a second sun – flooding the pan with an unearthly glow.

Ntwetwe must be the quietest place in Africa. Back in camp there were always natural sounds: the cluck of hornbills, keening jackals. Here there was nothing. Nobody spoke. Even the wind had died, and the sharp night air was cold and clean, like breathing pure oxygen.

I lay on my back and gazed up at the sky, where the torrents of the Milky Way fumed and glittered with an unbelievable brilliance. Listen, say the Kalahari bushmen, and on such a night you can hear the stars hunting. So I cupped my hands behind my ears, but all I could hear was the beating of my heart.

That was in the dry season; but visiting Jack's Camp during the rains is more like being in the Okavango Delta when the floods are up. The surrounding grasslands are alive with bullfrogs and half the tracks are under water as we slosh towards Ntwetwe Pan in Ralph's Land Cruiser.

In just three days here you can feel the Makgadikgadi taking hold of you: a kind of madness – desert fever some people call it. But then the Makgadikgadi is no ordinary desert.

Rimmed by islands of tall hyphaene palms, it is the ghost of a prehistoric lake, an inland sea twice the size of Lake Victoria. Into it once poured all the waters of the Okavango and Chobe rivers. Then, some 15,000 years ago, came a cataclysmic spasm of the earth's crust. The rivers changed course. The lake died, its vanished deeps replaced by a desolation of glittering soda pans.

Today the two main pans, Ntwetwe and Sua, stretch for more than 6,000 miles – the biggest in the world – and together with their satellite pans they cover an area the size of Switzerland. In the dry season you can explore them on quad bikes, as I had done the last time I was here. But in the rains they are accessible only to the flamingos that arrive by the thousand to gorge on brine shrimps.

On my last day we pack a picnic lunch and set off in search of the Makgadikgadi zebra migration. We drive deep into the national park, into the mosaic of flooded pans and treeless plains that lie beyond the palm groves. The first animals we see are a herd of oryx. With their cantering stride and horses' tails they look like a squadron of lancers on a mission as they splash across the pans, shattering the mirror images of blue sky and cumulus clouds.

And suddenly, there are the zebras all the way to the horizon. We drive for two hours and there is no end to them. In all, there must be at least 20,000, and nobody but ourselves to enjoy the spectacle.

Too soon, the light turns to gold. It's time to go, and as we drive back to camp I remember something Ralph had said to me the day we sat under Chapman's Baobab. "One day not far off," he had said, looking out into the desert beyond, "the world's greatest luxury will be space. That's why we are so lucky to live out here, where there is still room to be yourself, to sit under a tree and count the stars."

April 2009: The Secret World of Deception Valley

UNTIL recently Deception Valley was one of Africa's best-kept secrets, a place where adventurous, in-the-know aficionados could drive up from South Africa in their camper vans to sleep out in the vast emptiness of Botswana's Central Kalahari Game Reserve. The only alternative was to stay outside the reserve at Deception Valley Lodge, a good two hours' drive away, as I had done in 2006.

Kalahari Plains Camp has changed all that. Run by Wilderness Safaris, it means visitors can now reach this wildlife hotspot in 15 minutes, allowing plenty of time to track down the desert lions and other predators while they are still active in the first hours after dawn.

Every day in camp starts with the wake-up call of the red-billed francolin – the Kalahari alarm clock. At sundown, when the desert sky turns furnace red, there come the curious cries of barking geckos, and the nights echo to the sepulchral muttering of giant eagle owls.

My guide, Matt Copham, grew up in South Africa but has worked in Botswana for the past eight years and knows the Kalahari in all its moods. Tyres humming like angry bees, we skim by Land Cruiser down the soft sandy trail that leads directly to Deception Valley.

A dry weather wind is blowing, heralding the end of the rains, but the desert is still brimming with life and colour; with crimson-breasted shrikes, bee-eaters brighter than emeralds, and noisy parties of plum-coloured starlings.

Golden orb spider webs – "ten times stronger than steel," says Copham – glisten in the early morning sun. Pale chanting goshawks with salmon pink shanks glare at us from every tree and it soon becomes clear that the Central Kalahari with its wild flowers and monarch butterflies is no ordinary desert. Its endless sands and fossil dunes are buried under a shaggy pelt of grass and scrub, and it is only the heat and lack of water that places it among the earth's most unforgiving habitats.

For most of the year the Kalahari suffers. All through the long, hot African winter the grass withers and cruel mirages tremble in the heat-haze, creating the illusion of shimmering water that gave Deception Valley its name.

Then the rains come. They fall from December to March, mostly in the form of a few apocalyptic thunderstorms, transforming the Kalahari into a carpet of greenery pulsating with life. And at the heart of it is Deception Valley.

The valley is the giant footprint of a forgotten river system. In prehistoric times it might have flowed into what was once the world's biggest lake, where the Makgadikgadi saltpans now glitter from horizon to horizon. But what you see today is a river of grass, a faltering sweep of open savannah stretching for some 80 kilometres through the surrounding seas of fossil dunes.

During the rains its sweet grasses attract huge herds of gemsbok and springbok, and these in turn pull in the carnivores; not only lions and cheetahs but also smaller opportunists such as jackals and the rare brown hyena.

Marooned in the grasslands, acacia islands create closed canopies of shade. Under one of them, two American zoologists, Mark and Delia Owens, camped for seven years in the 1970s, and wrote *Cry of the Kalahari*, relating their experiences with two lions, Bones and Blue, and a brown hyena named Pepper.

The predators patrol the valley margins where open plains give way to bush, and it is here one morning that we find the lion king. In the Kalahari you have to work hard for your lions; but one of its black-maned pride males is worth ten lions anywhere else, and this one is huge.

He walks with the confident, almost insolent swagger that only the territorial pride males possess. His mane is so luxuriant that it reappears in thick tufts behind his front legs, and there is not a mark on him. Perhaps the blood of Bones and Blue runs in his veins? What I do know is that in a lifetime of watching lions he is the best I have seen.

But he is ruthless, too. When the camp opened in November two male cheetahs had taken up residence in the valley. In January he killed one of them and then to compound the felony he killed a brown hyena only a day before my arrival. We find its corpse in the afternoon, upside down in the grass and already stinking to high heaven.

Yet even without its top predators Deception Valley is a magical place. Three months of showers have laid the dust and the clear dawns ring to the far-carrying cries of jackals. Springbok live up to their name, leaping and bounding as if filled with the sheer joy of being alive, and herds of gemsbok with tribal masks and rapier horns canter over the plains like squadrons of lancers on patrol.

Soon the drought will begin to bite. Already the valley is acquiring the bleached hues of winter as the grass turns to gold. But in these first few days of April I see enough to convince me that during the green season it becomes one of wild Africa's most sublime arenas.

Chapter Ten

Lowveld and the Great Karoo

April 1999: Tracking with the Rain Bringer

F IRST light in the South African lowveld and the long grass is all around us as we cruise in our open-sided Land Rover across the Sabi Sabi Game Reserve. The reserve takes its name from the Sabi River, known to the Shangaan people as the 'River of Fear' because of its sinister man-eating crocodiles. But crocodiles are not on my mind right now as I look for tracks on the road ahead.

At the wheel in his broad-brimmed bush hat sits Andre van Zyl, our ranger-guide, and perched in the jump-seat on the bonnet is Patrick Mnisi, whose name means 'Rain Bringer' and whose keen eyes miss nothing. It's the start of a ranger-training experience, a three-day crash course in the ways of the wild, and this is Lesson One.

"Always listen out for alarm calls," says Andre as he stops the vehicle. "They could mean there's a predator not far off."

As if on cue, a jackal begins to yell nearby and moments later a spotted hyena comes rocking out of the grass. Alerted by the jackal's cry, the hyena knows there is always the chance of a free meal whenever the big cats are on the prowl; and sure enough, Patrick spots a leopard hiding under a bush.

Andre recognises her at once. "She's a young female I've seen recently with two young cubs," he whispers. "That's why she's nervous." In the standoff that follows, she wriggles her haunches, then mock-charges our vehicle before changing tack and vanishing into the tangled thickets of a dried-up riverbed.

Afterwards Patrick points out her tracks in the dust. "To track a leopard," he says, "you must learn to think like a leopard. You must become the thing you hunt, try to imagine where she might be going, what she may be doing next, and why."

Rhinos, I discover later, are easier to follow. On foot we pick up a set of their three-toed tracks where they have crossed the road – each cloverleaf footprint the size of a dinner plate. "Three rhinos have passed this way," Patrick tells me: "a bull, a cow and a yearling calf."

We inspect the spot where the bull has re-visited one of his middens – a pile of dung he has scented and scraped to lay claim to his territory. His urine is still wet on the ground and the trail he has made through the grass is so freshly trodden that even I can follow it, leading to a wallow, and beyond, a tamboti tree trunk still glistening with mud that the rhinos had rubbed off after bathing.

At one point the trail goes cold but we circle around and pick it up again, heading for dense bush where the family will lie up during the heat of the day.

We are getting closer now, treading more cautiously as we push on down a tunnel in the shadowy thickets, and I am glad Patrick is carrying a rifle. Rhinos have unpredictable tempers and I don't fancy climbing a thorn tree.

Suddenly Patrick freezes and points at the bushes ahead. And there, through the dappled leaves no more than 20 metres away, three ponderous horned shadows are slowly moving. Fortunately they are white rhinos, grazers with square mouths that should really be called wide-lipped rhinos, and are more docile than the notoriously grumpy black, or hooked-lip rhinos that also roam the Sabi Sabi.

Even so, white rhinos weigh a good three tons and run faster than an Olympic sprinter, and this trio know we are here. Short-sighted they may be but their hearing is incredibly acute and I can't help noticing how their ears have locked onto us and continue to monitor our presence as we slowly back away.

In the days that follow I will learn more from Andre and Patrick about what it takes to be a ranger. I will find out what it feels like to fire a .458 calibre elephant gun with a kick like a zebra, using bullets the size of chipolatas to blast holes in a target propped up on an anthill. I will discover how to make tea by brewing up seedpods of the magic guarri bush, and how to find water by following the movements of elephants or sandgrouse along dried-up riverbeds. But nothing else will match the spine-tingling intensity of meeting three rhinos on foot in their lowveld hideout.

September 2005: Land of Crooks and Tuskers

EARLY September in the Kruger National Park. It hasn't rained since April and the Luvuvhu River is shrinking daily. As the temperature rises, yellow leaves fall from the nyala trees, drifting idly in the windless air. Within minutes of arriving I'd seen two big bull elephants drinking at a bend in the river and, soon afterwards, I passed a sign by the roadside saying: 'Welcome to Makuleke, heart of the Great Limpopo Transfrontier Park'.

In the Kruger, this is the road less travelled. Most visitors concentrate on the south of the park, which is closer to the comforts of civilisation. The farther north you drive, the fewer vehicles you pass until at last you turn off the main highway into the Makuleke concession and find nothing but pristine wilderness.

Makuleke is the Kruger at its emptiest and most remote, how South Africa must have been a century ago, where the tarmac runs out leaving nothing but elephant trails winding across the lowveld to the hidden gorges of the Lebombo Mountains.

Its most recent inhabitants were forcibly removed by the former apartheid regime in 1969. Then, in 1997, in what was seen as a test case, the Makuleke people were awarded rights to their ancestral lands, but opted to keep them as a conservation area within the park and went into partnership with Wilderness Safaris.

The result is Pafuri, a luxury safari camp that opened in August 2005 with a stunning location on the banks of the Luvuvhu. Its 20 guest tents are linked to the thatched dining area by raised wooden walkways, tall enough for buffalo to wander beneath, and have shady decks overlooking the river.

In September the sweet-scented caper bushes are in flower, attracting clouds of butterflies. The riverside trees are festooned with flame creeper, and from now until the end of the dry season the Luvuvhu becomes Makuleke's lifeblood.

From dawn to dusk its trickling shallows attract a constant procession of thirsty animals; baboons and warthogs, greater kudu with spiral horns and shaggy-throated nyala bulls with painted heads like tribal masks.

There are birds, too: plovers, hamerkops, bee-eaters, spinetails. And sometimes, sudden moments of high drama, as when, disturbed by a sudden commotion in the riverbed, I look down and see a snake eagle in the act of killing a black mamba.

Above all, Makuleke is elephant country. Their giant footprints are everywhere. Their farmyard odour hangs in the breeze. Often, heading back to camp at dusk, our game drives become a game of Russian roulette played out with tetchy breeding herds in the winding tunnels of feverberry bush.

From end to end the Kruger has long been renowned for producing elephants with exceptionally heavy ivory. The most famous became known as the Magnificent Seven and included giants such as Mafunyane ('Grumpy'), whose tusks were so long that they dragged on the ground.

Sadly, having roamed the Kruger for more than half a century, the Magnificent Seven are no more. They all passed on in the 1980s, although only two met a violent end. The rest simply died of old age and their tusks are displayed in the elephant museum at Letaba Camp in the middle of the park.

But the tradition of the Kruger's giant elephants was continued by Mandleve ('Ears' in Tsonga), a ragged-eared monster that used to hang out in the south of the park. When he died in 1993 his tusks were found to weigh 152 pounds and 160 pounds respectively – the heaviest ivory ever carried by a Kruger bull.

Today the new king of the ivories is a Timbavati bull known as Mac. In May 2005 when he was anaesthetised and re-fitted with a new radio collar his tusks were estimated at 111 pounds and 105 pounds a side, making him the biggest tusker alive today.

Although the elephants I see are not in the same league as the Magnificent Seven, Andy Schafer, my safari guide at Pafuri, reckons there are still one or two big tuskers in the Makuleke concession, and the whole area is steeped in the history of South Africa's pioneering days when ivory poaching was a way of life.

❀   ❀   ❀

A century ago this remote northern tip of what is now the Kruger was known as Crooks' Corner and the reason is not hard to find. It lies between the confluence of the Luvuvhu and the Limpopo where three countries meet – South Africa, Zimbabwe and Mozambique – a place where outlaws could escape their pursuers by the simple expedient of stepping over the border.

I walk there one morning, following the trail that leads down to the Limpopo through ancient groves of leafless baobabs. In September the Limpopo is not great, grey-green and greasy as Kipling would have you believe, but a dry sand river with nothing to mark the place where three national boundaries collide except the skeleton of a fallen tree washed down on the last summer floods.

But nearby you can still see the foundations of a trading post built in 1910 when Crooks' Corner was in its heyday. The store became notorious as a meeting-place of the lawless, who came to sell ivory and stock up with food, liquor and ammunition before vanishing once more into the lowveld.

Among its regulars was Cecil Barnard, better known by his Shangaan nickname of Bvekenya ('He who Swaggers'), whose story is told in *The Ivory Trail* by T.V. Bulpin, a minor South African classic published in 1954.

Born in 1886 and imprisoned by the British during the Boer War, Barnard set off in 1910 to become an ivory hunter in what Bulpin calls 'this secluded and sinister wedge of land'.

Here, he became obsessed with tracking down an elusive elephant called Ndlulamithi ('Taller than Trees'), a lifelong quest that ended in 1929 when Barnard had the big bull in his sights but found himself unable to shoot it.

Now both are long gone, the hunter and the hunted, but that moment lives on as an inscription from Bulpin's book, on the stone placed in Barnard's memory not far from the spot where the old trading post stood. 'He saw the elephant's eyes, its weather-beaten face, the wrinkles in its skin, the tremors of its body, the waving of its ears with the ragged ends where the thorns had torn them. He saw the elephant in its strength and its wisdom, its savagery, patience and courage. He saw Africa, and he knew that he loved it. He put the gun down. "Let him live," he said.'

How amazed Bvekenya would be to see what is happening to his old hunting grounds. In 1927 when the Kruger first opened to visitors, only three cars turned up. Now it welcomes more than a million visitors every year and exciting changes are afoot that will expand the park to nearly twice its present size.

The plan is to drop Kruger's border fences, allowing the animals to spread far into Mozambique and Zimbabwe. When that happens, Crooks' Corner will become the epicentre of the Great Limpopo Transfrontier Park – a wildlife sanctuary bigger than Denmark – making it the world's largest national park.

At least, that is the dream. But while negotiations with Mozambique are going smoothly, a question mark hangs over Zimbabwe, where the adjoining Gonarezhou National Park has been ransacked during President Mugabe's years of misrule.

Meanwhile, the opening up of Makuleke has given the Kruger a new dimension. This is without doubt the wildest corner of the park and, as I discover, contains its most diverse habitats.

In one day you can pass through forests of fever trees with ghostly green trunks, drive deep into the Lebombo Mountains to emerge on the rim of Lanner Gorge, where black eagles drift in the up-draughts, or search for rare fishing owls that roost by day in the Luvuvhu's bankside jackalberry groves.

🐾   🐾   🐾

As for big cats, there is no better way to start the day at Pafuri than to be woken at dawn by a lion roaring in the riverbed. "Sounds like our local pride male," says Schafer when I join him by the campfire. We grab a quick coffee and hurry out to look for him.

It quickly becomes apparent that the lion has been following a large herd of buffalo whose dung lies freshly strewn in the trampled grass; but where is he now? Unlike the semi-habituated pussycats that obligingly pose for you in South Africa's glitzy private reserves, the Makuleke prides are still wild and elusive. That is why – when at last we pick up the lion's tracks and find him glowering on a grassy knoll – Schafer punches the air with joy. It is, as he predicted, the Pafuri pride male, six-years old and in his prime, with a gold mane turning black at the tips. Apart from an old scar on his muzzle he appears to be in perfect condition; but when he stands and stretches I can see a fresh horn wound behind his shoulder, picked up, perhaps, during a tangle with the buffalo.

Afterwards, when the lion has gone flat and closed his eyes, we drive on across Mangala ('the Place of the Man-Eater') to see if we can find a lioness Schafer had seen with two young cubs. We park the Land Rover under a baobab and set off on foot with Schafer carrying his heavy rifle.

By now the sun is burning hot. We walk in silence towards an escarpment where baboons keep watch from rocky *krantzes* and wait-a-bit thorns clutch at my shirtsleeves.

Suddenly, from a dense thicket ahead comes a warning growl that stops us in our tracks. It is the lioness, and her Clint Eastwood message is unmistakable: "Are you feeling lucky?"

We cannot see her, so we move on again with heartbeats doubled, crouching as we try in vain to pick her out in the thorny shade. Then she growls again, louder than before; a deep down rumble, dark with menace. In all my years in Africa, this is the most chilling sound I have ever heard. Schafer beckons with his hand and slowly, step by cautious step, we back away until we are safely out of range.

March 2007: The Leopards of Londolozi

EVEN in the South African summer when midday temperatures hit 35°C, the lowveld mornings can be sharp and cool. The dew has not yet dried and the sky above is a faultless blue, filled with the shrill cries of migrating bee-eaters bound for the distant shores of Europe.

We bump down a game trail in our open Land Rover, past leadwood trees with trunks rubbed smooth by passing elephants, and the dried-up bed of a seasonal watercourse called Manyeleti – 'the Place of Stars'. Our tyres swish over fresh lion tracks in the sand. "That'll be the Sparta pride," says Dave Varty, my guide.

Varty, lean and tanned after a lifetime in the wilds, is the owner of Londolozi, the private fiefdom whose fathomless sweeps of guinea grass and tamboti trees we are now traversing. This is where, at the age of six, he used to clean his father's precious Rigby 416 hunting rifle, and where, as a bush-wise 12-year-old, he tracked his first lion.

By now the sun is up, the air as clear as liquid amber, the bushveld echoing to a dawn chorus of francolins, shrikes and Heuglin's robins.

All around us impala, their coats still fluffed up against the chill, are snorting in alarm but it is not the distant roaring of the Sparta lions that is giving them the jitters. Deep in the surrounding thorn thickets, two young leopards, a brother and sister, are crouching in the shadows.

Varty has the low-down on this pair. "They are just over a year old," he whispers. "We call their mother the Vomba Female." And as soon as he mentions her name I feel a stab of recognition.

She was a leopard I saw here seven years ago. I'd seen her during a night drive, a gorgeous three-year-old, stalking a civet cat under the stars. Now it's her offspring I am watching as they loll in the bushes only metres from our vehicle.

This is the story of two families, one feline and the other human, whose lives at Londolozi in the game-rich Sabi Sand reserve have become inextricably entwined and, in doing so, have changed the face of wild Africa.

☙ ☙ ☙

It began in 1926 when a bankrupted cattle farm was bought site unseen by two big game hunters, Charles Varty and his friend Frank Unger. Together with Winnis Mathebula, an expert lion-tracker, they arrived on foot and set up camp in a jackalberry grove on the banks of the Sand River. Their original hunting camp is long gone but a campfire is still lit every night near the spot where Charles Varty pitched his tent 80 years ago.

By the 1970s high-end tourism was on the rise. Out went the old long-drop loos and the bush showers with a canvas bucket dangling from a tree, replaced by air-conditioned suites with luxurious bathrooms, teak decks and private plunge pools. Providing the impetus for these dramatic changes were Charles Varty's two grandsons, Dave and John. Dave is a visionary conservationist, John an acclaimed wildlife filmmaker, and together they set about transforming Londolozi into a big game sanctuary whose development became the blueprint for South Africa's emerging eco-tourism industry.

During the 1970s and 1980s the Vartys' guiding principle for Londolozi was to demonstrate the economic viability of wildlife in a land torn apart by racism, fences and division. To this end a share of all the profits still goes every year towards improving the lives of the Shangaan people who live and work around the reserve.

In 1994, around the time Nelson Mandela came to power, the game fences that had separated the state-owned Kruger National Park from the private reserves on its western border were removed, allowing wildlife to follow the old migration routes denied to them for so long.

The dropping of the fence lines was a powerful metaphor for the political changes taking place in South Africa at that time. Mandela himself became a regular visitor to Londolozi, describing it as "the dream I cherish for the future of nature preservation in our country".

For the past 14 years Londolozi has been leased to CC Africa, an eco-safari corporation the Vartys created and which now owns a string of five-star lodges all over the continent from the Eastern Cape to the Serengeti. But this year, in a move that surprised the safari industry, the lease was not renewed. Instead the Vartys decided to take back their flagship property and run it themselves.

Already its five lodges (each one discreetly hidden from the rest) are undergoing a thorough makeover. "It's a delicate task," says Dave Varty. "A lifetime of care has given Londolozi a sense of place we would lose at our peril."

When the work is completed in a couple of months it promises to be irresistibly stylish with lots of personal family touches to recall the pioneering days of the 1920s. "It's been a long journey," says Varty. "But we felt it was time to return to basics, to follow the dreams which have made this place so special. Now we are back where it all began. We're closing the circle."

🐾   🐾   🐾

And what of the leopards that are Londolozi's greatest luxury of all? Established more than half a century ago, the 63,000-hectare Sabi Sand reserve is sub-divided into a handful of smaller sanctuaries and now boasts more lodges per square mile than anywhere else in Africa. Among them are MalaMala, Singita and Richard Branson's Ulusaba. All promise close encounters with the Big Five (elephant, rhino, buffalo, lion and leopard); but Londolozi is the best of all for watching leopards round the clock.

On safari, the leopard is the animal that everybody wants to see. Leopards have charisma. They exude an aura of magic and mystery in the way they can suddenly materialise and then just as silently melt into the shadows. Of all big cats they are the most beautiful, the most cat-like in their movements and behaviour. But they are also notoriously elusive – except at Londolozi.

Leopards are plentiful all over the Sabi Sand lowveld, and Londolozi with its abundance of cover is leopard heaven. Here are dense riverine forests, shady *dongas* ('gullies') and marula trees with mottled trunks into whose lofty canopies a leopard can safely hoist its kill out of reach of lions and hyenas. Yet leopards were seldom seen. Their private lives remained a secret, even to the scientists who had tried to study them; and only once in a while would a tracker, perched in his jump seat on the bonnet of a game-drive vehicle, excitedly whisper the magic word *ingwe* – Shangaan for leopard – as a spotted cat streaked for cover. Then, one day in 1979, a mother with two small cubs was found near her den.

Slowly, and with infinite patience the Londolozi rangers established a relationship with her. Day after day they returned and soon began to get regular sightings. At first she was incredibly shy, but the rangers were always at pains not to frighten her; and whenever she and her cubs seemed agitated, the Land Rovers would withdraw and leave them alone.

Within six months, mother and cubs had become so completely at ease in the presence of vehicles that they would play in the open in broad daylight; and so began the remarkable bonding between the leopards of Londolozi and its rangers – a process that continues to this day.

Before she died in 1991, 'the Mother' as she was known, produced nine litters, and among them was another exceptional leopard called the Tugwaan Female.

Born in 1984, she survived for nearly 17 years – an incredible age for a leopard – giving birth to a whole dynasty of cubs whose lineage has been painstakingly recorded by Natasha de Woronin, a former Londolozi ranger.

Which brings me back to the here and now, to the early morning standoff between the nervous impalas and the two yearling cubs. This time their cover has been blown; but in a couple of months or so their hunting skills will be honed to perfection. By then they will be fully independent – the fifth generation of leopards in the Londolozi saga – and next time the impalas may not be so lucky.

April 2007: Tales from the Great Karoo

THE invitation sounded too good to pass up. "Come and meet Sibella, our South African television superstar." And what a glamour-puss she turns out to be; every inch a catwalk queen from her amber eyes to the black-and-white tip of her elegant tail.

The story of Sibella, now a resident of Samara Private Game Reserve in the Eastern Cape, had been widely reported in the South African media. Born seven years ago, she roamed free in the Northern Province until her capture in 2003. Badly hamstrung and mauled by dogs, she was tied up in a cage and left for dead.

Luckily, word of her plight got out. She was rescued by the De Wildt Cheetah and Wildlife Trust, underwent life-saving surgery and was then brought to Samara with two male cheetahs. Together they made history – the first cheetahs to be seen on the plains of Camdeboo for nearly 125 years.

But Sibella wasn't finished yet. A year later she produced a litter of five cubs and in 2006 went one better and gave birth to a litter of six, putting Samara on track to achieving its ambition of becoming the country's top cheetah reserve.

Just prior to my visit Sibella had been darted and taken to a holding pen to be fitted with a new radio collar. Now it is time to release her again and I have been invited to set her free. Quietly I open the gate of her enclosure, then step aside as she strides past with barely a glance to rejoin her new life in the Great Karoo.

It was the long-vanished Khoi-San people who called it the Karoo – 'the Dry Place where there is Nothing'. This is South Africa's Empty Quarter, a vast upland desert stretching for 30,000 square miles. Across the plains framed by huge skies of burning blue, stark mountains sprawl, like sleeping lions shutting out the rest of the world. To the south, only a couple of hours' drive away, lies the Garden Route – the tourist highway that hugs the coast from Cape Town to Port Elizabeth. But the Great Karoo, that ancient land of dinosaur bones and Stone-Age hand axes and Khoi-San cave paintings of extinct Cape lions, is passed by as if it never existed.

Among the most remarkable adventurers to explore this wild land were the naturalist William Burchell, the first European to discover the white rhino, and the French ornithologist François Le Vaillant who dressed in an ostrich-plume hat and shoes with silver buckles and travelled everywhere with 16 guns, a scimitar and a tame baboon.

As for the early settlers who trekked here by ox-wagon, only the hardiest and toughest survived. Most became sheep farmers, moulding their own bullets, fashioning shoes from springbok hides, living off biltong and even eating their donkeys when times were hard.

To this day the Karoo remains unforgiving, unsparing, and achingly lonely. And yet it has always had its devotees, people who are passionate about its sun-struck plains and boundless space.

Among them are Mark and Sarah Tompkins. He is an Englishman, a physicist by profession. Sarah, his South African wife, was a marketing product manager, and together they have demonstrated how hands-on conservation can transform 70,000 acres of clapped-out farmland into a hugely successful born-again wilderness.

"Ten years ago," says Sarah, "we were staying at Rorke's Drift Lodge in Zululand. There we met a man who filled our heads with magical tales of the Great Karoo, of the vanished creatures of the bushveld, the wandering cheetahs and the millions of springbok that once migrated across the plains of Camdeboo in such numbers that the dust raised by their passing took two weeks to settle.

"He told us there was a farm for sale and we went to see it. At first the land seemed desolate and devoid of life. But then we entered the Milk River Valley. We saw the buffalo grass and the indigenous trees, the vistas of mountains above and beyond, and were humbled by its beauty.

"It was a kind of delirium, like a love affair. We were living in Paris at the time and buying a farm in Africa made no practical sense whatsoever. But we went ahead and bought it."

That farm became the nucleus of Samara and today their crazy dream has become a reality. Since their first visit they have bought ten more farms, pulling down the fences to create one of the largest private game reserves in the country, re-stocked with species that roamed here before the settlers arrived; not only cheetahs but white rhinos, highly endangered Cape Mountain zebras and 15 kinds of antelope. Now, having converted the original farmhouse into a luxury lodge, visitors can enjoy a malaria-free safari in a part of Africa that has never been on the tourist map before.

A week or so before my arrival a storm had swept across the Karoo, dumping four inches of rain in the mountains and causing flash floods on the plains below. Now Samara is buried in grass, its red earth stippled with desert flowers. We drive from the airstrip through the green desert scrub and its thick aromatic scent travels with us, past flowering acacias with six-inch thorns and shepherds' trees with paper-white trunks.

The hillsides bristle with tall mountain aloes – strange plants that look as if they belong to another planet. Meerkats watch us with beady eyes, standing like ninepins around their burrows, and above us loom dolerite rim-rocks where black eagles breed. Then we enter a *kloof*, a valley leading towards the pyramidal summit of the Spitskop, splash across the stony shallows of the Milk River, and there stands the lodge, a desert oasis of gracious living with swallows swooping over manicured lawns.

The original farmstead, a low, single storey building in the colonial style of the previous century, has been immaculately restored with easy chairs set out on the *stoep* (veranda) under a blue-green corrugated tin roof.

There are three suites in the main lodge and three bungalow suites in the grounds, decorated with zebra-skin rugs and 19th-century lithographs by Cornwallis Harris. Close by is a swimming pool, a tennis court and a boma for dinners under the stars.

In the golden hour before sundown we go out on a game drive. We pass a lake where blue cranes are resting and as we watch, more fly in – gracious birds the colour of wood-smoke – filling the air with sweet-throated cries. A herd of gemsbok canter past, long horns held aloft, as if on parade.

To the north, the 7,000-foot crests of the Sneeuberg Mountains stand out sharp etched against the sky as the sun sinks through red reefs of cloud. It's time for a beer. We pull out the cool-box and watch the valleys fill with purple shadows. Then, our sundowners finished, we drive slowly back under the stars, shining a spotlight to search for the nocturnal animals of the plains.

Night in the Karoo belongs to the quick little bat-eared foxes, to the restless jackals whose feet hardly seem to touch the ground as they trot across the desert, and the aardvark or earth-pig, whose powerful claws can dig a three-metre-deep hole in the hardest soil to obtain its nightly feast of termites.

Next morning, awakened at sunrise with a tray of fresh-baked rusks and coffee in a silver pot, I draw back the curtains to see two male waterbuck sparring outside my window.

The dew is still heavy on the grass as we set off up the kloof, heading deeper into the hills where the elusive Cape leopard – smaller than its lowveld cousin – clings on like a legend. We're on our way to a mountain called Kondoa, struggling up bottom-gear tracks towards the summit 2,500 feet above.

Chacma baboons bark a warning at our coming, and two male kudu with corkscrew horns go crashing off through the *spekboom* ('elephant bush') thickets. Their arrow-shaped tracks are everywhere.

When at last we reach the summit we find ourselves on a high plateau of open savannah, a miniature Serengeti marooned in the sky along with its grassveld pipits and wild herbivores. Wherever I look there are animals; nervous blesbok with bold white blazes on their muzzles; black wildebeest cavorting over the grassy slopes; herds of eland with suede coats and swinging dewlaps; and most exciting of all, two family groups of highly endangered Cape mountain zebras trotting along the skyline.

The comparison with the plains of East Africa is uncanny. Even the oat grass spilling in green waves around us is the same species that grows in the Maasai Mara. "You're right," says Sarah proudly. "That's why we call this our Samara Mara."

It also reminds me of the Grands Causses, the limestone tablelands of the Cevennes. Islands of silence, the French call them, and the same profound hush holds Kondoa in its hand. But listen again and what you hear is pure unadulterated Africa; the whistling cries of redwing starlings, the curious yapping of the black wildebeest – so different from their Serengeti cousins – and the song of the wind running over the land.

Here, close to a viewpoint called Eagle's Rock, a picnic lunch had been arranged, with tables set out in the shade of a canvas pavilion. The food is exquisite; smoked duck-and-ginger consommé; carpaccio of eland. Even the sandwiches have been individually wrapped in brown paper and tied with blue ribbon. Glass of chilled Sauvignon in hand, I watch the cloud shadows on the plains below, crawling towards a horizon like the edge of the world.

Afterwards, having returned from the mountain, we go looking for two male cheetahs called Mozart and Beethoven. Both have been fitted with radio collars to make finding them easier in the dense scrub; but even so, if they lie down in a donga the signal is lost.

By now the temperature is soaring. Seen through the trembling desert air the summits of the Sneeuberg range dissolve into shimmering swirls of burnt sienna and iceberg blue. A secretary bird strides across the middle distance, its quills bouncing in time to each slow-marching step, and in all that immense heat-hazy space it is the only thing that moves.

All afternoon we search in vain and now the sun is almost down. Its last rays reach out across the grass, igniting the mountains until they glow like embers under red reefs of cloud. And only then, in the dying light, do we pick up a strong signal and find Mozart and Beethoven playfully stalking ostrich chicks on the darkening plain.

Chapter Eleven

Namibia

March 1990: From the Desert to the Deep

THERE is no road to Purros; only the ruts of old tyre tracks disappearing westward into the mountains and deserts of Kaokoland. Purros itself is nothing but a scattering of shacks and mud huts belonging to the Himba, nomadic pastoralists who dress in skins and roam the hills with their scrawny goats.

As we lurch down the dried-up bed of the Gomatum River, a tributary of the Hoarusib, the sky turns black and thunder rumbles in the hills. "Is it going to rain?" I ask. Sitting at the wheel of his Toyota Land Cruiser, my companion, the photographer David Coulson, looks up at the sky and shakes his head. "Not here," he says positively. "Not in the desert."

Coulson should know. He has been travelling around Namibia for years, recording its rich heritage of African rock art. But even as he speaks the first fat spots begin to fall and moments later we are in the thick of a ferocious tropical storm – and it is precisely at this moment that fate decides we should have a puncture.

There is nothing for it but to leap out into the lashing rain and change the wheel. Within seconds we are soaked to the skin.

When at last the wheel is fixed I unlace my desert boots and hold them upside down to pour the water out, and think to myself what an odd way this is to begin a journey into one of the driest and most inaccessible places on earth.

Namibia is the last great wilderness in southern Africa and much of it is desert. Some of its rivers do not run for years, and in some places no rain has fallen for almost a century.

To explore such demanding terrain requires local expertise, and that is why we are heading to Purros, to rendezvous with Louw and Amy Schoeman, who are going to take us to the Skeleton Coast.

The Skeleton Coast National Park is a strip of desert up to 25 miles wide, running south for some 300 miles from the Kunene River on the Angolan border to the Ugab River, near Cape Cross. When the park was proclaimed in 1971 it was decided to set aside the northern sector as a wilderness area where only limited tourism would be allowed; and in 1977 it was Schoeman, a practising attorney and one-time diamond prospector turned tour operator, who was awarded the concession to operate fly-in safaris there.

Since then he has flown, driven and walked all over the area and come to know it better than anyone. "Never underestimate the desert," he says. "It isn't hostile but it can be dangerous – even deadly if you don't know it. But I've been coming here for 30 years and it's just like moving around my own living room."

From Purros we follow Schoeman across what he thinks of as the most beautiful land on earth, traversing immense gravel plains with no sign of life except a few springbok and ostrich on the farthest horizons, until we come at sunset to his lonely camp on the edge of the Khumib River. The river had flowed a month ago after heavy storms in the mountains up country, says Louw; but now it is bone dry again.

The mess tent stands under the spreading branches of an ancient omumborombonga or leadwood, the holy tree of the Herero people, who believe it to be the ancestor of all life on earth; and at suppertime a pair of shy, spotted genets emerge from its branches to wait for scraps.

When I go to bed, ducking into my low-slung tent, I fancy I can smell the sea on the night breeze, even though the coast is a good eight miles away; and sure enough, when I awake in the stillness of dawn I can hear the dull roar of the Atlantic surf, like the distant drum roll of a passing jet.

After breakfast, before we set out I am given a hat, a legionnaire-style *kepi* with a flap to protect the back of my neck from the desert sun, although Schoeman insists on going hatless, even on the hottest days. With his grey hair and avuncular manner he has the look of a country doctor; but in reality he is one of Namibia's most experienced desert veterans, possessed of an endless store of knowledge gleaned from the barren world about us.

"We're paranoid about vehicle tracks up here," he says as we steer through the dune-fields towards the sea. "The desert is a fragile place, easy to scar and slow to heal. I can show you the tracks made in 1943 to rescue survivors from the wreck of the *Dunedin Star*. Even now they look as if they were made only last week; and there are other areas, on the coarser, more stable gravel plains, where tyre tracks will last for centuries."

We drive on through a desolation of barchan dunes – wandering sand-hills that crawl across the desert floor before the prevailing southerly winds at the rate of as much as 100 feet a year. At first glance these shifting sands seem utterly devoid of life; yet every slope bears a scribble of tracks – signatures left by side-winder snakes, scuttling lizards and fog beetles that collect the dew that condenses on their backs.

In places the sands are stained a rich maroon, as if someone has emptied giant vats of claret down the slopes. Louw hands me a magnifying glass and tells me to take a closer look. With my nose in the sand I squint through the glass and see that each polished grain is in fact a miniature gemstone. I am lying on a bed of garnets.

With Louw I learn the secret of driving in the dune-fields. You simply let down the tyres until they are like squashy balloons. Then, with the vehicle in four-wheel drive, you put your foot down and float through the soft sand with a sensation akin to skiing in powder snow.

As we come over the last crest of sand there is the glorious sight of the Atlantic below, with huge rollers crashing on an empty strand. Offshore lie two trawlers, rising and falling among the green hills of the sea. "Spanish, probably," says Louw. "They've robbed this country of billions of tons of fish."

We walk down to a beach that is knee-deep in spume: an extraordinary phenomenon produced by the rich blooms of plankton that thrive in the cold Benguela Current. Whipped up by the surf to the consistency of shaving cream, it covers the shore in thick, quivering blankets, slowly breaking up in the wind to roll away like tumbleweed.

Up and down the coast as far as the eye can see, the sands are littered with the flotsam of centuries; a tangle of ships' masts, planks and spars, with here and there the bleached skeleton of a great whale, butchered by the American whaling fleets a hundred years ago. Kelp gulls watch us at a distance and ghost crabs tiptoe away over the sands like shadows; but ours are the only footprints.

March 1990: Kunene

THE following day we fly up the Skeleton Coast on our way north to the Kunene River where Schoeman has another camp overlooking the Angolan border. Below us are scattered more masts, more ribs and vertebrae and giant jawbones of the vanished whales. We fly low over a colony of Cape fur seals hauled out on the beach and narrowly miss a flock of rare Damara terns that rise from the water like a white cloud in front of us and go swirling past our wing-tips. Had we hit them it would have brought down our small aircraft as effectively as any ground-to-air missile, but Schoeman appears unperturbed, and I learn later that among his friends he is known as 'low-flying Schoeman'.

At last we come to the wide brown mouth of the Kunene and follow it inland across a scene of utter desolation. To the south lies nothing but the glare of saltpans, a terrifying emptiness reaching away into the dunes and mountain ranges of Kaokoland. To the north rise the sun-scorched rocks of Angola. "Amazing to think that most of this country we've been flying over has never seen a human foot on it," Schoeman yells above the engine's roar. "Not even a bushman."

It seems impossible that there could be any safe place to land in this burnt and broken country; but eventually a strip appears and we touch down on a wide plain to step out into the blowtorch heat of late afternoon.

A vehicle is waiting to take us to camp. Recent rains have raised a faint flush of green grass from the red sand, but already it is withering in the unrelenting heat. To the south a range of nameless hills raise their granite heads. Rock kestrels whistle among the crags and larks fly up as we drive along the stone ridges in search of a safe place to descend to the river, but their cries are torn away on the hot wind.

By the time we reach camp the sun is setting. Shadows seep out of the ground like smoke, filling the hollows of the hills above the gorge in which the river is hissing and swirling in spate. There is a swimming pool among the rocks (the river itself is full of crocodiles), and although there is barely room enough to turn around, it is bliss to cool off and then sit with a cold beer and watch the lightning flickering in the mountains of Angola.

Somewhere in those forbidding hinterlands is where the Kunene has its source in the same giant watershed that gives rise to the Zambezi and the Okavango. But unlike them, the Kunene flows westward to the Atlantic, forming one of the loneliest frontiers on earth.

"Nobody comes here to see animals," says Schoeman. "It's not like the Etosha National Park. You come for the remoteness, the ruggedness. That's what the Kunene is all about. Mass tourism has no place here; but a lucky few will pay for the privilege of coming to such a wild area, and they need the kind of guidance we can provide because it's not a good place to get stuck in."

Next morning, Schoeman launches an inflatable boat powered by two giant outboard engines and we set off upstream, bouncing over the racing brown current in which fierce whirlpools spin and gurgle under our bows. After about a mile of this the gorge begins to narrow, causing the water to become even more turbulent as it tumbles towards us in a series of rapids. Here the river tries its best to unseat us but we cling on grimly as the boat bucks and turns beneath our feet.

Ahead loom towering walls of granite, closing in like the gates of hell. Somehow we squeeze through them and surge on past a chaos of sunless cliffs that have collapsed like a stack of giant dominoes, until our way is blocked by an enormous cataract and we can go no further.

Once we are out of the rapids, returning downstream is far more enjoyable. Goliath herons flap out of the reeds and brilliant green-and-yellow bee-eaters sit on the swaying branches of the winterthorns above luxuriant tangles of morning glory flowers.

Back at camp we laze over a late breakfast, then leave the Kunene to fly back to the Khumib. Once more that savage northern landscape unfolds below, the sands a smouldering Martian red, the blinding soda pans, the mountains flayed by wind and sun. I am glad I have been to the Kunene, but at the same time I cannot deny feeling a sense of relief to be escaping from its brooding hostility.

March 1990: Breakfast on the Skeleton Coast

AT the Khumib we say goodbye to Louw and Amy Schoeman, bump-start David Coulson's Land Cruiser and set off south down the Skeleton Coast. [I did not know it then but I would never see this remarkable man again. Sadly, Louw died of a heart attack in 1993, leaving his four sons to carry on his Skeleton Coast Safaris.]

After an hour or so we come to the mouth of the Hoarusib. There had been more storms inland and so the river is running. We wade across to see if it is too deep to drive. The water is below our knees but flowing strongly and still rising as we watch, coming down in sudden surges that spread out across the sand. It is now or never. Slowly we nose into the flood and drive across it obliquely with the water lapping at the bottom of the doors; luckily the riverbed is firm and with some relief we manage to reach the other side.

It is now late afternoon and springbok are feeding down on the shore, bathed in the golden Atlantic light. It seems incongruous to find them beside the sea; but sometimes, says David, desert-dwelling elephants follow the sand rivers down to the coast, leaving their giant footprints along the beach; and from time to time a desert lion comes wandering out of Damaraland to scavenge for seal carcasses in the surf.

Our destination is the ranger station at Mowe Bay where we stay two nights. With its bleached driftwood shacks and small gardens heaped with fishnets, whalebones, and other flotsam, the bleak little settlement is like the setting for a Steinbeck novel.

Yet despite its remoteness it seems to attract a succession of exceptionally gifted people. One of the shacks is the home of the wildlife filmmakers Des and Jen Bartlett, who have spent the past 14 years living and working in the Namibian parks, and over a breakfast of tea and kippers they explain how they have been using microlights to film the desert-dwelling elephants from the air as they migrate through the dunes.

Later we meet Garth Owen-Smith, the man who has done more than anyone to protect the elephants of Namibia's wild northwest. With his luxuriant beard and thousand-mile stare Owen-Smith has the look of a desert prophet, which is not far from the truth.

His has long been a voice in the wilderness, fighting the ignorance of government officials and their leftover views imported from South Africa's apartheid regime as he champions the rights of the indigenous Himba, Herero and Damara people. "I have always believed that involving the local people is the only way to save what wildlife is left," he says. "They want the wildlife but they also want to benefit from it, which is fair enough."

With him is his equally dedicated colleague, Rudi Loutit, who has been fighting to save the last of Namibia's desert rhinos. These are black rhinos that have evolved to cope with their arid surroundings, and his latest project involves dehorning them to deny the poachers the prize they seek. "People were very defeatist when we started," says Rudi, "They said the rhinos would be killed by lions if we removed their horns. But we went ahead and did it anyway because somehow we've just got to get these wonderful animals into the next century."

He pauses, a dark, good-looking man in his green ranger's uniform. "You know, my wife Blythe and I never had any kids because of the life we lead. We decided to dedicate ourselves to keeping the rhino alive, and it's ironic, really. We're keeping them alive for other people's kids to see."

After Rudi has gone I stroll down to the shore and sit on the beach and think about these extraordinary and solitary men who choose to spend all their lives in the wilderness and now are themselves a vanishing species.

A fog bank comes rolling in, heavy with the smell of kelp. The damp sea mist clings to my bare legs but I am not cold and I walk for miles, relieved to be out of the desert heat, listening to the gulls that remind me of home in faraway Dorset, beachcombing for agate pebbles among the jackal tracks and palest pink sea-urchin shells. It is hard to believe I am still in Africa, yet I know that inland, less than five miles away the sky will be a burning blue and the sand too hot to tread on.

April 1990: The Sheltering Desert

WE leave the Skeleton Coast National Park at its southern end below the Ugab River. A ranger opens the gates, adorned with sinister black-painted skulls and cross-bones, and we follow the Atlantic down to Swakopmund, a clean oasis of palm trees and old-fashioned buildings still locked in a dream of the Kaiser's Germany.

Swakopmund provides a brief interlude of hot baths, clean sheets and air-conditioned rooms; and then we are off once more to the desert, following the dried-up Kuiseb riverbed into the Namib-Naukluft National Park.

This is the true Namib – a sun-struck wilderness of gravel plains above which mirages of distant mountain-tops appear as rocky islands in a trembling sea of blue.

High rolling dunes march south with us along the western horizon, like the Sussex Downs painted red. Further south at Sossusvlei they reach a height of 1,000 feet – the tallest dunes in the world. There is no water anywhere but there are trees beside the Kuiseb, giant winterthorns from whose broad parasols of shade have fallen large seedpods with furry shells as soft as moleskin.

Here we camp at a place called Homeb, and when it is cooler in late afternoon we cross the riverbed and climb up out of the valley to watch the sun go down behind the dunes. We come to a stony plateau scattered with wind-blasted pebbles of clear white and yellow crystal that glitter in the sand like fallen stars. Nothing grows here except for a few sparse grey tufts of grass that creak and hiss in the wind; yet scatterings of old, dry spoor show that gemsbok and zebra have passed this way.

Back in camp, night comes swiftly. A full moon sails up over the horizon and in the clear desert air every detail of its cratered surface is visible through my binoculars. We barbecue the steaks we bought in Swakopmund and eat them with potatoes and onions wrapped in foil and baked in the embers, washed down with beers from the cool-box; and afterwards, stretched out in my sleeping bag, I lie on my back looking up at the brightest stars in Africa. From somewhere downriver comes the sepulchral hoot of an owl, and the jackals crying in the dunes. The last thing I remember before falling asleep is that today is Easter Sunday.

Deeper in the desert, while driving through the burnt-out badlands and labyrinthine canyons of the Swakop River, we come upon a stony valley upon whose slopes grow hundreds of *Welwitschia mirabilis*, one of the world's oldest and weirdest plants. Some of these living botanical fossils are said to be 1,500 years old; yet in their entire lifetime they produce only two leaves, which may attain a length of nine feet and split into leathery green fronds. I do not care for these unlovely relics. They lie in the sun like something out of John Wyndham's *The Day of the Triffids*, as if waiting to shoot out one of their sinister-looking leaves to grab you by the ankle, suck out your juices and then discard you like an empty paper bag.

Above Homeb, the course of the river cuts through a range of cindery hills into the desolate Kuiseb canyonlands, where two German geologists – Hermann Korn and Henno Martin – and their palindromic dog, Otto, hid for nearly three years to avoid being interned by the South Africans during the Second World War.

Afterwards, Henno Martin recounted the story of their Robinson Crusoe existence in a book, *The Sheltering Desert*, in which he graphically describes their solitary lives, shooting game, searching for water in the bottom of the canyons and coming to terms with the hardships imposed by one of the cruellest places on earth.

We visit one of their old hideouts, the place they called Carp Cliff, high above the Kuiseb Canyon. Here the two fugitives had built a shelter under the overhanging rim rock, living like Neolithic Man on whatever game they could catch. The walls they had built 50 years ago were still there, and a stone slab they had used as a table.

Mountain zebras had come this way not long ago. We find fresh spoor at the foot of the cliff and I remembered Henno Martin's account of how he and Hermann would shoot zebra and gemsbok, turn the meat into biltong, make the blood into sausages and sometimes enjoy a nostalgic feast of gemsbok liver dumplings and sauerkraut in the middle of the desert.

Distance lends these far-reaching barrenlands a surreal perspective, with the sharkfin shapes of mountain ranges thrusting over faraway horizons. Here, in the pitiless heat of the Namib, the earth's rocks are being tested to destruction, blow-torched by the sun, sand-blasted by the searing winds, broken down into fissured gullies and ravines in which the eye cries out for the sight of a green tree or a pool of water. In the emptiness of the Namib the earth is already a dying planet. This is the shape of things to come, and long after humankind and all other life has been extinguished from the face of the world, the inert carcase of this implacable desert will continue to roll through space.

All my life I have loved wilderness and wild places, but the Namib's unrelenting hostility has me beaten. In its furnace heat I can feel my spirit wilting like a dying flower. Only in the last golden hour before sunset and again in the first cool hour of dawn does the desert relent, allowing deep shadows to soften its harsh contours, transforming it into a silent world of unearthly beauty.

March 1998: The Cheetahs of Okonjima

AFTERNOON tea at Okonjima has to be one of my most memorable meals ever. Not just for the quality of Lise Hanssen's home baking or even the garden setting of tropical flowers smothered in butterflies. At Okonjima, a luxurious family-run lodge on a 15,000-acre farm in the middle of Namibia, you sit on the lawn and sip your tea while three full-grown cheetahs purr and prowl and rub their sinuous bodies against you.

These cheetahs, it must be said, are not dangerous. They are adorable orphans that have lived at Okonjima since they were cubs. Chinga, aged nine, was the first to arrive. "It all started with her in 1989," says Lise. "She was auctioned after her mother was shot. We bought her for 100 rand [£12]."

Chinga's two companions, Chui and Caesar, were the next to be rescued. Chui came to Okonjima when she was only six months old, having been found by the roadside with a broken pelvis; and Caesar had been kept as a pet in a 30-foot-long wire pen.

The cats seem to enjoy teatime almost as much as the guests. Cameras click and the cheetahs – leggy supermodels in spotted coats – stare back with smouldering amber eyes. But this is much more than a hands-on, bunny-hugging treat for Namibia's burgeoning tourist trade.

A stay at Okonjima brings visitors face to face with the harsh realities of conservation. For this is also the home of the AfriCat Foundation, founded by the Hanssens in a bid to find common ground between Namibia's farmers and the cheetahs and leopards that prey on their livestock.

Namibia's cheetah population – estimated at around 2,500 in 1998 – is the biggest in Africa. In a country four times the size of Britain, with fewer than 1.2 million people, you might think there would be plenty of room for them. Yet even in this vast land the cheetah is running out of space. The farms are so big, the land so dry. It takes 20 acres to keep one cow alive, and it is on these meagre grazing lands that most of Namibia's spotted cats are found.

Cheetahs and leopards thrive on farmlands because, unlike the cats in national parks, they face no competition from lions and hyenas. The bad news is that they are classed as vermin, to be trapped, poisoned or shot on sight. Between 1980 and 1991, Namibia lost 7,000 cheetahs – a tragedy for an endangered species. "In Namibia," says Lise, "the cheetah's biggest enemy is ignorance."

Yet Lise and Wayne, her husband, know they must work with the farmers if AfriCat is to succeed. "You can't just go in with an attitude," says Wayne. "Their lives are so hard that you have to feel sorry for them as well as the predators."

At the time of my visit 259 cheetahs and 209 leopards had come to Okonjima since the AfriCat Foundation began. Some have been returned to the wild or relocated in game reserves; but cheetahs such as Tyke, who has only three legs, will live out the rest of their days in a 400-acre compound funded by Tusk, the UK-based conservation charity.

"Many of our cheetahs come here as orphans," says Lise. "Since they have never learnt how to hunt they must stay on the farm until we have developed techniques for helping them to fend for themselves. Our next step is to build a 5,000-acre enclosure, stock it with game, then put in the cheetahs and see what happens. If they can cope, then maybe we can put them back in the wild where they belong.

The cheetahs may be the stars of Okonjima but they are not the only residents. Others who enjoy the run of the place include a pair of caracals, a warthog called Miss Piggy (actually a male), and Elvis the baboon, who loves to ride with Wayne in his Land Rover.

Elsewhere on the farm, held securely behind electric fences, are three orphaned lions. The biggest is Matata ('Trouble'), a 27-month-old male who arrived as a premature cub weighing only five pounds. His companions, Tambo and Tessie, were just skin and bone when they were brought to the farm, having been kept in a cage and fed on dog pellets. Now all three lions are sleek and healthy.

Midway through my stay a call comes through from a communal farm deep in the bush some 250 miles away. Two calves and a donkey foal have been killed. Now the raider – a leopard – has been caught in a box trap and the owners want it removed. Lise sets off to collect it and I tag along for the ride.

When the tar runs out we drive on down gravel roads that lead west towards the Skeleton Coast across the emptiness of southern Damaraland. Far away to the south I can see the Spitzberg, the African Matterhorn, beckoning across a furnace waste of burnt-out hills and stony plains; and somewhere out there lives a farmer called Nicodemus, the man who has trapped the leopard.

Eventually we find him. He squeezes into the front of Lise's *bakkie* and directs us for another ten miles down the waterless bed of the Omaruru River. At last we come to a deep gorge lined by shady camelthorns, and there is the leopard, a picture of fury, coughing and snarling in its trap.

Its muzzle is bleeding, having been rubbed raw on the wire sides of the trap in its vain attempts to escape. "A male," says Lise. "Not a big one but apart from his nose he's in beautiful condition."

Hurriedly she sets to work. First, she sedates the leopard with the aid of a blowpipe. Once the dart has struck home it takes about five minutes for the drug to work, but eventually he lies still. His eyes remain open but they see nothing as she hauls him out unceremoniously by the tail, and together we carry him to the bakkie. He lies heavily in my arms, limp as a sack of meal, and I cannot believe I am holding one of Africa's supreme carnivores. Fully awake, he would rip me to pieces.

"Are you going to give him a name," I ask. "We don't do that for all our animals," says Lise. Then she grins. "But I think we might call this one Brian."

Gently we lay my namesake on a blanket in the back of the bakkie, and Lise pulls back his black lips to expose his fangs. I place my hand beside them. His canines are as big as my thumbs. "When that boy wakes up he'll have a hell of a hangover," says Lise. "But he'll get over it."

Back at Okonjima, once he has recovered, he will be moved to a spacious compound for three months. Then, with luck, he will be fitted with a radio collar and released, so that Wayne and Lise can track his movements and probe deeper into the secret lives of these most shy and mysterious of cats.

Chapter Twelve

Monsoon Shores
(Lamu and Zanzibar)

December 1994: Where the Wind Blows

A BOULEVARD of midnight-blue water running through the mangroves is all that separates Lamu from the mainland. Yet this Indian Ocean island, just two degrees north of the Equator, seems to exist in its own parallel world. Nowadays you can fly there from Nairobi in 80 minutes; but from the moment I touch down on neighbouring Manda Island I feel as if I am stepping back into the age of Sinbad.

Here on the burning rim of Africa is a rickety wooden jetty, and at the end of it is a sailing dhow called *Pepo* ('Wind') waiting to take me on the ten-minute ride across the water. In the stern, as if too lazy to lift his hand, the skipper steers the tiller with his bare foot, heading out into the tideway towards Lamu's low-profile waterfront of coconut palms and flat-roofed houses.

Lamu time is measured not by the tyranny of clocks but by sun and tides, by the phases of the moon and the quavering voice of the muezzin summoning the faithful to prayer. Even the names of the fishing dhows rocking at their moorings reflect its mood of contented indolence: *Furaha* ('Happiness'); *Malaika* ('Angel').

The town itself is the oldest in Kenya, an exotic UNESCO World Heritage Site where two worlds collide, Africa and Arabia, creating a labyrinth of mosques, coffee shops and coral stone houses threaded by the narrowest of alleyways. Even in the main street, the Usita wa Mui, there is scarcely room for two donkey carts to pass. The rest of the streets have no names, but the various *mitaa*, or town wards, are known by evocative titles such as Pangahari – 'Sharpen your Sword' – and Mwana Mshamu – named after a famous Swahili poetess of the 19th century.

Other relics of earlier times can be seen in the town museum, including Lamu's famous brass *siwa*, a six-foot-long ceremonial horn made in about 1700 and inscribed: 'How often have you taxed yourself with journeys before sunrise and in the twilight... Don't despair, even though the search be long'. Side by side with this mighty relic is the great ivory siwa from Pate Island, and together they rank among the finest art treasures in Africa.

Historic it may be, but in truth Lamu is a raddled old town. Caught up in its web of airless alleys with their open drains and leprous walls, you may find yourself gasping for the ocean winds of Shela. Yet there is no denying its raffish charm. In the market square outside the 19th-century fort which served as a prison in British colonial times, old men dressed in traditional, ankle-length cotton *kanzus* and embroidered skullcaps known as *kofias* lounge on stone benches playing *bao*, an African board game of baffling complexity; and at dusk, when the coffee-sellers emerge with their conical brass pots, veiled women flit down the side-streets in black *buibuis* that reveal no more than a flash of almond eyes.

It is almost as if the Western World does not exist. There is no television, no sound of aircraft overhead, and no traffic except for a couple of old Land Rovers belonging to the district commissioner. For everyone else, life still moves no faster than the fishing dhows that set out each morning at *saa moja*, the first hour of daylight.

Even before the birth of Islam, Arab dhows were voyaging down the coast of the mysterious continent they called the Land of Zinj. They began to trade with the islanders of the Lamu archipelago, and it was these hardy seafarers, whose word *sawāhil*, meaning 'coasts', gave rise to a whole new culture as they intermarried with the local Bantu people.

Until the 1970s the dhow trade was still Lamu's lifeblood, after which it sank into genteel decay until tourism prodded it back to life; but Habu Shiri, a retired dhow captain, still remembers those long past glory days. I find him sitting under a tree on the waterfront, mending a sail with his fisherman friend, Hassani Mzee. "Many times I have crossed the Indian Ocean," says the old man with a faraway look in his eye. "From Zanzibar to India, going with the south wind, it would take us 30 days. Now that trade is ended. The big dhows stopped coming 20 years ago."

Today it is the tourist trade that keeps Lamu's economy afloat. Most of the fish Hassani catches are sold to the local hotels, but he is happy. "We are pleased to see the tourists," he says. "Without the *wageni* there would be many poor people in Lamu, and many sad hearts."

Like most of the small inshore fishing boats to be seen along the waterfront, Hassani's boat is a *jahazi*, built to a traditional local style with a straight-up-and-down bow, a wineglass transom and coconut matting strung along the gunwales to keep out the spray.

Behind the waterfront are the back-street furniture shops in which Lamu's elaborate hand-carved chests are made, and where ornate wooden doorways reveal tantalising glimpses of hidden courtyards. The finest of these Swahili houses date from the 18th century, Lamu's golden age. Built of coral limestone blocks, they are often three storeys high, with steps leading to a thatched rooftop eyrie where it is pleasant to sit at sundown and catch the breeze.

A mile-and-a-half beyond Lamu Town, where the channel curves to meet the open sea, the bone-white minaret at Shela village comes into view, and this is where I am heading now.

As we come alongside the jetty at the Peponi Hotel, small boys leap and dive into the clear water while barefoot villagers wearing wraparound *kikois* and ear-to-ear grins step forward to carry my bags ashore. "*Jambo! Karibu!*" they cry. "Hello! Welcome!" and I am reminded again what a melodious language Swahili is. Every word ends in a vowel, and on Lamu you will hear not the kitchen Swahili of up-country Kenya but the real thing. Even to my untutored ear I can make out every syllable. It is like the difference between, say, a London Cockney and the Queen's English.

The Peponi Hotel at Shela is one of the great landfalls of Africa, an oasis of coolness between the sandhills and the sea. Its name means 'Where the Wind Blows' and its position on the shore is designed to catch every last whisper of the monsoon breezes.

Now it is February and the *kaskazi* – the northeast monsoon that blows from mid-November until early March – is pouring through the hotel gardens, heavy with the sweet scent of frangipani. My room is as simple as a cave, with high, beamed ceilings and stone steps outside, leading past a terrace where the black snouts of ancient cannons still point across the water, and down to the beach. By day, the shrill cries of bee-eaters fall from the Nandi flame trees, and at night, when guests dine barefoot wearing their best kikois, bats flutter in and out of the lamplight, and at such moments you understand why decades of Nairobi ex-pats and up-country game wardens have flocked here to feast on the hotel's exquisite drunken prawns and tuna carpaccio.

For years, Lamu has been home to a colourful coterie of individualists: drifters and idealists, misfits from the outside world for whom the island's otherness makes it a perfect hideaway. Among them, I was told, lived an eminent London surgeon who, having been given only six months to live, decided to spend his last days in retirement on the island. Here, having informed the locals of his plight, he walked every day on the beach at Shela, swam in the sea, breathed in the pure Indian Ocean air and thrived so well on a diet of fresh fish and tropical fruit that he survived for years and became known to everyone as *Bwana Badu Kufa* – 'Mister Not Dead Yet'.

One of Lamu's most legendary denizens is Bunny Allen, the last of Kenya's old-time white hunters. Sitting barefoot on the roof of the rambling Arab-style house he built 30 years ago, Allen is a ghost from Karen Blixen's Africa, a gipsy with a ring in his ear and a string of leopards' teeth around his neck, who remembers the days when every thicket held a rhino and elephants with 100-pound tusks still roamed the savannahs.

As a young man he hunted with Denys Finch Hatton and Karen Blixen. "Ah, that Blixen girl," he sighs, "delicate as Chinese porcelain."

"Mind you," he adds with a wicked chuckle, "I always preferred Dresden myself. You know, rosebuds popping out all over the place."

As a professional hunter, he had escorted all kinds of celebrities on safari, including Ava Gardner; and even now, in his mid-eighties, his hooded eyes are sharp and clear and you can see why women adored him. But Kenya has changed, is changing still, leaving him beached in Lamu. Today, like the dhow fleets and the disappearing rhino, he belongs to the past, a part of that vanishing Africa in which it seemed that the game would go on forever.

March 2002: Beached on Mnemba Atoll

"WELCOME to our swimming pool," says the grinning boatman, gesturing at the pellucid shallows as I wade ashore on Mnemba Atoll to be welcomed with a glass of iced tea laced with African honey. "And there," he says, pointing to the deep purple shadows of submerged coral gardens, "is our house reef."

Once this scrap of coral lying off the northeastern tip of Zanzibar had nothing but a well, used by local fishermen who believed its waters were drawn from the very heart of Africa. Today it is a privately owned atoll and one of the most sought-after holiday spots in the world – the crème de la coconut crème.

Getting there involves a 15-minute speedboat ride from a beach where fishermen unload the day's catch from their outriggers, and then a wet landing.

The sand is almost too hot to walk on but the gift of shade is only a few steps away. Under the swaying casuarinas trees are ten beachfront cottages with hand-woven Zanzibari palm-frond floors and king-size beds as soft as sleep. There are no doors or windows but privacy is absolute as each cottage is hidden inside its own green tunnel of screw pines.

Barefoot casual is the Mnemba dress code. For dinner – the morning's catch of kingfish served with pineapple salsa and a lemongrass brulée for dessert – a Swahili cotton wraparound kikoi is perfectly acceptable. I find one laid out beside my bed, together with a straw hat and a guide to the 300 fish species that swarm around Mnemba's reefs.

At all times indolence rules. On my private veranda, I while away the hours playing *bao*, the world's oldest board game, on a slab of carved ebony with seeds as counters; and every cottage has its own beach bed, primitive but supremely comfortable, with a soft white mattress and palm-frond awning. It's an ideal piece of alfresco furniture on which to perfect the art of *pumzika* – snoozing.

The atoll itself is tiny. Twenty minutes is all it takes to stroll around it. But it is completely encircled by a dozen miles of pristine coral reefs, and at low tide the receding waters expose a glittering expanse of lukewarm pools and wave-ribbed sands where I feel I could walk forever and never reach the horizon. With its huge skies and flocks of crab plovers it reminds me of the North Norfolk coast – except that here the sands are powdered coral and the sea temperature is a blissful 28°C.

The tide lines are strewn with treasures of the deep: mottled cowries, strange starfish and the pink satin carapaces of ghost crabs. The light flung back by the burning sands is dazzling, intensifying the colours of the sea. Across the lagoon, a long thin line of white marks where the waves are breaking on the outermost reefs. Beyond it, sharp against the blue, are fishing dhows whose three-cornered sails have graced these waters since the time of Sinbad. And beyond them, nothing but a toppling wall of storm clouds coming down with the warm *kaskazi* trade wind.

When the heat becomes too much to bear, I cool off with goggles and flippers. Just off the beach in front of the lodge, shoals of fish are circling the house reef, slowly rising and falling as if riding an invisible carousel. Butterfly fish – their lips permanently pursed as if about to blow a kiss – glide past in stately golden convoys. Every species is a miracle of colour and design. There are angelfish with humbug stripes, Moorish idols like crescent moons, and parrotfish nibbling at the corals with an audible crunch. And between August and December it is possible to swim with whale sharks, the world's biggest fish.

In Swahili these beautiful animals are called *papa shillingi* – 'the Shark Covered in Shillings' – an illusion to their silver spotted backs; and despite their size they are harmless to humans, preferring to feed on the mantis shrimps that swarm off the East African coast at this time of year.

Everywhere at Mnemba, above and below the surface, there is life. At night, green turtles haul themselves ashore to lay their eggs in the sand; and one morning, immersed in a book, I look up to see a suni – an antelope no bigger than a hare – staring at me across my veranda.

After only two days here, Mnemba has me hooked. Almost against my will, I can feel its insidious lethargy taking hold. Not for me the activities on offer: diving, kayaking, windsurfing, deep-sea angling. Instead I loll and stroll, and the white band where my discarded watch had been is becoming as brown as the rest of me.

Lying in bed at night I hear the dull roar of the sea breaking on the distant reefs as the waves run before the *kaskazi*, and from much closer comes the wash of wavelets as they collapse on the beach and fall back with a gasp, like the untroubled breathing of a sleeper. A few more days of this, I decide, and I could end up in thrall to the barefoot life forever.

January 2003: Sailing with the Sons of Sinbad

TUSITIRI lies at anchor in a blue bay, opposite a crescent of coral sand on the shores of Pate Island. The only people living here are a handful of Bajuni fishermen who are building a dhow on the beach and will leave when the job is done.

At dusk, when the monsoon wind dies, a huge African moon appears, beating a silver path towards us across the water, and after a supper cooked on deck – fish soup, sweet mangrove crabs and coconut rice – I sleep out under the stars, waking only once in the small hours to see the constellations still glittering overhead.

Here, on the rim of northern Kenya lies a beguiling archipelago, whose Muslim inhabitants live closer to the age of Sinbad than the 21st century.

Theirs is a luminous world, half sea, half sky, divided by low horizons of dunes, mangrove creeks, deserted beaches and coral reefs running all the way to Somalia. Its clear waters are the haunt of turtles, pelicans, dugongs and whale sharks. There are no roads. Sometimes elephants and even lions make their way down to its lonely shores, and the only way to explore is on board a dhow such as *Tusitiri*, a vessel with a pedigree as old as Islam.

Every winter they came wafting down from the Gulf, the great ocean-going dhows of Arabia: Red Sea sambuks, double-ended booms from Kuwait and Iran, scimitar-prowed zarooks from the Yemen, all running before the *kaskazi*. At Lamu and Mombasa and Zanzibar they would arrive laden to the gunwales with sweet Basra dates, Shirazi carpets, Mangalore tiles and salt from Djibouti; and there they would remain until spring, when the northbound *kusi* blew them home again with all the romantic cargoes of Africa: coffee, amber, ivory and turtle shells.

Half a century earlier you might have seen as many as 200 dhows lying in Mombasa's Old Port. But in 1977 – the first year I visited Mombasa – only eight had made the journey south. I did not know it then, but what I saw was the last dying spasm of a trade that had lasted a thousand years.

Yet the local inshore dhow trade continues, as does the demand for fishing dhows, which are still built at Matondoni on Lamu Island and elsewhere in the archipelago, using methods that have not changed in centuries. Now, as then, dhows are born on fragrant beds of wood shavings. Slowly, as the months go by, the hand-hewn hulls take shape, like the rib cages of Jurassic monsters, coaxed from crooks of Malabar teak with axe, adze and bow drill – and no blueprint but the shipwright's unerring eye.

Such a vessel is *Tusitiri*, a 65-foot jahazi whose Swahili name means 'Something to be Treasured.' For nearly a century she was based in Mombasa, carrying cargoes of cement and mangrove poles. Then, 20 years ago she changed hands and was lovingly refitted for the charter trade.

Since then she has sailed as far south as Mozambique and is the only dhow I know that can undertake such lengthy cruises with any degree of comfort. On deck are heaps of soft scatter-cushions, hand-carved Lamu chairs and ornate brass-bound Zanzibari chests.

In the forepeak is the galley, where the crew conjure up miraculous seafood suppers, and down aft, suspended over the starboard quarter is a wooden coop with a hole in the floor and a seat over it – the traditional 'thunderbox' in which you can look down between your knees and see the waves flowing past.

Living space is not a problem. Beds are laid out on deck every night, and even with a maximum of ten passengers and a crew of eight to sail her, she still has room for two life rafts and tows a powerboat for scuba diving and snorkelling trips.

When I join *Tusitiri* she is lying at anchor off Shela village, a mile east of Lamu Town. I had flown there from Nairobi and now, less than two hours later, I am being welcomed aboard with the traditional offering of *kahawa chungu* – black coffee spiced with ginger and cardamom, poured into small cups from a conical brass pot, and served with *halua*, a sticky Swahili sweetmeat.

My shoes are placed in a wicker basket. I will not need them again unless I go ashore. For the rest of the voyage I will be living barefoot like the crew, who are already hauling up the anchor. Minutes later we are under way, motoring past Lamu's waterfront bars and hotels, making for the narrow channel between Manda Island and the mainland.

On both sides of us, green walls of mangroves tiptoe into the sea on spidery roots, and a procession of fishing dhows come drifting past like drowsy white moths. "Look," says Mark Eddy, our South African skipper, as we pass a gap in the mangroves. "That's where elephants still cross the water to reach Manda. Sometimes you can find their footprints on the beach."

Eddy is a professional yacht master, a blond, blue-eyed sea gipsy who has been living on boats since he was seven years old. Born in Durban, he left South Africa 15 years ago and has been sailing *Tusitiri* for the past three years.

On we cruise, across a dazzling bay beneath whose seemingly innocent waters lurk hidden sandbanks. Not that Eddy appears concerned. Unlike the old-time dhow captains who had only the stars to steer by, *Tusitiri* can feel her way unerringly through the hazards using radar, depth finder and a state-of-the-art GPS navigation system. But these, and her 120hp Ford Sabre engine, are the only concessions to the 21st century.

Her single sail, a giant shark fin of salt-stained canvas, is so heavy that it takes six sweating crewmen to haul it taut, but *Tusitiri* is a happy ship. Even at work, burnishing the deck with linseed oil until the entire vessel is steeped in its cricket-bat smell, the crew make up impromptu songs. "Oh *Tusitiri*," they chant, "we will make you beautiful."

Our route lies inside the reefs, taking us past the island of Uvondo, its beaches empty except for pelicans, and the dhow-building town of Ndau, one of the oldest settlements in the entire archipelago, with its waterside baobabs and fishermen's houses.

Ahead of us now, across the bay, I can see the sand hills of Kiwayu, a narrow island flanked on its seaward side by a 12-mile beach; and at the far end, overlooking a wide curve of sand on the mainland shore, rise the thatched roofs of Kiwayu Safari Village*, Kenya's most exclusive coastal hideaway.

Kiwayu and its idyllic lagoon mark the end of my three-day voyage from Lamu. It lies on the unspoilt shores of the Kiunga Marine National Reseve only 30 miles from the Somali border, and although accessible by plane from Nairobi it still feels gloriously remote, which is why arriving by dhow and wading ashore with my luggage on my head seems like the perfect way to turn up for breakfast.

---

*Sadly, Kiwayu Safari Village has closed indefinitely following a raid by Somali pirates in September 2011 during which a British visitor was shot dead and his wife abducted.

Afterword

L AST year I returned to Zambia's South Luangwa National Park for the first time in a decade and wondered why I had stayed away so long. This was my eighth Zambian safari, and with every visit I have found my allegiance to East Africa sorely tested. Somehow the Luangwa Valley has withstood the test of time. Its emphasis on walking safaris means there are fewer vehicles than you might see in the Mara or the Serengeti, and small, owner-run bushcamps are still the rule, providing unsophisticated but extremely comfortable accommodation and employing some of Africa's finest safari guides as well as offering a game-viewing experience second to none.

This time I stayed at Puku Ridge Safari Camp, overlooking an Arcadian scene that sums up the valley to perfection. Reaching away below my veranda lay a vast floodplain, enclosed by a distant wall of woodland and nibbled as smooth as a Home Counties lawn – a giant, natural theatre-in-the-round on which all kinds of dramas are played out.

The day before my arrival, lions had tried to kill a buffalo while guests were at breakfast, so in the afternoon we drove out to look for them. We found only one, but what a lion he was. The guides call him Shaka Zulu, and two years ago he was lording it over the local pride. Then, as is the way with lions, three feisty young strangers deposed him.

Now aged 15, his day was almost done, but he still managed to cut a regal figure as he strode towards us across the plain, and it was only then, as his pale yellow eyes met mine, that it occurred to me how lions have been the one continual thread running through my regular visits to Africa.

Over the years lions – and the land they live in – have become an obsession with me. Fellow big cat junkies will know the feeling. When you have been away from lions for a long time you long for a sight of them, and even now, 40 years on since the first time I heard a wild lion roaring, I lie awake in my tent at night, unable to sleep until I have heard them grunting in the darkness.

The leopard awakens similar feelings: the shadow-stepper, elusive, mysterious and without doubt the most beautiful cat of all in its sleek coat of midnight black rosettes. But it is lions that dominate my thoughts.

So many lion memories: of The Earl hunting tsessebe on Busanga Plain in Kafue National Park; the black-maned Kalahari pride males and the majestic old outcast I encountered on his stolen kill at Naabi Hill in the Serengeti. Above all I think of the Musiara males – Scar, Brando and Mkubwa – the coalition that ruled the Marsh Lions when Jonathan Scott and I were recording their lives three decades ago. They were the first lions I came to know as individuals, as instantly recognisable to me as my family and friends.

Some people may tell you lions are boring. Don't believe them. True, lions spend most of their days resting, lying belly up in the shade as they wait for darkness. But if you are patient and put in the time they will do everything for you, and you will be rewarded by the social behaviour that is so much a part of their eternal appeal.

Then, if you are lucky, you may witness them hunting; not the kill itself but the way the lionesses work as a team, fanning out through the long grass, waiting with infinite patience and then crawling belly-to-ground to get close enough for the final rush. As a spectacle it is surpassed only by those magical moments when the cubs come out to play, stalking each other or pouncing on their mothers' tails in the first light of dawn or in the golden hour before sundown.

Today, like all Africa's wildlife, lions face an uncertain future. George Adamson could not bear to see a lion that was not free, but I have an even greater worry. I cannot envisage a world without lions, but it is time to think the unthinkable. At some point in the future, when humankind's greed for horn and ivory has consigned the rhino and elephant to history, it may be the lion's fate to follow them. Then one day, perhaps not far off, the last lion will throw down his thunderous challenge in the stillness of the wide savannah. And the only reply will be the echo of his voice returning from the distant hills, to be followed by a silence that will last for all eternity. We must not let that happen.

Acknowledgements

SO many people have helped to ease my way across Africa down the years. Strangers when we met, I now think of them as good friends who helped to open my eyes and ears to the wonders of the natural world I have tried to portray in this book. All gave willingly of their time and expertise, with great generosity, and the days spent in their company has provided me with a lifetime of unforgettable memories.

Some of them will be familiar to you: Iain and Oria Douglas-Hamilton, who have devoted their lives to conserving the African elephant; the redoubtable Richard Leakey, founder of the Kenya Wildlife Service; Tony Fitzjohn, who learned his trade at Kora with George Adamson and emerged from the Old Man's giant shadow to become a leading conservationist in his own right at Mkomazi National Park in Tanzania; and the inspirational Ian Craig at Lewa, who set up the Northern Rangelands Trust.

Others I also fondly recall for being the catalyst behind some of my most hair-raising safaris, such as Don Hunt, whom I accompanied on a wild chase after Grevy's zebras in northern Kenya, and Marcus Russell, who took me into Tsavo to report on the ivory wars of 1988 when the park was a no-go area overrun by poachers.

Equally memorable are the many happy days spent collaborating on *The Marsh Lions* with Jonathan Scott in the Maasai Mara, as are the safaris shared in Namibia with David 'Mrefu' Coulson, co-founder of the African Rock Art Foundation, in the Aberdares with Colin Church, the former chairman of the Rhino Ark Charitable Trust, and with Kuki Gallmann, author of *I Dreamed of Africa,* at her idyllic home on the Laikipia Plateau.

Nor will I forget Kay Turner, the widow of Myles Turner, who accompanied Jonathan Scott and me on a poignant safari around the Serengeti where she and Myles had lived when he was the park's legendary head warden, or Randall J. Moore and Abu, his wise and gentle elephant bull who together gave me some of the high points of my life at Abu's Camp in Botswana.

Looking back down the years I also realise what a debt of gratitude I owe to those whose camps and lodges have provided comfort and hospitality to a degree I can never repay. Foremost among them are the late Aris Grammaticas and his family who always managed to find a bed for me at Governors' Camp in the Maasai Mara. Many others have been equally generous in the Mara, notably Jake Grieves-Cook at Porini Lion Camp and Ol Kinyei, the Beaton family (Ron, Pauline, Gerard and Rainee) at Rekero, and Paul Goldstein at Kicheche.

Elsewhere in Kenya my heartfelt thanks go out to Mikey and Tanya Carr-Hartley, Riccardo Orizio, Peter Sylvester, Simon ole Kinyaga at Il Ngwesi, and Luca and Antonella Belpietro at Campi ya Kanzi, their stunningly beautiful home in the Chyulu Hills.

In Tanzania I would particularly like to thank Aadje Geertsema for the unfailing hospitality shown towards me at Ndutu Lodge, and the same goes for Chris Fox at Mwagusi in the Ruaha National Park and to the staff of &Beyond for their outstanding mobile safari camps in the Serengeti.

In South Africa I will always be grateful to Dave Varty for the luxury – and leopards – that are part and parcel of a stay at Londolozi, and to Sarah Tompkins at the Samara Game Reserve in the Great Karoo. In Namibia my thanks are due to Lise Hanssen and Dave Houghton for glorious days in the company of Okonjima's rescued cheetahs, and in Botswana to the charismatic Ralph Bousfield at Jack's Camp in the Makgadikgadi, and Dave Dugmore at Meno a Kwena on the Boteti River.

As for Zambia, seldom have I felt more at home in the bush than when flying down to this friendliest of countries, whose owner-run camps are some of the best in the business. Happy are the days I have spent in the Luangwa Valley with Robin and Jo Pope, Phil Berry and Babette Alfieri, and Rod and Guz Tether; and the same goes for Grant Cumings at Chiawa and Old Mondoro on the Lower Zambezi.

Indispensable to the success of any safari is a good professional guide – especially if you intend to go walking – and I have been fortunate to travel with some of the very best. Chris Fox, Ralph Bousfield, Robin Pope, Phil Berry and Grant Cumings I have already acknowledged for the superlative camps they run, but they are also at the very top of their game as safari guides, as are Jock Anderson, Jackson ole Looseyia, Richard Bonham, Alex Hunter, Mark Jenkins, Anthony Russell and Ngatia Sempeta (all in Kenya); Richard Knocker, Paul Oliver and Sandor Carter in Tanzania, Mike Penman and Brent Reed in Botswana, Lexxon Munana and Jacob Shawa in Zambia, Dennis van Eyssen and Ian MacDonald in Zimbabwe and Andy Schafer in South Africa.

To this list I must add the specialist tour operators, based in the UK and in Africa, who have expertly tailor-made the safaris I have undertaken since my first visit to Kenya 1974. In no particular order they are: Stefano and Liz Cheli of Cheli & Peacock Safaris, Wilderness Safaris, Bill Adams at Safari Consultants, Geoff Kent at Abercrombie & Kent, Chris McIntyre and Richard Trillo at Expert Africa, Nick van Gruisen at The Ultimate Travel Company, Henrietta Loyd at Cazenove & Loyd, John Spence and Richard Smith at Aardvark Safaris, Jane Durham at Okavango Tours & Safaris, Will Jones at Journeys by Design, John Burdett at Africa Exclusive, Albee Yeend and George Morgan-Grenville at Red Savannah, Jemma Hewlett at Audley Travel, Marc Harris at Tanzania Odyssey, Nicola Shepherd at The Explorations Company, Scott Dunn, Steppes Travel, J&C Voyageurs, The Bushcamp Company, Robin Pope Safaris, Gamewatchers, Uncharted Africa Safaris and Tim Best.

Almost all the accounts featured within this book have previously appeared in one guise or another as newspaper or magazine articles, and in this regard I should particularly like to thank Graham Boynton, Michael Kerr and Charles Starmer-Smith at *The Daily Telegraph*, as well as Christine Walker for her unstinting support at *The Sunday Times*, and Craig Rix at *Travel Africa*.

Sadly, many of the legendary figures it has been my privilege to meet are no longer with us, but I would like to pay tribute to George Adamson, Norman Carr, Hugo van Lawick, Julian McKeand, Jeff Stutchbury and Louw Schoeman, all of whom have made a lasting contribution to the Africa whose wildlife and wild places they fought so fiercely to conserve.

Other individuals, each in their own very different ways, have contributed so much to my understanding of Africa. Among them are Steve Stephenson – one of Tanzania's most distinguished wardens – and his wife Yvonne; Niels Mogensen of the Naboisho Lion Project; Robin Bachelor – balloon pilot extraordinary, and Humphrey Carter – helicopter pilot without equal. I would also like to thank Stephanie Dolreny for taking me lion tracking at Ol Donyo Wuas, Lindsay Swan for arranging my first visits to Zambia, and Patrick Orr and Gloria Ward for helping to organise a string of trips to East Africa.

Extract from *The Marsh Lions*
by Brian Jackman, Jonathan and Angela Scott

To a casual eye it was a serene and shining landscape, as peaceful as an English park. There was no malice in it, no hint of suffering or hostility. Orioles called with clear voices from the dappled shade of forest figs. Hippos chuckled in the river, and bou-bou shrikes chimed their monotonous xylophonic responses from the heat-drugged thickets. The sounds of summer lulled the senses; but the world of the plains animals was a constant paradox. Nothing was ever what it seemed. Tranquillity was an illusion behind which stalked old familiar spectres: hunger, thirst, disease. The golden vistas, outwardly so innocent and benign, were full of sudden, violent images. The pristine plains were a charnel house of skulls and bones, half-eaten zebras, bloated vultures. Hidden in the tall grass, slovenly hyenas raised gory muzzles from a shipwreck of ribs, and hungry lions tore at their kills with paws encased in gloves of blood.

When night fell, lightning flickered along the horizon and thunder rumbled in the distant hills. The short rains were coming. The animals felt it, and the waiting made them restless. The Talek mother sensed it as she nursed her cubs in the riverine forest, but her growing unease was not due merely to the sultry weather. Ever since she had isolated herself from the pride to give birth eight weeks earlier, she had become increasingly aware of the presence of other lions. The newcomers were nomadic strangers, outcasts from the Talek prides to the east, and footloose males who had come north with the wildebeest. They feared the intimidating figure of Scar, whose nightly challenge reverberated across the Marsh; but they did not disperse.

In the morning, anxious for the safety of her cubs, the lioness led her family back to the Marsh. Startled waterbucks ran off as she approached, high-stepping through the grass, then stopped to turn and stare once they realised she was not hunting. Cautiously she crossed the clearing, her big flat paws raising puffs of dust which made the cubs sneeze and grimace in her wake. At the edge of the forest she found a pool which still held water, and paused to drink while the cubs wriggled to lick the drops from her whiskers.

Skirting the fig-tree forest she came at last to the two ancient figs that grew at the edge of the plains. There she sniffed at the base of the bigger tree, exploring the bark for news, and found Scar's pungent presence still fresh from the previous night. Then, satisfied that no alien lions were lurking in the immediate vicinity, she slumped in the shade; the three cubs, exhausted by their long march, snuggled against her and fell asleep at her nipples. Neither she nor the cubs had seen the watchful leopard concealed in the canopy of the fig-tree forest.

He was a handsome animal, not as old or as heavy as the wall-eyed male of Leopard Gorge. His ears were not yet scabbed and battle-scarred; his nose was still a youthful pink and his whiskers stood out like porcupine quills. In colour, too, he was strikingly different from the wall-eyed tom, whose spots and rosettes were a dusky olive brown, like the colours in an old tapestry. His own markings were distilled from a deeper darkness and blossomed as soft as soot on his lustrous coat.

Now he lay in his tree and waited, dozing intermittently; one forepaw supporting his head, the other hanging down. There was no hurry, and his patience was infinite. Occasionally his eyes opened and his chilling stare would rifle through the curtain of leaves. During the afternoon he awoke to see Scar resting with his lioness. At first the cubs were awed by the formidable presence of their father. Later, when they had overcome their fear, one of them even tried to play with him. The big lion did not growl, but merely raised a crooked lip; the sight of the huge canine tooth was enough to send the youngster scurrying back to its siblings. All this the leopard observed as the sun passed down and the shadows of his forest spread like a dark stain towards the sprawling lions.

As for the book itself, I would like to pay tribute to Jonathan Truss for the superb illustrations that grace every chapter. At the same time I would also like to thank the immortally beautiful Virginia McKenna, who played the part of Joy Adamson in *Born Free* and went on to establish the Born Free Foundation, for having provided the most generous foreword; and of course nothing could have been accomplished without the invaluable assistance of Jonny Pegg, my agent, the unerringly keen eye and encouragement of Rachel Fielding, my editor, and the full support of Adrian Phillips at Bradt for taking on this project in the first place.

And finally, words cannot express how lucky I am to have been blessed with a wife such as Annabelle, who accepts my long hours at the computer screen and is, if anything, even more passionate about Africa than I am.

Travel the world from your armchair...
Up the Creek
An Amazon Adventure
JOHN HARRISON
The Urban Circus
CATRIONA RAINSFORD
A·TOURIST·IN·THE ARAB·SPRING
TOM·CHESSHYRE
MICHAEL PALIN · BEN FOGLE
The IRRESPONSIBLE TRAVELLER
TALES OF SCRAPES AND NARROW ESCAPES
SIMON CALDER · JONATHAN SCOTT
THE TWO-YEAR MOUNTAIN
PHIL DEUTSCHLE
A Nepal Journey
savannah diaries
brian jackman
The Leopard's Tale
JONATHAN &
ANGELA S
Connemara Mollie
An Irish journey on horseback
Hilary Bradt
Dingle Peggy
Further travels in Ireland on horseback
Hilary Bradt
Madagascar the eighth continent
LIFE, DEATH & DISCOVERY IN A LOST WORLD
PETER TYSON
The Marsh Lions
The Story of an African Pride
A Glimpse of Eternal Snows
A Journey of Love and Loss in the Himalayas
Jane Wilson-Howarth
FAKIRS, FELUCCAS AND FEMMES FATALES
E.T. LAING
Bradt